The
EVERYTHING™
HOME
IMPROVEMENT
BOOK

The EVERYTHING™
HOME IMPROVEMENT BOOK

Everything you need to know to keep your home
looking—and working—better than ever!

Tom Philbin

ADAMS MEDIA CORPORATION
Holbrook, Massachusetts

An Everything™ Series Book.
The Everything™ Series is a trademark of Adams Media Corporation.

Published by Adams Media Corporation
260 Center Street, Holbrook, MA 02343

ISBN: 1-55850-718-3

Printed in the United States of America.

J   I   H   G   F   E   D   C   B   A

Library of Congress Cataloging-in-Publication Data
Philbin, Tom.
The everything home improvement book / Tom Philbin.
p.   cm. — (Everything Series)
Includes index.
ISBN 1-55850-718-3
1. Dwellings—Maintenance and repair—Amateurs' manuals. I. Title. II. Series.
TH4817.3.P446   1997
643'.7—dc21   97-6617
CIP

This publication is designed to provide accurate and authoritative information with regard to the subject
matter covered. It is sold with the understanding that the publisher is not engaged in rendering legal,
accounting, or other professional advice. If legal advice or other expert assistance is required, the services of
a competent professional person should be sought.
— From a *Declaration of Principles* jointly adopted by a Committee of the American
Bar Association and a Committee of Publishers and Associations

Many of the designations used by manufacturers and sellers to distinguish their products are claimed as
trademarks. Where those designations appear in this book and Adams Media was aware of a trademark
claim, the designations have been printed in initial capital letters, e.g. Sheetrock.

INTERIOR ILLUSTRATIONS BY MARY NAGIN AND BARRY LITTMANN

This book is available at quantity discounts for bulk purchases.
For information, call 1-800-872-5627 (in Massachusetts, call 617-767-8100).

Visit our home page at http://www.adamsmedia.com

Contents

Introduction

This book is designed to help home-owners repair, maintain, and improve their homes—and then some. I see it as an encyclopedia for the home, containing information that one will consult again and again.

Many home repairs are covered, and often we need a little help to get all the details right, even though we might have followed everything to the letter the first time. There are also checklists of things to do to maintain your home—not only for such things as clearing gutters and the like, but also hints to make your house impregnable to pests such as bats and rodents.

There are a variety of simple home improvements to do and information on ones you may not want to do because they would be too difficult. The facts are here so you can make an intelligent choice.

In compiling the contents, I tried to think of every area that the average home-owner would be interested in, a soup-to-nuts menu except instead of soup and nuts we talk about nails and paint. I also gave careful thought to the home-improve-ment skill level of the person who will be using this book, and the accent here is on helping the neophyte—those who want to learn how to wire a Nike missile better go elsewhere.

In providing that detailed help, I aimed to make the instructions as clear as possible—a job infinitely aided by artist Mary Nagin's line drawings, which will fill in the gaps when my golden words fail.

I was also very, very conscious of saving money—your money. Sprinkled throughout the book is, collectively, a bucket of tips on how to save on every-thing from buying washers to buying win-dows. Indeed, what one can potentially save is, in my opinion, quite significant.

I have also tried to write in a style that will be a bit entertaining while being informative. In my view there's no need to write in a dry, punishing, boring way when a lighter style will do the same job. On the other hand, I did not strive to be Henny Youngman, which wasn't hard.

All in all, I think the book will serve you well for many different repair, mainte-nance, and home-improvement jobs and be, hopefully, everything you need—*The Everything Home Improvement Book.*

—Tom Philbin

CHAPTER

It's handy to know not only how your home is built but also how the systems in it work. Besides being of practical value when you want to work on it or when a contractor comes in to talk about making changes in it, it simply takes the mystery out of some problems you'll have. And your house should not be a mystery.

Following, then, is a look at how homes are built and how the systems in it—plumbing and electrical—work.

Anatomy

The wood skeleton of a home sits on a foundation made of concrete or masonry blocks. There are basically three kinds of foundations: slab, full, and crawlspace. A slab foundation is a solid slab of concrete, usually 4 inches thick, set directly on the earth. Under the slab edges, as with any foundation, there are footings, or walls of concrete or block that help support the slab. The footings are wider than the wall (like feet are wider than ankles) to support the load better. The bottoms of the footings go beneath the frost line, or the depth at which the earth hardens when it's cold. If this were not the case, the earth, which swells when frozen, could push the foundation out of alignment.

Frost lines vary. If you live in Florida the earth may never freeze; however Nome, Alaska, would be another story.

A full foundation is really a large hole in the ground. (Very reassuring, right!) Walls are built—either of poured concrete or block—around the sides of the hole, and the bottoms of the walls are supported by footings. A home with a cellar uses a full foundation.

A crawlspace foundation is simply a smaller version of a full foundation. When the house is erected, there is literally only room under it for crawling (except if you're very short).

Balloon or Box Frame

Homes are commonly balloon or box framed. Balloon framing can be found in construction of older homes. (It was dubbed "balloon," when it was invented in the 1800s, because it was light and airy in contrast to the heavy timber framing used earlier.) Here, the studs—the vertical wall members—are house height, going all the way from the foundation to the roof. At various points between studs, there are firestops—horizontal boards designed to stop the spread of fire. Otherwise, if the studs went clear to the roof, they could act as flues during a fire.

Box framing has been used more frequently in the last fifty years. In this type of construction, the studs are only room height (8 feet, usually), and their bottom ends are set on an assembly of heavy wood members called joists. The joists form what amounts to a shallow box— hence the name.

A Closer Look

Let's take a closer look at the anatomy of the house.

The first level in any kind of house skeleton is the sill. It is commonly composed of double 2 x 6's laid flat on top of the foundation walls and overlapped at the corners. (Note: When lumber sizes are given, the first number refers to thickness; the second refers to width.) The sill is secured to the foundation by means of bolts anchored in it. (With slab foundations, a sill is not used. Rather there are 2 x 4's—called shoes—bolted to the slab edge. Joists are not used, either.)

The average house also has a girder, which is the main supporting beam of the house. This is set across the middle of the foundation walls, with the ends notched into the walls, and the top edge flush with the sill.

Girders

Various materials can be used for girders: Steel I beams—a length of steel shaped like the letter I in cross section; a 6 x 8 made by nailing three 2 x 8's together; or 2 x 10 and 2 x 12 boards. The girder is supported along its length by lally columns. These are cement-filled iron posts with steel plates welded to each end. They are commonly installed 7 feet apart. In an older home, you may find locust posts instead of lally columns. Locust posts are made of an ironlike wood that is impervious to damage from decay and termites.

Joists

Joists are set on edge on top of the sill. Normally, joists are 2 x 8's, but this depends on the span—the length of the joist. For spans over 14 feet, they are usually much thicker.

In box-framed construction, joists are usually 16 inches on centers; that is, 16 inches from the center of one to the center of adjacent ones. If balloon framed, the centers may not be exactly 16 inches, because years ago framing was not so standardized and carpenters were not that concerned with centers. Also, the joists are spaced differently and specially framed when they have to allow plumbing pipes to pass through from the basement to upper floors. Wherever there is to be a wall, good framing requires that the joists be doubled—two joists set flush against each other—for proper support.

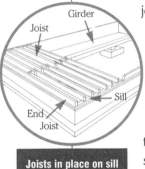

Joists in place on sill

Keep Those Joists Upright

To keep joists from falling over (a good idea!) and to help distribute the weight above properly, "bridging" is nailed on between joists. These may be solid boards, boards in an *X* shape, or strips of metal.

The subflooring, or deck, goes on top of the joists. It may consist of 4 x 8 sheets of plywood, tongue-and-groove boards (one board has a lip that fits into a groove or recess on the adjacent one), or another material. Tongue-and-groove material is usually installed diagonally. (It is not used much today because it is labor intensive.) Finish flooring is installed at right angles to the joists on top of the subflooring.

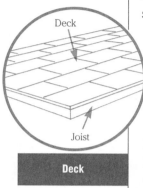

Deck

Joist

Deck

The walls are erected on top of the deck. Each wall consists of a bottom 2 x 4 member, called a shoe, which is nailed to the subflooring; 2 x 4 studs, which are nailed to the shoe, 16 inches apart; and doubled-up 2 x 4's nailed across the tops of the studs, called a plate. As previously mentioned, the height is normally 8 feet.

Walls, of course, are also framed for doors and windows. Wherever there is a doorway, the shoe is cut out and framed with jack studs—which are simply flanking studs cut shorter than regular ones—and a header, or horizontal cross member, forming the top of the doorway. Its purpose is to support the wall weight above. Windows also use jack studs and a

header. Also, to allow for nailing Sheetrock—the brand name for drywall—or other wall material to walls, special corner stud assemblies consisting of three boards and short blocks of wood are used to join the walls at the corners.

Partition and Load Bearing Walls

All conventionally framed homes have what are characterized as load bearing and partition walls. Load bearing walls, which support house weight, normally include exterior walls and a main wall running down the center of the house, which is aligned with and sits on top of the girder. You might consider this assembly the spine of the house.

Partition walls do not support weight. They are built like load bearing walls, except that the plate used is usually only a single 2 x 4, not a double.

Second-Floor Framing

If a home has a second floor, it is framed like the first floor. In box framing, joists are extended across the tops of the plates. (In older homes, joists are secured to the studs.) Decking, or subflooring, is installed on top of the joists, as on the first floor, and walls are erected on top of these, also as on the first floor. The main load bearing wall that runs across the first floor is continued on the second floor, that is, erected directly over the first; and, if there is a third floor, the wall is continued there as well.

Ceiling Material

Ceiling material for the first floor is secured to the bottom of the joists. In this situation joists are sometimes called ceiling beams, but these are separate members, smaller than joists (usually 2 x 6's). They are used on the top floor of the house. Like joists, they are laid across the tops of walls and secured to the wall plates and to the rafters.

Rafters

Rafters are installed with one end notched, or given a "bird's mouth"—it looks like the wide-open mouth of a bird—so that it fits against the wall plate or a special shoe on top of the ceiling beam; the other end is notched to fit against the so-called ridge rafter, a main rafter running down the center of the house. Collar beams—short boards nailed between and near the tops of rafters—are added to give the framing rigidity.

Most homes have gable ends, that is, narrow triangular-shaped sections of the roof (remember *The House of the Seven Gables?*). This area is filled with—what else—gable end studs. These are simply

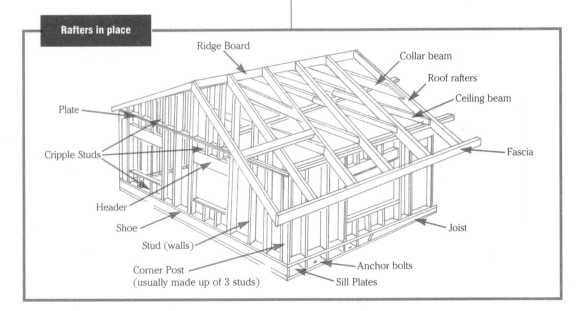

Rafters in place

Ridge Board · Collar beam · Roof rafters · Ceiling beam · Plate · Cripple Studs · Fascia · Header · Shoe · Joist · Stud (walls) · Corner Post (usually made up of 3 studs) · Anchor bolts · Sill Plates

studs cut to fit between the rafters and the plate below. If the house has been conscientiously framed, these studs will have half their thickness extend beyond the rafters so that the 2 x 4's can be secured to them as a convenient place for securing Sheetrock.

Sheathing

The walls and roof of a house are also sheathed, that is, a sheet material base for siding or roofing material is installed. Wall sheathing can be any of a variety of materials: In older homes it might be 1 x 8 tongue-and-groove boards; 1 x 8 ship lap (the board edges overlap); or a sheet material such as plywood or oriented strand board, which is made from wood scraps and sawdust or sheathing grade plywood.

The sheathing is installed so that it completely covers the framework. If boards are used, it may be installed horizontally or diagonally. If boards are installed horizontally, wind braces will have been installed in the walls. Wind braces are boards—usually 1 x 6's—that are nailed diagonally across studs and are notched into them.

Roof sheathing, which is technically known as decking, is usually made of plywood. It is installed in a fashion similar to that of sheathing for siding.

Tar paper (15 pound felt) or a similar product is used to cover both siding and roof sheathing to make them wind- and watertight. The roofing or siding is applied over this.

How a Plumbing System Works

Residential plumbing actually consists of two systems: the fresh or potable water and the drainage system, as well as the fixtures and appliances that the systems serve.

Water

There are three possible sources of water: a municipal water works, a spring, and a well. Water that starts its journey to your house in a water works is purified there; it then travels through a series of pipes until it enters a single main service line (usually $3/4$-inch diameter) into your house. As it enters, it goes through a meter, which records its use. From there it branches out into a pair of narrow pipes (usually $1/2$-inch diameter) that travel side by side throughout the house and terminate at the appliances or fixtures that use the water. One of the lines is for cold water and one is for hot. The water becomes hot by first being routed through the hot water heater before it begins its journey through the house.

All fresh water travels under pressure, because it is pumped to your home. That's why it gushes out when you turn on a faucet. In a sense, the

water is always ready to go—the faucet simply directs the pressure where you need it.

Different names have been given to water pipes. Those that travel vertically at least one floor are called risers. Lines that travel horizontally to fixtures and appliances are called branch lines.

Valves

At various points on the pipes there are valves, which are faucetlike devices for shutting down the water supply to the pipes. This way, when repairs are needed, you don't have to shut down all the water. Valves are on runs to control specific lengths and are usually (or should be) under sinks and toilets: hot and cold valves for the sink, plus one valve for the toilet tank.

Valves are also located at the bottoms of risers; these are used to drain the pipes. Additionally, homes usually have one or two main valves at the water meter. One is called the meter shutoff and is on the street side of the meter; the other is called the main shutoff and is on the house side.

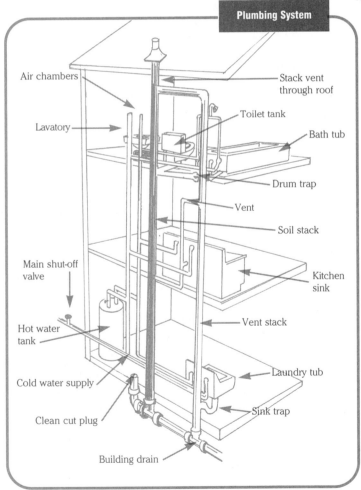

Plumbing System

Air chambers

Lavatory

Main shut-off valve

Hot water tank

Cold water supply

Clean cut plug

Building drain

Stack vent through roof

Toilet tank

Bath tub

Drum trap

Vent

Soil stack

Kitchen sink

Vent stack

Laundry tub

Sink trap

Turning either of these valves will stop all water flow to the house.

Air Chambers

Every plumbing system should have air chambers (though not all systems do). These are vertical pieces of capped pipe that jut up from water supply pipes at the point where the pipe enters the fixture. In essence, an air chamber is a shock absorber. When the pipes are handling excess water, the excess enters the air chambers; otherwise, the pipes could start vibrating, a malady called waterhammer, and possibly loosen or leak from the shock.

Fixtures

There are three kinds of water-related fixtures in the house: sink, tub, and toilet. Outside faucets, also known as sillcocks, may also be considered fixtures, but they are called, like other faucets, fittings.

The Drainage System

The second part of a plumbing system is the drainage system, technically known as a "DWV" system to describe what it does: It *drains* away *wastes* at the same time as it *vents* them. The DWV system is composed of waste pipes, a soil stack, traps, and vents.

How a DWV system works can be illustrated in the way a sink operates. Waste runs out of the sink to a series of pipes that lead to the waste pipes, usually pipes with a diameter of $1\frac{1}{2}$ or 2 inches, which are sloped to empty into the soil stack. The stack is a large pipe, usually 3 or 4 inches in diameter, that runs from the lowest point in the house to the highest and emerges about 6 inches through the roof. (The stack is affectionately known in the trade as a "stinkpipe.") In older homes cast iron was commonly used; in newer homes copper and plastic are used. From the stack, the waste goes to the building drain, a horizontal pipe that runs across the house and leads to the sewer line and to the disposal system—sewer, septic tank, or cesspool.

Traps

Traps are safety devices. They are shaped to trap water (hence their name), and thus they're constantly filled with water so that gases and vermin can't back up into the house through sink or tub drain holes. Sink traps are separate pieces of tubing; toilets are shaped to trap water. In addition there are drum traps for tubs and a trap and fresh air inlet where the soil pipe leaves the building.

From Toilet to Stack

Pipes that go from the toilet to the stack are called soil pipes. There are no branch lines here. The soil pipe drains into the soil stack directly. Drain lines only carry sink waste; soil pipes only carry toilet waste. The entire system operates by gravity.

All water fixtures are connected to the soil stack. However, if the distance between fixture and stack is too far, there may be additional stacks. These also are vented. In essence, a stack has two purposes: It functions as a waste line and a vent line. It's a waste line below the fixture and a vent line above.

Cleanout plugs are located at the bottom of each soil stack and wherever the waste pipe changes direction, because that's where blockages often occur. These plugs can be removed and a cleanout tool (snake) inserted for clearing the blockage.

Vents

Venting is required to release gases. However, it has another important function: It keeps the air pressure in the system equalized. This prevents water from the drain or waste lines from backing up, by a siphoning action, into the fresh water system.

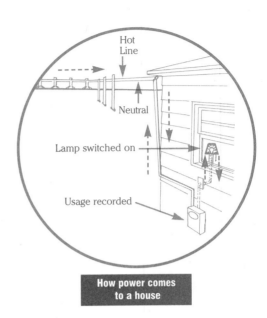

How power comes to a house

How an Electrical System Works

A home's electrical system is like its plumbing system, but instead of water flowing through pipes, electricity flows through wires. In order to flow, electricity requires a circuit—a closed loop that goes around and around. When this circuit is broken, the electricity stops flowing.

The circuit starts at the power company, where electricity is generated by the action of huge magnets. From there it flows through high-tension wires to a service line that leads into the home. (This line is called the service entrance cable; it goes through the electric meter, which records its use.) Electricity continues to flow to the fuse box or circuit breaker panel. From there it flows through house circuit wires to receptacles where the power is tapped off by electrical devices. Like water, electricity is always under pressure, ready to surge out when you turn on a switch or plug something in.

Power coming through the circuit is either 120 volts or 240 volts. One black wire, or hot leg, carries 120; if there is another hot wire, and there almost always is, it is colored red and also carries 120 volts, for a total of 240 volts. The wire that carries 120 volts is connected, for example, to lamps or similar devices; high voltage—240 volts—is connected to major appliances.

The Path of One Circuit

From the circuit breaker or fuse box, the electricity flows through a black wire (usually called the hot leg), through the device—for example, the filament of a light bulb—then back along the neutral or white wire to the circuit breaker or fuse box, and then to the power station. All this happens instantaneously.

Grounding

For safety, all electrical systems must be grounded—that is, connected to the earth. The *ground* is simply a separate metallic path for the electricity to the earth, in case the device you are using, such as a toaster or appliance, develops an electrical leak. If a leak occurred and there were no grounding system, electricity would electrify the appliance. If you touched it, you'd get a shock.

Bare Ground Wire

Clamp

Ground rod

2 ft.

How an electrical system is grounded

Fortunately, though, metal is a much better conductor, or carrier, of electricity than a human body. Thus, if a metallic path is open to the electricity, it will travel through it.

Electrical systems are grounded in a variety of ways. There may be a separate wire (made of copper) connected to the receptacle or switch that runs to and is attached to a grounding bar in the fuse or circuit breaker panel box. A copper wire or rod leads, in turn, to another metal object—usually the water meter—that is in contact with the ground; or it may be a metal rod buried in the earth.

In other cases the path to the earth is along the outside of the metal cable—the BX electrical cable, for example. If a leak developed in the device, the errant electricity would flow from it through the receptacle, which would in turn be connected to the BX cable. Normally, then, errant electricity would go back to the fuse box or circuit breaker panel, which is connected to the earth. It should be emphasized that the same electrical device can be grounded in various ways; all of them work fine. As long as there is that metallic path—and you won't become that path—one method is as good as another.

Safety Tip

Electricity, of course, can be dangerous, and there are a number of things you should observe when dealing with it. First, no matter what you are working on (except a portable device that you unplug), turn off the current at the fuse box or circuit breaker panel. Before doing this, plug a light into the receptacle. When you turn off the circuit, the light should go out.

Calculating Circuit Capacity

It's a time-consuming process, but it's an excellent idea to know the capacity of the various circuits in your home. Knowing the total capacity of each will enable you to use electrical devices and not overload the circuit.

To do this, first turn on all the lights in your house and plug lamps into outlets normally used by small appliances such as toasters. At the fuse or breaker box, usually located in the basement, turn off one breaker or unscrew one fuse. Then check to see which lights around the house go off. Mark them down (a floor plan of your house showing receptacles helps), showing the wattage of each device used on that circuit; remember to mark down the wattage of appliances that have been replaced by lights. The wattage is usually listed somewhere on the appliance casing.

When you've added up all the wattages, label this circuit "number 1" and mark the total wattage after it. If, for example, the circuit is 15 amperes and totals more than 1,650 watts, that circuit is just about overloaded, because 15 amps times 110 volts has 1,650 watts capacity. A 20-amp circuit should not handle more than 2,200 watts, assuming that everything is turned on all at once.

Repeat the procedure for the other circuits (the average house usually has nine or ten). When you're finished, you'll know exactly what you can or cannot add, as long as you know the wattage of each device used.

In some cases, the wattage will not be marked on a device. Rather, you will get the amperage. To convert it to wattage, just multiply by 110 volts.

It should be remembered that what you are calculating is the total capacity of particular circuits. It may well be that not every receptacle or light switch will be on at one time. So, for example, if you know that your number 1 circuit only normally has two lights used on it, then you could likely use a small-wattage appliance without overloading it.

Keep the capacity records handy. The best place is down by the fuse box or circuit breaker panel. You'll know instantly what the capacity of a circuit is when you want to add a device.

Building Codes

Homes and the electrical and plumbing systems in them must conform to what are known as building codes, which are specifications on what is and is not allowed. Codes vary, but the ultimate authority is your local building code authority. Before you launch any major remodel—or your contractor does—the plan should be checked with them for compliance.

Terms

A number of terms are used when talking about electricity:

Volt. This is the unit used to measure the pressure at which electricity flows through wires. In normal house wiring, it would be 117-120 volts, commonly referred to as 110; or 240 volts, commonly referred to as 220 volts. The lower figures are used because in practice voltage can vary, but normally the lower amounts come into the house.

Ampere. Also referred to as amps, or amperage, this describes the rate at which electrical current flows through a circuit. A normal circuit for lights is 15 amps; larger appliances use 20 to 50 amps, and one entire circuit may be needed for just one appliance. You might think of amperage as the amount of electricity that is used and voltage as the push behind it.

Watt. This is the unit that measures electrical power drain, in terms of both voltage and amperage. Wattage describes the amount of electricity one uses. To determine how much electricity is used, you multiply the number of volts a device uses by its amperage. For example, a toaster might be rated at 6 amps, and if the voltage is 110, it would use 660 watts. To calculate your electrical bill, the utility company charges so much per watt per hour—1,000 watts for one hour equals 1,000 watt-hours, which equals 1 kilowatt-hour.

Circuit breaker. This is a safety device that shuts off the flow of electricity if the wires are carrying too much current. It becomes overloaded when the electricity being used by the total number of devices in operation exceeds the amperage capacity of the circuit. A fuse serves the same purpose. If the current flow were not shut off, the excess current could burn up the wires and start a fire.

Electric service panel. This is the common name for the fuse box and circuit breaker panel.

Short circuit. This occurs when, for some reason, the circuit the electricity takes is shorter than it should be. That is, it doesn't travel all the way through the hot wire, into the device, and back to the panel.

Overload. This occurs when wires carry too much current—overloaded wires can burn up (as in the common expression for someone under stress: "Their circuits are overloaded").

Alternating current. This is the type of power used in all farm and home wiring systems. It is commonly called AC.

CHAPTER

2

The home handyperson (or one who would venture into these uncharted waters) should have a variety of tools in his or her arsenal for home repair, maintenance, and improvement projects around the house. Following is a basic lineup, tips on use, and, of course, that extraordinarily interesting subject, safe use of tools. (Other sections of the book suggest specific tools you might use when doing a particular project, such as painting or hanging wallcoverings.)

Choosing and Using Tools

Claw Hammers

The main use of the carpenter's hammer is to drive or draw (pull) nails. The hammer has either a curved or a straight claw and comes with a slot in the claw for pulling nails. It is available in various weights; lift the tool at the store to see what size you can handle.

> ### Money-Saving Tip
> $ It pays to shop around for tools. Just recently I priced tape measures, and the same model cost anywhere from $8 (home center) to $22 (local hardware store).

Using a Hammer

Except for light blows, hold the handle close to the end with four fingers underneath and the thumb along the side or on top of the handle. The thumb should rest on the handle, not overlap the fingers. To drive a nail, hold it down near the point and straight on the surface. Give it a few light taps to get it started (holding the hammer closer to the head). Then follow with full-force blows, whipping your wrist

for maximum power. If you don't want to risk damaging the work, drive the nail to within a fraction of the surface, then drive it the rest of the way with a nailset. A nailset looks like any extra thick nail with a small blunt end.

The way to hold a hammer

Pulling Nails

You can pull small nails simply by slipping the claw of the hammer over the head and prying backward. For large nails, however, you can get extra leverage if you place a small block of wood under the hammer before pulling back.

> ### Safety Tip
> If the hammer is made of wood, make sure that the head is on tightly. Also, don't strike metal with the hammer—metal chips could fly.

Saws

Wood-cutting handsaws come in a variety of types. The most useful for the DIYer (do-it-yourselfer) is the so-called crosscut saw, which is for cutting boards across or at an angle to the grain of the wood.

Saws come with varying numbers of teeth per inch. The more teeth the saw has, the smoother the cut will be. For general use, one with eight teeth per inch will serve well. A 26-inch blade is a preferred size. To tell quality, look for a springy, well-finished blade.

Using a Saw

Before using a saw, be sure that there are no nails or other objects in the line of the cut that can destroy the teeth of the saw. When sawing out a strip of waste, do not break out the strip by twisting the saw blade. Doing so dulls the saw and may spring or break the blade. A saw that is not being used should be hung up or stored in a toolbox.

Correct angle to hold saw

> ### Money-Saving Tip
> If you have a good saw that has become dull, don't throw it out. It can be sharpened. Check your Yellow Pages for a sharpening company.

Be sure that the saw will go through the full stroke without striking the floor or some object. If the work cannot be raised high enough to obtain full clearance for the saw, you must carefully limit the length of each stroke so the blade doesn't bang into anything. When possible, use a sawhorse or something else that can elevate the material being cut and clear it from obstacles. Short boards stock are more easily cut when they are held in a vise.

Hold the saw in the right hand (or the left hand, if you are left handed) and extend the first finger along the handle. Grasp the board and take a position so that an imaginary line passing lengthwise along the right forearm is at an angle of approximately 45 degrees with the face of the board. Be sure that the side of the saw is *plumb*, or at right angles, with the board face. Draw a line on the board where you want to cut, and place the heel of the saw on the edge of the mark. Keep the saw in line with the forearm and pull it toward you to start the cut.

To begin sawing, take short, light strokes, gradually increasing the strokes to the full length of the saw. Do not force or jerk the saw. The arm that does the sawing should swing clear of your body so that the handle of the saw passes your side rather than in front of you.

Use one hand to operate the saw. You may be tempted to use both hands at times, but if your saw is sharp, one hand will serve you better. The weight of the saw is sufficient to make it cut. If the saw sticks or binds, it may be because it is dull, the wood has too much moisture in it, or the blade is off the cutline.

Keep your eye on the line rather than on the saw while sawing. Watching the line lets you see instantly any tendency to leave it. A slight twist of the handle and taking short strokes while sawing will bring the saw back. Blow away the sawdust frequently so that you can see the line.

Final strokes of the cut should be taken slowly. Hold the waste piece in your free hand so that the stock will not split when you take the last stroke.

Money-Saving Tip

$ Buying tools by catalog can be much cheaper than going into a store, and the quality is good. Some catalogs I've used successfully include Trendlines, Tool Crib, Tools On Sale, and Harbor Freight Tools. Call the 800 number directory assistance for more information.

Screwdrivers

A screwdriver is the most basic of hand tools. It is also the most frequently abused; it is used for everything from prying to scraping. Thus, it rapidly becomes an ex-screwdriver.

Standard screwdrivers are classified by size, according to the combined length of the shank and blade. The most common sizes range in length from $2\frac{1}{2}$ to 12 inches. There are many smaller and some larger for special purposes. The diameter of the shank and the width and thickness of the blade are generally proportionate to the length, but again there are special screwdrivers with long thin shanks, short thick shanks, and extra wide or extra narrow blades.

Screwdriver handles may be made of wood, plastic, or metal. When metal handles are used, a wooden hand grip is usually placed on each side of the handle. In some types of wood- or plastic-handled screwdrivers, the shank extends through the handle; in others the shank enters the handle only a short way and is pinned to it. For heavy work, special types of screwdrivers with a square shank are made. They are designed in this way so that they may be gripped with a wrench, but these types are the only kind on which a wrench should be used.

Using a Screwdriver

When you use a screwdriver, it is important to select the proper size (so that the blade fits the screw slot properly) and to keep the blade perpendicular. A regular screwdriver has a straight slot, and the blade fits into a straight-slotted screw.

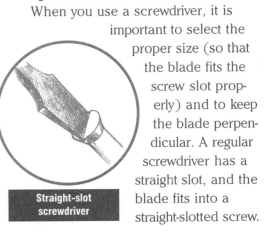

Straight-slot screwdriver

Another type of screwdriver is the Phillips (named after Henry Phillips, who invented it in the 1930s). The head of a Phillips-type screw has a four-way slot into which the screwdriver fits. Three standard-sized Phillips screwdrivers handle a wide range of screw sizes, and

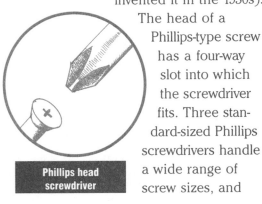

Phillips head screwdriver

their ability to hold helps to prevent damage to the slots or the work surrounding the screw.

Wrenches

A wrench is a basic plumbing tool that is used to twist bolts, nuts, studs, and pipes. There is a variety of types available, but for the DIYer a few will serve.

Adjustable open end. This type of wrench is commonly known by one brand name, Crescent. It has smooth, adjustable jaws and comes in a variety of lengths. The longer the tool the wider the jaws open.

This tool is particularly good for turning nuts that are smooth and for surfaces where

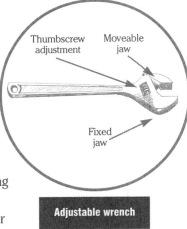

Thumbscrew adjustment · Moveable jaw · Fixed jaw

Adjustable wrench

you don't want to leave scratches, such as on faucet chrome. A 10-inch size should serve quite well.

Pipe Wrench. Also known as a Stilson or monkey wrench, this wrench comes in various sizes and has grooved adjustable jaws. It is generally for turning pipes, but is also good for a variety of other jobs in which a concentrated turning force is required. A 10-inch size is about right.

Using a Wrench

Correct use of a wrench can be summed up in a few rules, the most important of which is to be sure that the wrench properly fits the nut or bolt head (it should be good and snug). When you have to pull hard on the wrench, as in loosening a tight nut, make sure that the wrench is seated squarely on the flats of the nut. Pull on the wrench—do not push. Pushing a wrench is a good way to skin your knuckles—the wrench can slip or the nut can break loose unexpectedly. If it is not possible to pull the wrench, and you must push, do it with the palm of your hand and hold your palm open.

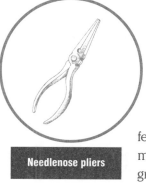

Needlenose pliers

Pliers

Pliers are made in many styles and sizes. They are used to perform many different operations, but mainly to hold and grip small objects in

situations where it may be inconvenient or impossible to use your hands.

Slipjoint pliers

Long-nosed pliers are less rugged, and break easily if you use them on heavy jobs. They are useful for holding small objects in tight places and for making delicate adjustments.

Slip-joint pliers have straight, serrated (grooved) jaws, and the screw or pivot with which the jaws are fastened together may be moved in two positions in order to grasp small- or large-sized objects better. To spread the jaws of slip-joint pliers, first spread the ends of the handles apart as far as possible. The slip-joint, or pivot, will move to the open position. To close, again spread the handles as far as possible; then push the joint back into the closed position.

Money-Saving Tip

$ Garage sales can be great sources of cheap tools. And if you think you'll only need a tool once, you can usually rent it from your local hardware store.

Vise-Grip Pliers

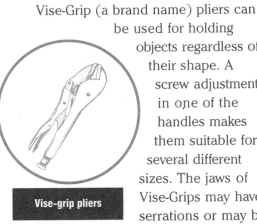

Vise-grip pliers

Vise-Grip (a brand name) pliers can be used for holding objects regardless of their shape. A screw adjustment in one of the handles makes them suitable for several different sizes. The jaws of Vise-Grips may have serrations or may be the clamp type. The serrated kind works best for general use.

Vise-Grips have an advantage over other types of pliers in that you can clamp them on an object and use both hands to apply turning force; a nut or bolt that wouldn't yield to one tool will yield to Vise-Grips. Vise-Grip pliers should be used with care, since the teeth in the jaws tend to damage the object on which they are clamped. Do not use them on nuts, bolts, tube fittings, or other objects that must be reused.

Water-Pump Pliers

Water-pump pliers were originally designed for tightening or removing water-

Land groove

Water-pump pliers

pump packing nuts. They are excellent for this job, because they have a jaw adjustable to seven different positions. The inner surface of the jaws is a series of coarse teeth adapted to grasp round objects. However, they can also be used on nuts, bolts, and the like. A big advantage is that their jaws open quite wide. Channel-lock (a brand name) pliers are another version of water-pump pliers.

Hacksaws

There are two parts to a hacksaw: the frame and the blade. Hacksaws have either an adjustable or a solid frame. Adjustable frames can be made to hold blades from 8 to 16 inches long; those with solid frames take only the blade length for which they are designed. The adjustable type is recommended.

Hacksaw blades are made of high-grade tool steel, hardened and tempered. There are two types, the all-hard and the flexible. All-hard blades are hardened throughout; only the teeth of the flexible blades are hard. Hacksaw blades are about $1/2$ inch wide and have from 14 to 32 teeth per inch (the more teeth the smoother the cut). They are from 8 to 16 inches long and have a hole at each end that hooks to a pin in the frame. All hacksaw frames that hold the blades either parallel or at right angles to the frame are provided with a wing nut or screw to permit tightening or removing the blade.

Using a Hacksaw

Good work with a hacksaw depends not only on proper use of the saw but also on the type of blade used. Coarse blades with fewer teeth per inch cut faster and are less liable to get stuck with chips. However, finer blades with more teeth per inch are necessary when you are cutting something thin.

The way to hold a hacksaw

To make the cut, first install the blade in the hacksaw frame so that the teeth point away from the handle. Tighten the wing nut so that the blade is under tension; this helps make straight cuts.

Place the pipe or object to be cut in a vise. (Metal that is too thin to be held in a vise can be placed between blocks of wood.) A minimum of overhang reduces vibration, gives a better cut, and lengthens the life of the blade. Have the cutting line outside of the jaw of the vise so that the line is visible while you work.

Grip the hacksaw so that your forefinger points straight and rests on the frame. When cutting, let your body sway back and forth with each stroke. Apply pressure on the forward stroke, which is the cutting stroke, but not on the return stroke. From forty to fifty strokes per minute is the usual speed. Long, slow, steady strokes are best.

Safety Tip

The main danger in using hacksaws is injury to your hand if the blade breaks. The blade can break if too much pressure is applied, if the saw is twisted, if the cutting speed is too fast, or if the blade is loose in the frame. Additionally, if the work is not tight in the vise, it will sometimes slip, twisting the blade enough to break it.

Chisels

Chisels are used for chipping or cutting metal (or wood). They are made from a good grade of tool steel and have a hardened cutting edge and beveled head. They will cut any material that is softer than that which they are made of.

The kind of chisel most commonly used is the cold chisel. It is used to split nuts; chip castings; cut rivets, thin metal sheets, and cast-iron pipe; and, most importantly, repair concrete.

Using a Chisel

As a general rule, hold the chisel in the left hand (assuming you're right handed), with the thumb and first finger about one inch from the top. It should be held steadily but not tightly. The finger muscles should be relaxed, so that if the hammer strikes the hand, the hand can slide down the tool, lessening the effect of the blow.

Cold chisel

Safety Tip

When using a chisel for chipping, always wear glasses or goggles to protect your eyes from flying chips.

Files

There are a number of different types of files in common use, and each type may range in length from 3 to 18 inches. Files are graded according to the degree of fineness, and they come in different shapes.

Protect file teeth by hanging your files in a rack when they are not in use or by placing them in drawers with wooden partitions. Files should not be allowed to rust—keep them away from moisture. Avoid getting the files oily. Oil causes a file to slide across the work and prevents fast, clean cutting. Files that you keep in your toolbox should be wrapped in paper or cloth to protect their teeth and prevent damage to other tools.

Safety Tip

Never use a file unless it is equipped with a tight-fitting handle. If you use a file without the handle and it bumps something or jams, the tang (the part the handle fits onto) may be driven into your hand.

Vises and Clamps

Vises are used for holding work when it is being sawed, drilled, shaped, sharpened, riveted, or glued. Clamps are used for holding work that cannot be satisfactorily held in a vise, either because of its shape and size or because a vise is not available. Clamps are generally used for light work.

Although there are various kinds, a machinist's bench vise works well. It is a large steel vise with rough jaws that prevent work from slipping. Most of these vises have a swivel base with jaws that can be rotated. A similar light-duty model is equipped with a cutoff. These vises are usually mounted on a workbench.

C clamps

Clamps are in the same family, and for the handyperson the most important is the "C" clamp. (It is shaped like the letter *C*.) As you turn the screw, the ends of the "C" clamp hold onto the item.

Electric Drills

There is a wide variety of portable and stationary power tools the DIYer can use, but the one essential power tool is the electric drill. Electric drills come cordless and corded. The former runs on battery power or has been electrically charged; the latter has an electrical cord to plug into an electrical outlet while in use.

Drills are characterized according to "chuck" size, which refers to the diameter of the largest drill bit that can be accepted. For DIYers, this is commonly $3/8$ inch or $1/2$ inch, with the $3/8$ inch preferred. The $1/2$-inch size is for heavy work. Electric drills accept various bits, for drilling a variety of holes in different materials and driving and pulling (by setting the drill on reverse) screws.

I favor the cordless drill for light use. It has enough power for most jobs around the house, and you don't have to worry about an outlet to plug it into. For heavy use, the corded type is best; you can use it indefinitely.

Drills come insulated to protect against shock. They also come in various qualities. For the home, a 7.5 horsepower drill is about right.

Electric drill

Opens More than Beer Cans

A hook-type beer can opener is an excellent do-it-yourself tool. It can be used for digging out old caulking, opening up cracks for plastering, as well as for opening up paint and other cans.

Measuring Tools

Steel Tape. For long measurements, use a 12-foot steel tape. It is nice and compact, and very seldom do you have to lay it out more than twice on one measurement. (Very few rooms run more than 24 feet long. In cases where you are measuring something extra long, you can use a 50- or 100-foot tape and measure it all in one shot.)

Framing square

For small carpentry work, such as marking off boards or molding up to 8 feet long, a folding wood ruler is convenient and has certain advantages over a tape—it's stiffer and will brace against a wall. I don't recommend a yardstick when accuracy is important.

Squares. There are three different kinds of squares used in carpentry. The framing square is an *L*-shaped piece of flat steel, 16 inches on one leg and 24 inches on the other. It's made to this size for convenience in laying out 16-inch centers, a common distance between frame members, such as roof rafters. Its large size is an advantage for various other kinds of layout work.

Tri-Square. Another kind of square is the tri-square. It comes in various small sizes up to 12 inches and consists of a metal blade and a wooden section. It's good for 45- and 90-degree angle checks. It's also good for checking the end of a board to see if it's square. It's easier to hold tight against the edge of the board to mark than a framing square, which you must hold down at a little angle and thus risk not being exact.

Adjustable Square. This is similar to the tri-square in that you can check 90- and 45-degree angles, but the blade can slide back and forth. As such, you can set the blade for an exact size: Set a pencil on the end of it and, by moving the square along the board edge, make a line exactly parallel to it.

For accurately marking 45-degree angles on big pieces of wood, the framing square is better than the adjustable. To use the adjustable, you have to lay the nonblade section on the edge of the board; a bit of grit or sawdust could throw it off. With a framing square, you just align numbers on opposite legs of the square with the board edge and

Adjustable square

draw your angle. As long as those numbers are accurately aligned on the edge, you can't go wrong.

Chalkline. This is the tool for marking straight lines. It consists of a string coiled in a chalk box. To mark a straight line you pull the string out, place one end over one mark and the other end over another mark, pull the string tight in place, and then snap it. A perfectly straight line is marked.

Level. This is another essential tool. There are wood and metal levels. I have no particular preference. Some have the bubble vials fixed; some more expensive ones have adjustable bubble vials. I don't know if that's necessarily an advantage, except that you can correct the level when it's wrong, which can happen if it gets jarred.

When leveling, place the level horizontally and vertically on the piece, turning it

Chalkline

Level

end for end each time. It should read correctly in all directions, with the bubble perfectly centered. If it doesn't, the work isn't level—or your level is inaccurate.

Always wipe the surface of the level clean before use. Even a speck of sawdust can throw it off.

Plumb Bob. This is a tear-drop shaped, pointed weight on a string. One of its major uses is to help you mark perfectly vertical lines on a wall.

To do this, hang it with a nail from the ceiling (or have a helper hold the end), so that the bob is just clear of the wall at the floor. The string shouldn't touch anything, either. (A bump on the wall can throw it off.) When it's perfectly still, stand directly in front of the string, look at the wall, and mark directly behind the string—one mark close to the ceiling and one close to the floor. Then close one eye and sight the two marks behind the string; the string must obscure both marks simultaneously. If this is the case, and one mark is

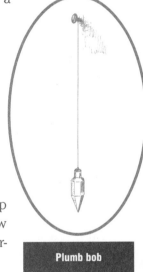

Plumb bob

Measuring in General

When measuring anything, you should always take an overall measurement. Then add up component sizes and see if the figures are the same. Also, measure two ways and see if you get the same figures twice.

If you're building something that requires precise measuring, such as a cabinet, a good way to avoid problems is to lay things out so that all the openings come out in even inches, making up the odd amounts on the widths of the wood members. You can't always do that, but it's good to keep it in mind.

It's also a good idea to know the exact sizes of components before you start to build. For example, if you're going to use ready-made shutters as doors on a cabinet, find out just what size the shutters are before you buy. That way you can adjust your cabinet size to the shutter you have to buy.

On some jobs, no tape or ruler is needed. Knowing component size allows this. For instance, you can measure roof shingles from the ground by just counting them. Shingles are 5 inches "to the weather" (each shingle course is exposed 5 inches). Just count across the edge of the roof, multiply by 5, and divide by 12 to know how many feet of width you have. Shingle tabs are 1-foot long, so you count them across the face of the roof to figure out the length. If you are measuring for ceiling or floor tiles, you can do the same thing. When ordering the material, add a little for waste.

directly below the other, simply draw a chalkline across the marks and snap it. Your line will be perfectly straight.

You can also use the plumb bob for long distances, such as establishing a vertical line down a second-floor stairwell. You can use it to check if a wall itself is plumb. Just hold the line at the ceiling so it hangs down an inch or so away from the wall. If there is a bow or bump, the string will pass closer to the wall. A plumb bob also comes in handy for lining up wallpaper or paneling strips.

For making straight lines for short distances, you don't necessarily need a plumb bob. Instead, you can use a long (4 feet) level. You can also use a straightedge and a level.

First position

Second position

Ways to use a level

CHAPTER

3

Useful Fasteners

In the course of human events—and doing it yourself—it is well to have some basic facts at your command regarding common fasteners used around the house. The following is a potpourri, plus some useful tips.

Nails

Nails are generally available in sizes that range from 1 to 6 inches long; as the nail gets longer, the diameter gets correspondingly thicker. When speaking of size, nails are referred to by weight and number. Weight is expressed by the letter *d* and stands for pennyweight (the way nails used to be sold), with sizes running from 2d (1 inch) to 60d (6 inches).

There are many different kinds of nails available, some of which can serve a variety of purposes; others are more specialized in their use (roofing nails, for example). There should be no reason why you can't use a nail that is ideally suited to the job at hand.

Common Nails. As the name implies, this nail is used for a wide variety of fastening purposes. Most people use common nails for general construction-type work—framing and the like. The common nail comes in a wide range of sizes and has a large, flat head that provides a good-sized hitting surface and acts like a washer in holding the nail in place. Common sizes are 4d, 6d, 8d, and 10d.

Box Nails. A variation of the common nail is the box nail. It is like the common type, but thinner, and good to use where a thicker common style might split the wood.

Finish Nails. The finish nail is perhaps the second most popular nail. It is thinner than the common type, but its main feature is its small head. The nail is designed for assembling work where you don't want the nailheads to show. After the nail is driven flush with the surface, a nailset is used to sink (technically known as countersink) the cupped head beneath the surface of the wood, and the cavity above it is filled with wood putty. When sanded and finished, it is difficult to determine where the nail is. In the very small sizes, usually up to 1½ inches long, finishing nails are called *brads*.

Casing Nails. A variation on the finishing nail is the casing nail. It gets its name from its primary use on case molding, or rough trim. It is thicker and stronger than the regular finish nail and, though the appearance is similar, its head is flat rather than cupped. As such it is not designed to be countersunk below the surface, but instead is driven flush with the surface and then simply painted over.

Common and finishing nails generally come without a finish—they're just plain steel. But both types are available in a galvanized finish, either coated or hot dipped. Both common and finishing nails are also available in a blued finish, which is not rustproof.

Ornamental Nails. Ornamental nails have large, fancy, oval heads and are mainly for securing upholstery. The finish is commonly either brass or chrome plated.

Tacks. Tacks commonly come in various sizes but are usually classified by number. They are generally available in a blued finish or in copper; copper tacks are impervious to weather. Although the latter are commonly used in marine applications, they also have good uses around the home, such as for securing webbing to patio furniture. Tacks are usually called carpet tacks, which describes their main function of securing rugs and carpets to floors.

Roofing Nails. A roofing nail has an extra-large head and a barbed shank. It is designed to hold shingles, roofing paper, and the like to roofs without damaging the material (the large head prevents the roofing from pulling loose through the nailhead). They come in various sizes; the most common are $3/8$ inch, $7/8$ inch, and $1^{1}/4$ inch. The size you use depends on the thickness of the material being installed.

Drywall Nails. For securing Sheetrock, the drywall nail has a countersunk head (depressed in the center) and a partially barbed shank; the barbed part is down near the end. When the nail passes through the drywall, the part that bites into the stud grabs fast. It is available in a few sizes so you can get them deep enough to go through whatever thickness of Sheetrock you are using. The drywall nailhead also dimples the paper covering on the drywall so that when a joint compound is applied, it covers the head, leaving no trace of it.

Spiral Nails. This nail is also known as a drive screw. It has a spiral shank that rotates when you drive the nail and gives the nail a tremendous grip on the wood, probably the greatest of any nail. The nail is normally used for securing flooring, but it can be used on any kind of rough carpentry.

Masonry Nails. Masonry nails come in a variety of sizes and lengths. The size you use depends on what you want to fasten or support.

The nail is made of tempered, case-hardened steel. It has to be; it is designed to be driven into masonry. (You must use a heavy hammer, and, as one might guess, it's important to protect your eyes against flying masonry chips.) A common application for the masonry nail is to hang studding (2 x 4's) on a block wall.

Panel Nails. You can buy small, colored nails to match the paneling you're using. This saves the job of having to countersink brads and fill depressions with wood putty. Just tap the nail in place and its head color will not be noticeable.

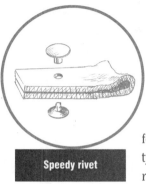

Speedy rivet

Miscellaneous Fasteners

Speedy Rivets.

These fasteners (Speedy is a brand name) are for joining various types of soft materials such as canvas or leather and canvas. To install one, a hole is punched in the material, and the riveted portion of the fastener slipped through. The other section is then placed over it, and the rivet is whacked with a hammer, joining the material. Some kinds of Speedy rivets require a special clamping tool for joining, instead of a hammer.

Tee Nut Fasteners.

A situation may arise in which you need a threaded core in wood for a machine screw. For example, you may want to join a pair of 2 x 4's this way. For this kind of job, use a Tee Nut fastener. It is mounted in a drilled hole in one of the boards; a machine screw is then passed through a drilled hole in the other 2 x 4 and into the threaded core.

Pop Rivets.

In the past, sheet metal screws were used to connect gutter sections and fittings. Today the blind rivet gun—more popularly known by the brand name of one gun, the

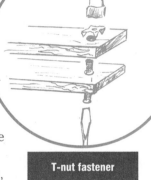

T-nut fastener

Pop Rivet Tool (by the USM Company)—is used extensively. It is faster and just as secure.

To use it, the shank of a rivet is stuck into the nose of the gun; the rivet itself protrudes. The rivet is then stuck through the hole, and the tool handles are squeezed; the rivet compresses, locking the parts together. When the rivet

Gun

Pin

Pin snaps off

Pop rivet — Rivet inserted into hole, handle squeezed to lock in place

is fully compressed, the shank is clipped off by the tool.

The beauty of this tool is that it installs blind rivets. You don't need access to the two sides of an item in order to be able to rivet it—as you would, for example, if you wanted to put two parts together with a nut and bolt.

Many metal items can be repaired this way, including toys, bikes, and appliances. The tool can also be used for joining fabric.

Rivets are available in a variety of sizes. When using them, two things should be remembered: The hole drilled (punched) must be the same diameter as the rivet, and you must use a rivet that is large (deep) enough to join whatever it is you want joined.

Nail Tip

When using a nail, there are a couple of points (no pun intended) to keep in mind: When fastening two objects together, the nail should penetrate approximately ¾ of the way through both. Choose a nail length accordingly. And, if you are working on very hard wood, there is a danger of splitting the wood with a thick nail. To avoid this, give thought to using two smaller, thinner nails. You can get the same (or better) holding power without the risk of splitting the material.

Money-Saving Tip

You can buy nails carded, loose, and in brown paper bags and boxes. The worst way to buy nails is carded. They are much more expensive this way than buying them loose. In fact, you should never buy anything carded.

Nuts and Bolts

Nuts and bolts are for assembling things where you need great strength. In such cases, screws or nails simply aren't strong enough.

Lag Screws. A lag screw is for use in wood. It is partially threaded, like a screw, and tapered; and its head is most often square in shape, though it may be hexagonal.

Lag screws are very strong fasteners. They are used mostly in the small sizes (½ to 6 inches long) for a very practical reason: They must be turned with a wrench—either an adjustable wrench or a socket wrench (which may be used on those with hexagonal heads). In

Lag screw

the very large sizes, they would be simply too big to turn.

You can think of a lag screw—in bigger sizes—as a screw that takes over for a regular screw when real holding power is required. It is heartily recommended that you drill pilot holes and shank holes for lag screws.

Carriage Bolts.

Carriage bolts get their name from the fact that they used to be the fasteners for assembling horse-drawn carriages. To install one, a hole is drilled the diameter of the shank. The bolt is slipped through the hole until it reaches a point directly under the head where the shank is square. The bolt is then driven into the wood with a hammer, thereby countersinking it and locking it in place so that it can't turn. A washer or nut can be threaded on the protruding end without having to hold the bolt. You can use carriage bolts in wood in operations where an exposed head is not going to be in the way.

Machine Bolts. A machine bolt has a large square head and is installed like a carriage bolt, except that there is no

Carriage bolt

square portion under the head, and it must be handheld when the nuts are run on it. It comes in various sizes. Machine bolts may be used on metal and wood items. It is possible to exert good tension on a machine bolt because it is tightened with wrenches—one on the nut and another on the head.

Carriage and machine bolts come in two styles: rolled and cut thread. The cut thread is better. Here, the manufacturer cuts the thread right into the steel shaft. In making the rolled kind, the thread is rolled onto the shaft separately. The reason is that less metal is used. In the smaller sizes, it doesn't matter. However, in the larger sizes a problem can occur: The shank, or smooth part of the bolt, may fit the drilled hole perfectly, but the rolled (threaded) part may not. And, if you drill a hole for the threads to fit, the shank becomes a loose, sloppy fit.

Nuts are used on both machine and carriage bolts. Washers should be used on softwood, where you don't want the nut to dig into the wood or damage it. A common use is in hardwood outdoor furniture. If a carriage or

Machine bolt

machine bolt has a tendency to work loose, use a lock washer under it. Once tightened, these washers won't move.

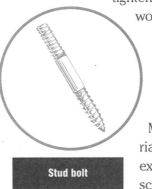

Stud bolt

All three kinds of bolts—machine, lag, and carriage—are available in a variety of finishes. Machine and carriage bolts are more expensive than lag screws, so if you have a choice, use a lag screw whenever possible.

Stud Bolts. This device has lag screw threads on one end and machine screw threads on the other, with a smooth portion in between. It is commonly used to assemble furniture: The lag screw portion is screwed into the frame of the piece; the machine screw portion screws into a threaded socket in the leg.

Hence, when the leg gets loose, you can turn the nut to tighten it.

The practical value of a stud bolt for the do-it-yourselfer is for hanging fixtures. For example, in a garage

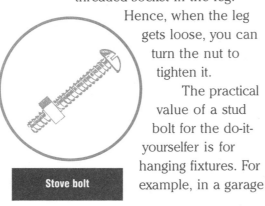

Stove bolt

the lag screw portion could be sunk into a joist or ceiling beam, and the fixture, which has a threaded hole, could be screwed onto the projecting machine screw part.

Eyebolts. The bolt is classified by shank size; the eye size is fixed. These bolts are commonly used for hanging clothesline and are used with nuts. They come galvanized or zinc plated.

Stove Bolts. A stove bolt is used to join pieces of metal. It is slotted and is commonly used in the smaller sizes, for example, $1/8$ inch. Stove bolts are also used in assembling metal shelves.

Double-Nutting

If you want to create greater tension on a machine or carriage bolt, use two nuts (a practice referred to as double-nutting). Double-nutting is used when assembling the components of a workbench, which is subject to a lot of vibration. Lock washers are also good in this situation.

Other Nuts. In addition to the standard nuts used on carriage and machine bolts, there are a few other common ones you should know about. One is the cap nut, also called an acorn nut, which is used where looks count. Another is the wing nut, which is used when you expect to periodically disassemble something. Another useful nut, called an elastic stop nut, has a pylon insert and is self-locking. It acts like a double nut or lock washer and provides a higher degree of tension or holding power.

Screws

Screws are on a par with nails in terms of usefulness to the do-it-yourselfer. However, they are stronger than nails and have the advantage of removability—you can disassemble the job at will.

There are four things to consider when selecting a screw for the job: finish, length, weight or gauge, and head. They can be plain steel, blued, and dipped.

Screws range in size up to about 4 inches. When you get beyond 4 inches, they become difficult to turn. In such cases, consider using a lag bolt, which is turned with a wrench. The length you use depends on the thickness of the material you're using. The screw should be about $1/8$" shorter than the total thickness of the material you're driving it into.

Screws are also classified according to the diameter or gauge, commonly ranging from no. 5 to no. 14, though larger sizes are available. The gauge refers to the diameter under the head. Because the screw tapers, the gauge gets smaller as the screw gets thinner. Screws of the same gauge are available in different lengths. Screw sizes are always given in terms of length and gauge, for example, $1/2$ inch x no. 8.

Screws have three head styles: flat, round, and oval. Flathead screws have a countersunk head, meaning that they are tapered to be recessed or sunk flush into the wood. To do this, you first drill a pilot hole that is as thick as the threaded part would be without the threads.

Roundhead screws are easier screws to turn down tight. For greater holding power you can put washers under them. Because their heads are meant to be left exposed, roundhead screws are often used in utility work where appearance is not a concern.

Ovalhead screws have heads that are partially recessed. They are decorative screws and, as such, normally come with a brass or chrome-plated finish.

Head styles may also vary in turning design. There are many different kinds, but the most popular are the straight slot and the Phillips. The slotted head has just that—a slot across the head of the screw. The Phillips head has crisscross slots and is turned with a Phillips screwdriver. The latter is supposed to allow more turning power to be applied, but in home application this isn't a factor. The straight slot works just fine.

Machine Screws. These screws are completely threaded and have flat ends and heads that may be either round or flat. They come in noncorrosive materials, such as brass and chrome plate, and also plain steel. Machine screws, so called because their original use was in metal machinery parts, are generally used with items that are threaded. For example, they are commonly used with hollow wall anchors (Mollies).

They come in various gauges—nos. 4, 6, 8, 10, and 12—and the larger the gauge, the heavier the diameter.

Machine screws are also characterized by the number of threads per inch. They may have either 24 or 32 threads to the inch. The former is called the National Coarse Thread, the latter the National Fine Thread. Screws are designated by gauge and threads. For example, a 10-32 screw is one that has a no. 10 gauge and 32 threads to the inch; an 8-24 is a no. 8 gauge with 24 threads to the inch. The finer the thread a screw has, the better it will grip.

Machine screws come in lengths of from $1/2$ to 4 inches. They are not very strong screws and are generally used in fastening lightweight materials. If you are fastening something like thin-gauge sheet metal, the screws should be used with washers and nuts. Machine screws come carded and by the box.

Sheet Metal Screws. These differ from wood screws in a number of ways, but chiefly in that there is no smooth shank part: The screw is threaded all the way from the tip to under the head.

Sheet metal screws are designed to drill their own thread. They are for use in thin-gauge sheet metal, for example, for holding parts on aluminum storm doors. Head styles vary, but the panhead with the single slot is the most popular and is adequate for most purposes.

Pilot hole

Slightly smaller than screw

Pilot hole

Pilot Holes

Pilot holes should be drilled for all screws driven into hardwood. Otherwise, you will have great difficulty driving them, and the wood may split. In softwood, such as pine, pilot holes are not required. When drilling pilot holes, make sure that they are slightly thinner than the screw to be placed in them. This job can be greatly simplified by using one of the commercially available countersinking devices, such as Stanley's Screwmate.

Loosening a Balky Whatever

To loosen a frozen nut, screw, bolt, or other threaded fastener, try tapping it with a hammer a bit, and then try to turn it; or spray WD-40 on it; or, if safe, heat it.

Staples

Carpentry staples (as opposed to the ones used for electrical wire) are *U*-shaped with pointed ends and are driven in place with a hammer. When the staple is driven, the legs spread, giving it better gripping action.

Staples are commonly available in galvanized finishes only. This is because they are designed for exterior use—for anchoring cable, securing fencing to posts, and the like. Sizes commonly are in the $7/8$-inch to $1^1/4$-inch range, though much larger staples may be purchased.

Corrugated Fasteners

These fasteners are small pieces of metal in corrugated form with one edge sharpened. They are strictly for joining wood edge to edge—jobs where nails would be unsuitable or difficult to use. For example, if you wanted to create a 24-inch wide board and couldn't buy it in that size, you could lay two 12-inch pieces edge to edge and join them with corrugated fasteners driven in from the top.

Wall Fasteners

Wall fasteners are useful where screws or nails can't work—that is, where there's no solid surface, such as a stud, for the nail or screw to bite into. These devices can also be used on ceilings.

At first glance there is a bewildering array of fasteners. However, there are three basic kinds: expansion shields for masonry, toggle bolts, and hollow wall anchors.

Expansion shield

Drilled hole

Shield inserted

Item screwed on

How expansion shield is used

Expansion Shields for Masonry. The expansion shield is for hanging things on masonry surfaces. It consists of a sleeve and a screw. To use it, a hole the diameter of the sleeve is drilled in the masonry. The sleeve, which may be lead, fiber, or plastic, is then slipped into the hole. A screw—either a lag screw or wood screw, depending on what you're hanging—is then slipped or driven through a hole in the item to be fastened and into the sleeve, and then tightened. As it is, it cuts its own thread, expanding the sleeve and locking it into the wall. It should be noted that the size screw used should be long enough to be able to pass through the item to be hung and penetrate beyond the end of the sleeve.

An exception to this screw-in type of installation is the kind of device that is hammered into place. One such device is the Tampin (Star). Here a machine screw is used. A hole the diameter of a prethreaded sleeve with a lead section on the bottom is drilled. The sleeve is slipped into the hole; then the machine screw is slipped through a hole

Toggle bolt is slipped into hole

in the item to be fastened and screwed down in the sleeve. The head is whacked with a special setting tool, and the lead mushrooms, locking the sleeve into place. This type of fastener is useful if you are hanging something that is threaded to accept a machine screw; the lag or wood screw, of course, wouldn't work.

Expansion shields are available in a wide variety of sizes. The bigger the device, the heavier the weight it will support.

Toggle Bolts. If you want to hang something on hollow wall construction, chiefly drywall (Sheetrock) but also on wood and plaster where there is space inside the wall, a toggle bolt may be used. There are two kinds of toggle bolts. Each consists of a machine screw with collapsible "wings" threaded on it. On one the wings are spring loaded—when squeezed together and released, they open; on the other type, the wings are not spring loaded (these are cheaper).

To use a spring-loaded toggle bolt, a hole is drilled in the wall, one large enough so that the toggle bolt, with its wings folded back, can be passed through. The wings are removed from the screw, the screw slipped through the item to be hung, and the wings screwed back on. The wings are folded back and the fastener slipped through the hole in the wall. Inside the wall, they pop open. The screw is run down by hand, then tightened

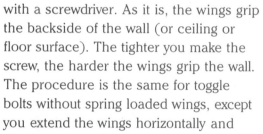

Inside, wings snap out

with a screwdriver. As it is, the wings grip the backside of the wall (or ceiling or floor surface). The tighter you make the screw, the harder the wings grip the wall. The procedure is the same for toggle bolts without spring loaded wings, except you extend the wings horizontally and slip them through the hole; inside the wall the wings open automatically.

It is important to remember to pass the screw through the item before slipping the toggle into the wall. Once the wings

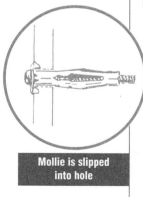

Mollie is slipped into hole

are inside, you can't back out the screw without the wings dropping off inside the wall, rendering the fastener useless.

Make sure that the wall cavity is deep enough to accept the toggle bolt. Toggle bolts come in very long sizes; if one is too long, the end of the screw will jam up against the backside of the other wall before you can run the screw all the way down.

There is a limit to how much weight you should put on a toggle bolt. If you are hanging something from a plaster or plaster-board wall, do not exceed 50 pounds per toggle bolt. But if you are hanging something from a plaster or plaster-board ceiling, each

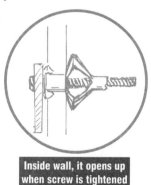

Inside wall, it opens up when screw is tightened

toggle should hold only about 5 pounds. Otherwise, the weight of the item could pull the fastener through the material. Instead, you should use woodscrews sunk in studs.

Hollow Wall Anchors. A toggle bolt is for one-time use. A fastener that can be used and reused but is also for hollow wall construction is the hollow wall anchor, commonly called a Molly (the brand name of the USM Company).

This fastener has its wings built on; it comes with a machine screw. To install the fastener, first drill a hole in the wall, slip the fastener through the hole and tap it with a hammer, and then tighten the screw. As the screw is tightened, the wings expand and eventually grip the backside of the wall. The screw is then removed, slipped through the item to be hung, and screwed back into the threaded sleeve in the wall. Thus, if you want to remove the item and replace it with another item, all you need to do is take out the screw.

Hollow wall anchors come in various sizes; they are based on the diameter of the machine screw used. The heavier the item, the larger the fastener must be.

When installing hollow wall anchors, remember that the hole drilled in the wall must be clean and the same diameter as the fastener. Otherwise the little prongs under the head may not be able to bite into the wall tightly when you tap it with a hammer; and as you turn the screw, the fastener will go around and around—it has no solid material to grip—and the wings won't expand. Use the drill bit size recommended by the manufacturer. If the fastener still goes round

and round, there is a tiny tool you can get free at the hardware store to hold it stationary.

Also, the size of the flange (the smooth area just below the head) must be equal in depth to the wall thickness—if the wall is $1/4$-inch thick, for example, the flange must be $1/4$-inch deep. If it isn't, the fastener will not be able to grip the surface properly.

Money-Saving Tip

In selecting hardware items, pay careful attention to the finish and metal used. Although some are better than others, it is the final application that should count. For example, you will pay about twice as much for a galvanized machine bolt than a plain one. In hardware, there can be too much of a good thing.

Hardware Finishes

Many items come with no finish at all—just a plain steel. Other items, such as bolts, are "oiled" (given a black oil-like coating). (In no way should oiled items be considered weather resistant.) However, confusion can reign when it comes to picking fasteners or hardware in general, especially in regard to the metal or finish used in making it. Following is some information that should clear things up.

Brass and Brass-Plated Finish. Many hardware items are made of pure brass. Brass is a fairly soft metal, but it is weatherproof. It may be used inside or outside the house. However, it has to be used with care around salt water, which causes corrosion.

Brass plated refers simply to steel that has been coated with brass. It is not weatherproof.

Bronze and Bronze-Plated Finish. Bronze is also available in pure form, and as such is weatherproof. Items made of it can be used inside or outside the house. It does not corrode; indeed, it is often used in marine applications. Bronze is also a very strong metal.

Bronze plated, like brass plated, refers simply to steel that is coated with bronze. Unlike pure bronze, however, it will not stand up to weather.

Galvanized Finish. *Galvanized* refers to a special kind of finish applied to steel items. The galvanizing may be hot-dipped or coated—technically, electroplated. The hot-dipped galvanizing is by far the superior of the two. Both are weatherproof. Most outdoor items are galvanized.

Zinc- or Cadmium-Plated Finish. (The terms *zinc* and *cadmium* are really synonymous.) Zinc- or cadmium-plated refers to a wash coating that is given to hardware that makes it rust resistant but not rustproof. Galvanized items are far superior to ones with a zinc or cadmium finish.

Blued Finish. This is not a finish but refers to a treatment given to items to keep them from rusting in the box while waiting to be sold.

Japanned Finish. This refers to a baked enamel finish. It is only about as weather resistant as items that are blued.

Chrome-Plated Finish. This refers to a highly polished finish used on cabinet hardware and many plumbing items. It is highly resistant to corrosion and quite good looking.

Construction Materials

A number of materials dominate when it comes to doing it yourself, materials that are used over and over again. Following is a look at these materials, as well as facts that will enable you to make better selections based on your needs.

Lumber

First of all, lumber is divided into softwoods and hardwoods. Both types follow different grading systems. Lumber is ordered and paid for according to nominal dimensions. Their actual dimensions are smaller due to the effects of milling and drying. Lumber prices are usually calculated by board foot, which is based on the size of the piece of lumber. Softwood lumber is manufactured and sold in standard sizes; hardwoods are milled in random lengths and widths to take advantage of every fractional inch of usable materials.

Softwood.

Softwood accounts for the greatest share of lumber sold. It is used for virtually every type of construction, from rough framing to interior trim to projects. Southern pine is the dominant species in use today; others include "whitewoods" like fir, spruce, and hemlock. Specialty softwoods, such as cypress, redwood, and cedar, are frequently used for exterior construction because of their natural resistance to decay. Pressure-treated lumber, an ideal choice for maintenance-free outdoor pro-

1 — Furniture Grade (clear)

2 — Common

3 — Construction Grade

Grades of lumber

jects, is softwood (usually pine) that has been chemically treated to resist weather, rot, and insect damage.

Hardwood. This is milled from slow-growing deciduous trees, such as birch, mahogany, and oak. Hardwood lumber is known as the premium lumber. More expensive than softwood, hardwood lumber is used primarily for cabinetry, furniture, millwork, trim, and fine flooring. Most lumberyards generally stock a limited assortment of hardwood species. So, for the best selection, buy from a yard specializing in this product.

Lumber Grades.

Experts consider lumber grading both an art and a science. (And sometimes it seems more complicated than training in brain surgery.)

Softwood lumber grades are based on visual and strength properties. Classifying softwood boards into two broad grading categories—select and common—makes it easier to choose the wood best suited for the project at hand.

Money-Saving Tip

$ Try to design projects so there is little waste. Lumber is available in even lengths (8 feet, 10 feet, etc.). Therefore, design projects according to those lengths rather than odd-number lengths, which will result in waste.

Use select lumber (grades B and Better, C, and D) for trim, cabinetry, and anywhere else that appearance is a primary concern. Use common lumber (nos. 1, 2, 3, and 4) for general-purpose carpentry. And use 2 x 4-inch stud-grade lumber for framing applications.

Structural lumber is graded according to strength for specific engineering applications. Lumber grade is based primarily on the number of defects on the surface of each board. The "clearest" boards (those most free of knots and other mars) are FAS (Firsts and Seconds) Grade, followed by Select Grade, no. 1 Common, and no. 2 Common.

Lumber Surfaces. Lumber is also classified according to the surface treatment it receives

before it leaves the mill. Rough lumber is not dressed (surfaced), although it is sawed, edged, and trimmed on all four surfaces. Dressed lumber is planed on the edges, on the sides, or both, to produce a uniform surface. The designation "S2S" refers to a board surfaced on both sides; S2S1E indicates a board surfaced on two sides and one edge.

Money-Saving Tip

$ Sometimes there is a very good sale on lumber. If this is the case, and you think you might have use for it in the future, buy it and store it.

Plywood

Plywood is another staple material. It comes in 4 x 8 foot sheets and consists of a sandwich of thin veneers or plies of wood bonded together for strength. It comes in $1/4$-, $1/2$-, $3/4$-, and 1-inch thicknesses. Unlike lumber, the nominal size of plywood is its actual size. A 1-inch thick sheet is exactly 1 inch thick.

Plywood

Plywood is also available for interior and exterior use. The latter uses exterior glue to bond the plies; the former uses interior glue.

Like lumber, plywood is graded:

Grade A does not have any defects on the face.

Grade B allows some defects and patches of defects.

Grade C allows small knots and knotholes.

Grade D allows large knotholes.

Grade and type are marked on the panel. Grade AC, for example, would mean that one side is defect-free and the other side has small knotholes.

When buying plywood, you should only buy the grade that you need. If the plywood is going to be painted, for example, you don't need to buy Grade A material—and then cover it with paint. Pick the grade that's suitable for the job.

Money-Saving Tip

You can buy plywood in scrap pieces that are often big enough for your project, at a greatly reduced cost.

Particleboard

Like plywood, particleboard comes in 4 x 8 sheets and in various thicknesses. It is made from wood scraps bonded together into sheets at high pressure. You might consider particleboard the "poor man's plywood" because it costs half as much. However, it is a good material, although it can't be used outdoors. It is twice as heavy as plywood and is murder on a blade saw. Moreover, it can't be stained or finished (just painted), and it doesn't accept nails on the edges. Still, it is a good building material for shelves and many other things, as long as you understand its limitations.

Drywall

Variously known as drywall, plasterboard, and gypsumboard, it's most commonly referred to by one brand name, Sheetrock. It comes in various sizes, but mostly 4 x 8 sheets and in $3/8$-, $1/2$- and $5/8$-inch thicknesses.

Plasterboard consists of gypsum sandwiched between two layers of tough paper. Before it came along, there was only "wetwall," or plaster. Drywall revolutionized building because everything became much faster to build. It comes in two grades of quality—visibly good and visibly bad.

Plaster is still the better wall. However, the craftsmen—bowlegged Old World men smoking malodorous cigars—are literally a dying breed.

When being installed on walls and ceilings, it is nailed to framing members. Then the seams or joints are covered with joint toe; and this, in turn, is covered with multiple coats of joint compound. Drywall is very cheap, and an excellent material. It is also great for patching holes.

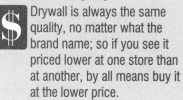

Money-Saving Tip

Drywall is always the same quality, no matter what the brand name; so if you see it priced lower at one store than at another, by all means buy it at the lower price.

CHAPTER 4

Although there are a number of repairs the homeowner should embrace with the same passion reserved for bubonic plague, there are quite a few that anyone can do, even those of us with more than the usual complement of thumbs. And the good news is this: The house is like the human body; things that go wrong with it are usually minor.

The ability to fix the minor things can result in great savings. Potentially costly visits to your home by carpenters, plumbers, electricians, and other tradespersons will be that much less frequent. Following is a potpourri of repairs that most anyone can do.

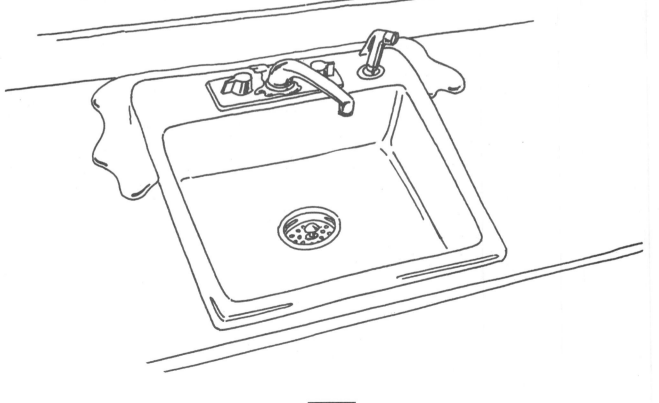

Plumbing Maladies

Leaking Faucet

One of the most common maladies in the home is the dripping faucet, something that seems to occur most often in the middle of the night. Before making the repair, it's a good idea to understand how a faucet works.

There are various types of faucets, but the most common group are those with *washers*. Here, the exterior faucet handle is attached to a shaft, called a spindle, and has a threaded part that screws down and covers a hole inside the faucet body—the part that's secured to the sink. Water is constantly ON—being fed through pipes and up into the faucet. But when the faucet is turned OFF, the bottom of the spindle acts like a cork—water pushes up against it but can't pass. When the faucet is turned ON, the spindle screws up and out of the hole, and water flows.

The Key to It All. The thing that really seals off the hole is the washer at the bottom of the spindle. This is made of a rubber or soft plastic material, and it looks like a tiny donut. It has some give, or softness, so that when it contacts the edges of the hole, it seals well; water can't slip up around the edges of the spindle. As time passes, however, the washer wears down and eventually loses its perfect seal. Just a little water gets by—and goes drip.

One's first inclination is to turn the faucet tighter, and, at least in the beginning, this will do the job. But eventually, no matter how hard you tighten, it will not seal completely.

No Brain Surgery Required. Making the repair is simple: Just replace the washer. First, though, you must turn off the water (remember, it's always flowing). This is usually simple to do. Under the sink or lavatory (bathroom sink), you will see two wheels projecting from the wall. These are the valves that control the water flow to the

Spindle

Washer

Exploded view of faucet

faucet. The one on the left controls the hot water; the one on the right controls the cold water. If the drip is cold water, just turn the right wheel all the way to the right; if hot water, do the same thing with the left wheel.

In some cases there won't be any valves under the sink. If you tried you could find valves on other pipes in the basement (or elsewhere) that control the flow, but it's a lot easier to turn the main water shutoff valve. This is located next to the water meter. Just turn it clockwise all the way and the water will stop. If you don't know where it's located, you should learn. Your water company will tell you, or even have someone come over and show you.

Taking It Apart. How you take the faucet apart will depend on what kind you have, but essentially it is a series of "things" that look like they can be unscrewed or turned and the faucet comes apart. There's no great mystery involved. One type of faucet has a big fat chrome nut. You can remove this with wrench jaws that open at least an inch wide and with flat jaws that grip the "flats" on the nut so you can turn and loosen it with a counterclockwise motion. If you don't have an adjustable wrench, pliers can sometimes be used, but the nut must first be covered with tape, or even Band-Aid™, so the plier jaws don't scratch the chrome.

Up and Out. Once the big fat nut is loose, you turn the handle, and the spindle and the assembly will come up and out. The washer is on the end of the spindle, held on by a screw. Grip the assembly in one hand and turn the screw out with an ordinary screwdriver, its tip size corresponding to the size of the screw slot.

Plumber's Secret

Most of the time the screw will turn out easily. If it doesn't, a good trick is to use a screwdriver to dig the washer out, exposing the screw head fully. Then, use a pair of pliers to turn it out. If it still balks, you can douse the screw with a penetrating oil (WD-40 is one brand name); the oil will work its way down and into the screw threads, breaking up any corrosion that's locking the screw in place.

New Washer. Washers can be bought singly and in small boxed assortments, which also contain a few brass screws of various sizes. Buy the box. Washers do wear out, and it is convenient having the right sizes around.

To determine the size needed, simply try various sizes until one fits neatly. Then secure it with a new brass screw, and screw the faucet back in place. Make sure—ask the dealer— that the screw is brass, not steel colored to look like brass; steel can corrode; brass will not. Screw the shaft down into the faucet body, and tighten the big fat nut. Do it

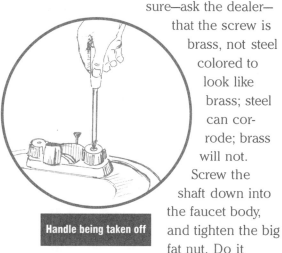

Handle being taken off

slowly—don't force—and keep the nut and shaft straight as you go.

Turn on the water and see if the drip stops. Sometimes a few turns are necessary before this happens.

Another Type of Faucet. There is another type of faucet that does not have a big fat nut on the outside. The handle covers the shaft, or spindle. For this type, first remove the handle. Do this by

Unscrew spindle washer at bottom

unscrewing the so-called Phillips screw that holds it on to the top of the spindle. Once this is out, you will see a large nut. Put your adjustable wrench on this, and turn counterclockwise until loose. Then, put the handle back over the top of the shaft, and turn it as if you were turning the faucet on. The whole thing will come up and out. On the bottom, of course, you'll see the washer.

There are other types of faucets, but the trick is the same. Turn what looks like it can be turned until you can get at the washer.

Other Leaky Faucet Maladies

If replacing the washer doesn't stop the leak, it usually means that the seat, the part that the washer presses

Fat nut being loosened

down against, is worn. Fixing this is not brain surgery either, but you first have to determine if the seat is replaceable or not.

To do this, remove the spindle. Then, shine a flashlight down into the faucet body hole. If you see a round hole, it means that the entire faucet may have to be replaced. However, if you see a hole with—you guessed it—flat edges, it means that there is a tool, called a *faucet seat wrench*, that can be used to remove it so that you can insert a replacement.

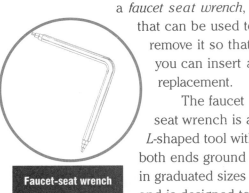

Faucet-seat wrench

The faucet seat wrench is an *L*-shaped tool with both ends ground flat in graduated sizes and is designed to be able to be poked down into the hole, fitting snugly against corresponding flats in the seat. Turning the tool counterclockwise loosens the seat, which is screwed in place, and you can lift it up and out.

Finding a Replacement Seat. One wonders who figured out replacement seats. Whoever did should be institutionalized, because there are literally hundreds of different sizes. Fortunately for the do-it-yourselfer, however, there is an easy way to get the right size: Just bring the old one into the store. Hardware stores, home centers, and plumbing supply stores all carry replacement seats. The dealer should be able to furnish you with a replacement.

To install the new seat, slip it over the end of the faucet seat tool, and then push the tool into the faucet until it

sticks by friction. Keeping the seat straight so that its threads correspond to threads on the faucet, screw it in place. Now you have a smooth new surface for the washer to seal against.

Round Seat. If your investigation shows that the seat has no flats on it, but it is round, it may mean, as mentioned, that the entire faucet needs to be replaced. But before doing this, you should obtain a *faucet seat reamer*. This is a tool for grinding down the seat so that the washer will fit snugly. The device hooks onto the faucet body and has a shaft with a rough end, which is used to grind away the rough portions on the seat. Consult the instructions that come with the tool for more details.

Round and hexagonal seats

Valves Need Their Exercise Too

Water shutoff valves will last longer if every now and then—say every six months—they are turned from OFF to ON and back again. Reason: Turning tends to grind away rust or corrosion that can build up, creating a fresh surface where the working parts of the valves meet.

Washerless Faucets

Another common group of faucets are the washerless ones. Instead, the faucet contains a plastic or metal ball with holes in it. The ball is manipulated with a single handle, and there are corresponding holes in the faucet body. When the holes in the ball align with those in the faucet body, the water flows.

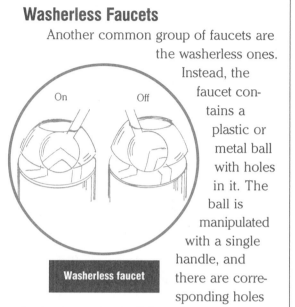

Washerless faucet

Although these are not washers in the conventional sense, the holes in the ball do have washers of a sort; and these can go bad. If there is a problem, tell the dealer exactly what type of faucet you have, and he can furnish you with a kit that contains all the parts needed, including a tool for installation.

Handle Puller

Some faucet handles are so corroded that not even dousing the parts with penetrating oil will enable you to turn them. When this is the case, you should buy a *handle puller*, a device that can be hooked over a handle and the handle pulled off, working like the wheel puller on a car. The device costs only $6 or $7, which is a bargain when compared with what a plumber might charge.

Stopping the Noise

If a faucet is dripping in the middle of the night and it's inconvenient to make the repair, you can at least silence it temporarily. To do this, find a shoelace or a long piece of string. Wet the string thoroughly, and then tie one end to the faucet nozzle, letting the rest hang down into the drain. Fiddle with the tied-on end until the dripping water runs down the string. This will carry it noiselessly to the drain. And that's it. If you don't have a string or shoelace handy, use a sock, rag, or towel, first wetting the item thoroughly.

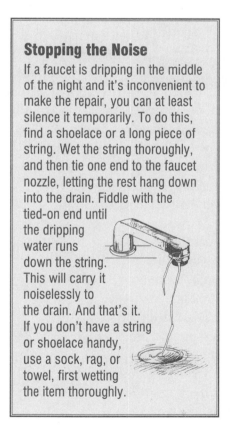

Stopped-Up Sink

Another common plumbing malady is the stopped-up sink. This is a problem that can usually be solved with a plunger, also known as the handyperson's helper, or force cup. It consists of a handle with a rubber cup.

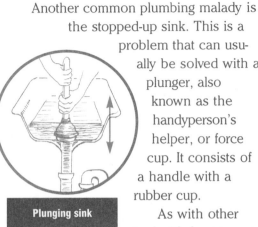

Plunging sink

As with other tools, it's best to get quality. One made of thick rubber with a retractable bulb, which is useful in clearing a toilet clog, works well.

To use the tool, first make sure there is enough water in the sink to cover the cup. Then, start plunging, pressing the cup down, and then lifting it up about an inch off the drain. Every now and then pull up hard.

When the water retreats, turn on the faucet full blast to see if the water goes down freely. If it does, this means that the blockage has been knocked loose and is heading for the sewer line. As a final treatment, turn on the hot water for a few minutes or pour boiling water into the drain. This will help dissolve any grease that may have accumulated where the blockage was.

If the sink has an overflow outlet, this should be plugged with a wet rag while the plunging is being done. Or, if you're plunging one of a pair of sinks, you must plug the other sink's drain. If you don't plug the opening, the suction you're creating by plunging will escape—you won't get much result.

If you find that the plunger doesn't work after three or four minutes, it means you have to take sterner measures.

Take Off the Trap. The next step is to take off the trap, a *J*-shaped pipe section that is under the sink. The trap's purpose, as mentioned earlier, is to trap a little water, which itself acts as a seal against gas from the sewer line flowing into the house. But the trap also catches such things as knives, forks, toothbrushes, spoons, rings—you name it. Debris clings to and collects on these items, and a blockage ultimately results.

Lavatory tall pipe

Take up

Slip joint nuts

Trap

Drain pipes, trap

So, take a wrench of big enough size and turn counterclockwise each of the nuts that are at the top and bottom end of the *J*. Slip these nuts up and off, and then gently remove the trap. When you do, it is likely that whatever is causing the blockage will plop out, along with accumulated water, so have a pan or pail under the trap.

Probing trap

Some traps have a plug on the bottom that can be unscrewed. Just use a wrench to turn this off. Then you may be able to fish out whatever is causing the blockage. With the blockage out, reassemble the pipe, and run hot water to help remove grease.

Snake. If the above ministrations fail, it's likely that the blockage is in the pipe somewhere beyond the trap. Many times this can be cleared with a *snake*, so called because it is a flexible wire cable that bends relatively easily. One end is pointed and has a hook on it; the other has a handle and a crank that enables the snake to be turned.

If it's not already off, take off the trap or the plug on the trap. With your hands, feed the snake into the pipe that goes into the wall. When it's firmly implanted, slide the tubelike handle down along the cable until it's a couple of feet from the pipe opening, and lock the crank in place by turning down on the little screw. Then push the snake in, at the same time turning the tube handle, which will turn the snake.

If the snake becomes stuck, it may mean that it's jammed in a bend in the pipe; but it also may mean that you've located the blockage. Push, pull, and twist. If it feels like it's really stuck, pull all the way out. The hook may have caught on the blockage, and you may be able to drag it out. If not, repeat the procedure.

As you feed the snake into the pipe, keep sliding the handle down and setting it in position. If the blockage is not cleared by the time you've fed all of the snake into the pipe, it's time for a plumber.

What about Caustic Cleaners?

A number of caustic or acid-based drain cleaners are sold, and the advice is to periodically pour them down a drain, or to use them to help clear a clog. Most commercial drain cleaners are considered caustic. I think it's okay to use them periodically, or to use them to clear a sluggish drain; but I wouldn't suggest they be used when a drain is totally stopped. If the chemical doesn't work, it means that the trap has to be taken off, which will then be filled with water and caustic chemicals.

Don't Work in the Nude if You Have a Cat

The funniest story I ever heard vis-à-vis taking a trap apart (I haven't heard that many!) concerned a woman who dropped her wedding ring down the drain. She awakened her husband and said he'd have to get up and take the trap off to retrieve the ring.

A few minutes later the husband was on his back, half in and half out of the kitchen cabinet, taking the trap off. And the family cat was on its haunches nearby, carefully observing a certain part of the man's anatomy, a part that the cat apparently started to regard as prey.

The cat leaped, and the man banged his head on the trap and was knocked unconscious. He recovered, but the fate of the cat is unknown.

Stopped-up Toilet

The first thing to know about a clogged toilet is how to turn the water off quickly. Otherwise, the clogged bowl can fill up with water and overflow. Take the lid off the tank, and pull up the thin metal rod that the copper or plastic float ball is attached to. As will be detailed later, this turns off the valve and stops flow instantly. Once you pull up the rod, you can wedge something under it or tie it to the nearest cabinet knob (or something else to hold it

in position). You can also stop water flow by turning off the water supply valve under the tank.

Next, try to clear the blockage with a plunger. The 6-inch one with a retractable bulb works well. This bulb fits snugly into the hole in the bottom of the bowl and allows better suction.

Plunge as You Would a Sink. Just plunge the bowl as you would a sink. Place the plunger into the hole in the bowl, and press forcefully down, compressing it.

Pull up about an inch, then press down again. Go up and down in a steady rhythm, every now and then pulling up hard. If you see the water starting to go down, continue to plunge until it is all gone. As a final test to see if the blockage is cleared, flush the toilet.

Plumber's Secret

If the bowl is filled to the brim with water before you start plunging, take an old pot or pail and ladle out some of it, bringing it down about 6 inches. Otherwise, the water will spill on the floor when you start to plunge.

Sterner Measures. If a few minutes of plunging doesn't work, you have to take sterner measures. You will need a *closet auger* or *snake* that is especially designed for clearing toilet blockages. It gets its name from the "water closet," the name the toilet tank was first called, and is still called by professionals.

A closet auger is similar to a snake, as described earlier. It's a cable with a pointed, hooked end. But in this model, the cable is thicker and less flexible and has a crank handle. It also has a rubber section that keeps it from scratching the bowl.

To use the tool, feed the end into the toilet hole with your hands. When it's inside, push it upward. Like sinks, toilets have traps built into them, and the idea is to have the auger drive through the trap to clear anything that might be lodged there, and into the pipe beyond.

All the Way In. You should push it in as far as you can with your hands, and when enough of it is solidly wedged in place, turn the handle, at the same time pushing. This will turn the end.

If the auger becomes stuck, it may mean that you've contacted the blockage. Push extra hard, also turning. If it feels as though the hook on the end has caught onto something, pull out hard. Of course,

Toilet cross section

Water supply

Drain

Closet auger

it could also mean that the auger is wedged solidly into a pipe bend.

If the auger doesn't clear the blockage, the toilet can be dismounted and the trap checked. This is easier than it sounds. In most cases, all you need to do is disconnect the water supply and free the toilet from the floor bolts, on which it is mounted. More than once, a child's missing toy has been discovered there.

Flush Tank Problems

Other problems with a toilet usually occur because something goes wrong in the flush tank. The flush tank is the squarish box above the toilet; it holds the flush water.

It's a good idea to get thoroughly familiar with how a toilet works before doing any repairs. So, carry this book into the bathroom and let's check it out. Refer to the numbered drawing (on page 60) as we go along.

First, lift off the top of the tank. Do this carefully. If you drop it, it could chip or break. Set it aside and look down into the tank. Looks like a hopeless jungle of piping, doesn't it? It's really not complicated.

Turn the tank handle (1) just a little. When you do, you'll see that it moves a vertical rod (or chain) (2) upward. Turn the handle fully to flush the tank. See what happens? The rod (or chain) lifts a rubber valve (3) that's resting in a hole in the bottom of the tank. When the valve is lifted out of the hole, the water in the tank runs out into the bowl, flushing it. Then the tank fills up again, automatically.

Flush the tank again and watch what happens to the float (4). As the water runs out, the float—which of course is floating—goes down with the water level.

The float does two jobs. First, when it gets near the bottom of the tank, the end of the rod it's on opens a water inlet valve, or ballcock (5), and new water starts to rush into the tank. At the same time, the valve at the bottom of the tank, which has been held up by water rushing past it through the hole, drops down and closes the hole, because there's no more water to keep it open. Second, as the water level rises, the float rises, and the end of the rod it's on gradually closes off the water inlet valve. So the float turns the water on and off.

While the tank is filling, a little tube (6) shoots water into the overflow tube (7) and fills up the bowl itself. If for some reason the incoming water flow is not shut off, the water will flow out the overflow tube into the bowl. There is no way that a toilet tank can overflow.

There are other parts to a toilet tank mechanism, but knowing those already mentioned will enable you to make the majority of the repairs required. Now, let's cover the common problems.

First, if you have a problem, take off the tank top so that you can see what's going on. If, after flushing, water keeps on running into the bowl and yet the tank

Flush tank cross section

Labels: 5. Ball cock; 6. Trip lever; 2. Lift rod; Float; 1.; Overflow tube; Rod guide; 4. Float Ball doesn't fill up all the way, it usually means that the little rubber valve at the bottom of the tank is defective: It is not plugging up the hole completely.

Replace Valve.
The cure is to replace the ball. First, shut off the water to the tank. This is done by turning off the water supply to the tank. You can do this by turning off the valve either below the tank or somewhere on the bathroom wall. An easier way, however, is by simply lifting the rod that the float is on as high as you can, then tying it in that position to something above the tank (like a cabinet doorknob). As you may remember, this closes off the inlet water valve.

Flush the tank, emptying it. When it's empty, hold the rod (or chain) that the valve is on and unscrew the valve with your other hand. Place it aside and gently wipe off the edges of the hole the ball rests in with fine-grade steel

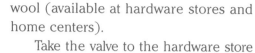

Lift rod

For valve to seat properly, lift rod must be straight

wool (available at hardware stores and home centers).

Take the valve to the hardware store and ask for one just like it. If, when you took the ball off, you noticed that the rod it was attached to was bent, get a new one of those, too. A bent rod can keep the ball from going in straight and plugging the hole completely.

With the rod in place, screw the new valve onto it. Untie the float rod or turn the water supply valve back on. Flush the toilet. If the water still runs out of the tank and the tank doesn't fill all the way, the valve is not fitting into the hole properly. This can be because the guide arm (8) that the rod fits through may not be properly positioned. Just turn off the water supply again, loosen the little screw holding the arm to the overflow tube, and jiggle the arm back and forth until the ball drops into the hole perfectly. Then tighten the screw to hold the rod permanently in that position.

In some cases, the outlet hole may be so damaged that snug sealing by the valve is not possible. Here, you can get a kit (from the manufacturer Flusher Fixer) that allows you to epoxy a new seat over the hole.

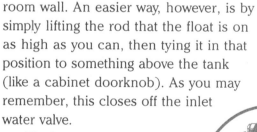

Flusher Fixer kit

Water Keeps Running. Sometimes the tank fills up all the way but the water continues to run until it goes out the overflow tube. If this is happening, you'll not only see the water running out the overflow pipe but also hear a hissing noise. This indicates that something is wrong with either the water inlet valve or the ball float or its particular rod.

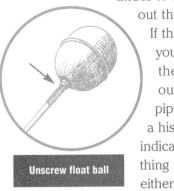

Unscrew float ball

Lift up the float. If the hissing noise stops and the water stops flowing, it means the trouble is with the float or the rod. Flush the toilet, emptying the tank. Tie the rod as before to shut off the water, or turn it off by turning off the water supply valve.

Unscrew the float and shake it. If there is water inside, the float must be replaced. Simply trot down to your local hardware store and get one just like it. Screw the new float in place, untie the rod (or turn the water supply valve on), and flush the tank. The tank should fill up but not overflow.

If you find when you take off the float that it doesn't have water in it, the problem is with the rod. To correct this, screw the rod in tightly, and then bend it downward with your hands, so the float is another half inch or so down into the tank. Flush the toilet. The float should be positioned so the water stops about an inch from the top of the overflow pipe. If it doesn't, bend the rod a little more to achieve this.

Money-Saving Tip

$ Buy a plastic float ball instead of a copper one. It costs a lot less and lasts longer.

If lifting the rod up does not shut off the water flow, it means that something is wrong with the water inlet valve. For this you can get the Flusher Fixer Kit (mentioned previously). It is inexpensive—under $10—and contains instructions on how to remove the ball-cock mechanism, which the inlet valve is part of, and replace it with the valve.

Bend down float rod

Erratic Faucet Spray

Many faucets are equipped with a little strainerlike device that screws onto the end of the faucet. Its purpose is to aerate the water so it doesn't splash when it hits the sink. When one of these gets clogged with soil, the water starts to jet—and splash—rather than flow in a soft, smooth stream.

To cure the problem, first remove the device from the faucet. Sometimes you can do this by simply turning it to the left or right—whichever way the thing goes—with your fingers. If necessary, use a pair of pliers, first wrapping a little tape around the device to protect its shiny finish from the jaws of the pliers.

Remove the little screens (or screen) from the device. You can poke them out with your finger or pick them out with the point of a knife. Note where each goes, so you can reassemble them properly later.

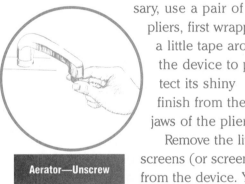

Aerator—Unscrew

Using an old toothbrush and a little hand soap, brush the screens thoroughly, even if dirt isn't visible. Rinse them thoroughly, replace them, and then screw the device back onto the faucet and tighten carefully. (Some screens may not come out, so just brush the exposed screen vigorously. That usually does the trick.)

Money-Saving Tip

$ If you need a new aerator, buy plastic instead of stainless steel and save half the price—and plastic works well.

Erratic Shower Spray

If a shower head ejects water in a hard stream, it probably means that inside is a soil buildup. Some of the little holes where the water comes out are clogged; so the water is virtually fired out of the other ones.

First, grip the shower head in your hand and turn it counterclockwise. It should come right off. If you need help, use a wrench or pliers.

Using a flashlight, look down into the hole in the back of the head. You'll likely see some foreign matter. If you hold the head to the light, you'll see that some of the holes are blocked.

Soap up a Q-Tip or a toothpick with cotton on the end and work down inside the shower head, clearing the holes and wiping the entire inside. After a few minutes, discard the Q-Tip and run hot water through the head until it emerges from the little holes. Repeat the procedure four or five times until a Q-Tip emerges as clean as it went in.

Screw the head back on the shower and turn on the water. If it doesn't come out properly, repeat the Q-Tip procedure as needed.

Leaky Water Pipes

You may be surprised to learn that you can probably repair a leaky pipe. You might not be able to fix one that's spewing water—that's usually a job for a plumber. However, you can repair the

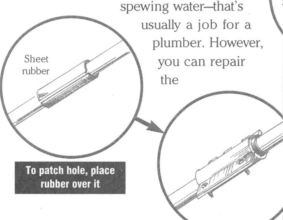

Sheet rubber

To patch hole, place rubber over it

Tighten with clamps

pinhole or small-hole leaks that drip or even spray a fairly steady stream of water.

The first thing to do is to turn off the water. As with a faucet, there are valves controlling water flow through particular pipes; ideally, you'd simply turn off the valve that would stop water flowing

through the damaged pipe. If you're not sure which valve controls what, you can turn off the main water valve, as described earlier. As you know, however, this will turn off both hot and cold

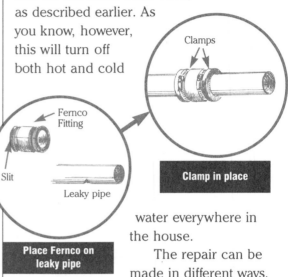

Clamps

Fernco Fitting

Slit

Leaky pipe

Clamp in place

Place Fernco on leaky pipe

water everywhere in the house.

The repair can be made in different ways. One way is by patching the leak with an epoxy putty, such as the kind Oatey makes. Just press the material over the hole. It dries as hard as steel.

Another way is to use a clamp-type patch obtainable at hardware stores. It comes with a rubber patch that looks like a bicycle tube patch. Place this patch over the hole, then slip the clamp device over the patch; tighten the clamp with the bolts provided. This presses the rubber hard against the hole, and water can't get out. You can turn the water on right away; it's a five-minute repair that will last awhile.

Another solution is offered by the Fernco Company. They make repair collars that you slit, press over the tube, and tighten on with steel clamps.

If you have a hole in a trap, take off the piece and replace it. (Check the section on clearing a clogged sink regarding how to remove and replace the trap.)

Furniture Fixes

Furniture, especially wood furniture, is subject to attack from various sources, from budding Michelangelos with ballpoint pens to guests who don't appreciate the fact that wet glasses can leave rings. The following is a roundup of these problems—with solutions. It should be emphasized that some damage cannot be corrected so that it is absolutely invisible—in these cases only complete refinishing can do that. However, you can repair a blemish to the point where only close scrutiny will reveal it.

Scratches

There are wood colorants you can buy that come in Magic Marker–like applicators. Just pick the color that's right and dab it on the scratch. Or, you can also use homemade colorants. All liquid colorings, be they homemade or commercial preparations, should be tested first on an inconspicuous portion of the furniture. Testing will enable you to make as close a match as possible.

On walnut furniture, try rubbing the meat of a walnut or Brazil nut or butternut into the scratch. Then wax the piece, and buff.

If the wood is red mahogany, ordinary iodine sometimes colors it properly. Apply it to the scratch with a Q-Tip or, preferably, an artist's brush. Be careful not to drip the iodine on any surrounding surface. When the iodine is dry, wax and buff the piece.

For brown or cherry mahogany, iodine that has turned dark with age sometimes works. For maple, dilute the iodine about 50 percent with denatured alcohol.

Even shoe polish can be used to hide minor scratches. Shoe polish is only good if the finish is shiny, because when you wax and buff, the polish will shine. You can use a brown shade for walnut, a cordovan shade for mahogany, a tan shade for light finishes, and black for black lacquered (very shiny) wood. Apply the polish with a Q-Tip or with a toothpick that has a little cotton wrapped around the end. If the color is too dark for the wood (or too light), you can remove it with *naphtha*, which is a petroleum-based solvent and available at paint stores.

Deep Scratches

Deep scratches, or gouges, require filling, to be effectively concealed. As with minor scratches, there is more than one method at your disposal.

The simplest solution—the least permanent, too—is to use wax sticks. These look like crayons and come in a wide variety of colors to match wood tones.

First, clean out the scratch with a razor and wipe it clean. Rub the stick along the scratch, filling it and working it level with your finger. Wipe it with a soft cloth and the job's done.

If the scratch is very deep, you can use colored wood putty. (There are various kinds of wood putty available. Get the kind that can be sanded.) Scoop out the material and apply it with a putty knife. The putty will spread like butter, but it dries hard. When the scratches have been filled, wax the piece.

Ink Stains

It's almost a waste of time to write about removing ink, because it's often impossible. The only answer is to completely refinish the piece of furniture.

However, if ink does spill, immediately blot up as much of it as you can with a blotter, paper towel, or bathroom tissue. Then pat the stain with a damp cloth. Don't rub. Keep turning the cloth so that you're constantly blotting with a clean section. If all the ink doesn't come off, try *rottenstone* (an abrasive powder available at paint stores), and oil, as explained under "White Marks."

Stains on Tile-Top Tables

Things made of tile require instant attention if something is spilled on them. Any spillage can seep into the material, and if there's grout—the stuff between the tiles—it is especially difficult to clean.

If you know what the stain is from, removal is very simple. For coffee, tea, fruit juice, and food stains, cold water and Spic and Span® floor cleaner usually works. If it doesn't, use laundry bleach.

Spic and Span® and cold water work on blood stains, too; blood stains can also be bleached out with hydrogen peroxide. For ink stains, use laundry bleach or peroxide. Grease spots yield to a mixture of one part tri-sodium-phosphate (or more commonly known as TSP) to nine parts water.

When you don't know what the stain is from, first, try Spic and Span® and cold water. No luck? Try turpentine or white vinegar. If these don't do it, graduate to laundry bleach. If this doesn't make it, use 20 volume hydrogen peroxide or ammonia. But never use bleach and ammonia together. The two combine to form a chemical with vapors that can literally kill you.

Just wipe on one of the cleaners mentioned, and give it half an hour to do its work. Then clean the area thoroughly with hot water, and dry it immediately with a cloth. To protect your hands when using cleaners, wear rubber gloves.

If none of the cleaners works, try rubbing the stains away with some sort of abrasive—but not on glazed (shiny) tile, as abrasives can scratch the finish. Indeed, it's very important to test any remover on an inconspicuous spot first. Otherwise, the cure can be worse than the malady. Try a mild treatment first, rubbing with fine-grade steel wool and a scouring powder such as Comet (with cold water). If this doesn't do it, rub with fine-grade sandpaper and Spic and Span®.

Stuck Paper

Sometimes, if you put a hot object on top of paper that is resting on a wooden piece of furniture, the paper will stick. Damp newspaper will also stick. To remove either, wipe ordinary olive oil on the paper. Give it a chance to soak through—a half hour—then rub off the paper and any remaining stain with a clean cloth.

Burns

Some furniture blemishes, as you've seen, are removed in unusual ways. But nothing compares with the way you handle a slight burn—by rubbing with cigarette or cigar ash or toothpaste. Actually, there's method behind the apparent madness. The ashes or toothpaste act as an abrasive and scour away the charred portion.

To fix, dampen your finger and rub ashes or toothpaste over the burned area. When all the blackening is removed, wipe clean and apply a touch of wax.

If a burn is particularly deep, use a more conventional method. First, remove as much of the charred area as you can by scraping it off with a knife or single-edge razor blade held perpendicular to the surface. Try not to scratch the surrounding area. Follow the scraping by wiping the area clean with a cotton swab dipped in naphtha. Smooth by rubbing with extrafine-grade sandpaper, and complete the face-lift by following the same method used to handle deep scratches.

Dents

A dent is a small area of the wood that has been compressed rather than actually gouged or cut. The idea here is to steam the wood so that it swells up back into shape. This can take awhile, but it does work.

First, use a wet cotton swab and some Soilax to remove the wax and polish from the dent. Place several layers of cheese-cloth or a plain folded cloth on the dent. Place a metal bottle cap, top down, on the cloth and directly over the dent. Press a hot iron on the bottle cap. This concentrates the steam. Keep the iron on the cap only a few seconds at a time, to avoid scorching the wood.

Fixing a dent

White Marks

There are two kinds of white marks that you may have to deal with: the white rings left by drinking glasses and the blotchy, cloudy patterns left by hot objects. You can follow the same removal procedure for both.

First, gently rub the mark with a dampened finger and cigar or cigarette ash; ordinary toothpaste can also be used. Follow the grain of the wood as you rub, and wipe clean when the stain disappears.

If the mark doesn't go away, it means that you need something more abrasive than ashes—namely, rottenstone, an abrasive powder available at paint stores. Shake out some rottenstone into one saucer and pour a little cooking oil or linseed oil into another. Fold a small piece of felt or flannel cloth into a small pad. Dip the pad in the oil, then in the rottenstone. Rub the blemish, again following the wood grain. Use light pressure. If the finish comes off in the process of removing the mark, you can repair it later by applying a dab of the appropriate finish with a small brush.

Hold ice cube against wax

Removing wax

Candle Wax

Wax is easier to remove if you harden it first. To do this, hold an ice cube against it for thirty seconds. Wipe away the melted water, and then use a dull knife (such as a butter knife) to pick off as much wax as you can without touching the wood. Then, very gently, scrape away the portion that is sticking to the furniture. When all the wax is gone, rub the area briskly with furniture wax and wipe it dry with a clean cloth.

Milk Stains

Anything containing milk can leave a bad blemish on furniture, because the lactic acid eats through the finish. If some sort of milk product spills, immediately wipe away as much of it as possible, and clean off as much of the remaining stain as you can with furniture wax. Then follow with the removal method given for "White Marks."

Damaged Veneer

Some pieces of furniture are covered with a beautiful wood "skin" called veneer. A number of things can go wrong with veneer, all repairable.

A common problem is that it becomes loose, and it separates from the piece of furniture proper. If this

happens, simply glue the veneer back in place with white glue. First, clean out all old, hardened glue and any food particles or other soil that may have worked under it. Because veneer invariably loosens at the edges of a piece, this shouldn't be a problem. Just take a nail file, a knife, or some other thin-bladed instrument, and scrape the old glue and soil out. If you don't do this, the new glue may not be able to hold the veneer properly.

When the area under the veneer is clean, use a sliver of wood or a toothpick to spread new glue. Press the veneer in place, then pile heavy objects—a handful of hardcover books will do—on the veneer until the glue has dried thoroughly. As you press the veneer down, some glue will likely squeeze out. Clean this off immediately with a rag. If a little remains, no sweat—white glue dries clear.

WHITE GLUE

Blister

Blistered veneer

Split Veneer

Another problem with veneer is it can blister, or bubble. Sometimes the bubble is split; other times it's not. If it's split, poke into the opening with a damp Q-Tip to clean it out as well as you can. If there's no split, make a small incision along the length of the blister with a single-edge razor blade.

Smear white glue under the raised veneer. Place a piece of wax paper over the veneer, then place very heavy books or some other weight on it to force it down into position.

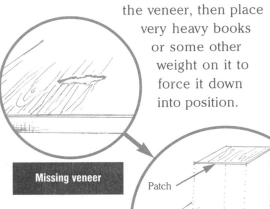

Missing veneer

Patch

Cut through patch and existing veneer, glue patch in place

Veneer patch

If you can see that the veneer is not lying flat, apply a damp rag to it until it becomes more pliable.

After the glue dries (overnight is more than enough time), pick and sand away the wax paper, using medium-grade sandpaper. Then wax and buff the entire surface.

Sometimes veneer on the edge of a piece of furniture chips off. If you're lucky enough to recover the broken piece, just glue it back in place. Then use wax paper on top of which you've piled books or other weights to force it down into position (as described previously).

It is likely, however, that you won't recover the piece that broke off. If this is the case, you have to make a patch with new veneer.

New veneer may be obtained from old pieces of furniture at junkyard dealers, or from another part of your piece of furniture where it won't show. If the patch needed is very large, you can buy a whole sheet of new veneer at a lumberyard. One source, Constantine's, of Bronx, New York, also sells veneer samples that can be used for patching. The key is to get a veneer that matches the color and grain of the wood in the existing furniture as closely as possible, so that it blends unobtrusively.

Cut a patch big enough to cover the spot where the veneer is missing. The patch may be cut in a rectangle, a triangle, or any other shape with straight lines.

Place the patch over the spot where veneer is missing and, using a steel ruler or other hard straightedge and a razor blade, carefully cut around the edges of the patch through the existing layer of veneer. Then simply remove the cutout material and glue the patch in place (as previously described).

Structural Furniture Problems

Wooden furniture is subject to a variety of maladies that have to do with the structure of the particular piece. Following are some of the things that can go wrong and how to cure them.

Loose Chair Rung

All parts of chairs are susceptible to loosening, but this is especially true of horizontal leg braces or rungs. The problem usually occurs in the winter. The low humidity, combined with house heat, evaporates the moisture in wood fibers, and the wood shrinks. In the case of rungs, which are usually secured in their

sockets with glue, the ends shrink and vibrations from using the chair ultimately break the glue seal. Hence, a loose rung. It's always easier to fix the rung if you can remove its end from the socket. Sometimes there's enough "play" —looseness—to do this. But don't try and remove it if it's in pretty tight. In the process you could loosen other parts. If you can get the rung out, follow this procedure.

Glue tourniquet

Using a small knife, scrape away all old glue, from the rung and inside the socket, down to clean, bare wood. Apply a coat of white glue to both the rung and the socket; a cotton swab works well here.

Immediately after applying the glue, stick the rung back into its socket. Wrap a length of clothesline around the chair. Tie a knot, then slip a stick under the cord and turn the stick so the cord winds up and acts like a tourniquet, pulling the rung and the part it fits into tightly together.

Then tie or position the stick on the chair so the cord doesn't unwind. Check around the socket for forced-out glue and wipe it off with a rag. Let the glue dry overnight, then take the cord off.

If there was a real gap around the rung, say an eighth of an inch or more, glue alone probably won't work. In this case, clean off all old glue as before. Apply fresh white glue to the rung end; then tightly wind a string around it. You are actually making the rung thicker with the string. Then, coat the socket with glue, and force the end into place. Make a cord tourniquet as before and then, with a single-edge razor blade, trim off any string sticking out of the socket. Let dry.

Of course, it is highly likely that you won't be able to get the rung out without making other chair parts loose. If this is the case, you can buy products like Locktite® that you inject into the socket to swell the wood, in effect making a tighter bond.

Sticking Drawer

Did you ever notice that drawers usually stick during the summer or in damp weather? The reason is that humidity is high and moisture gets into the wood and swells the fibers—in effect, the drawer becomes a wee bit too big for the compartment it fits into.

Usually, a little lubrication is all that's needed. Just apply candle wax, paraffin, or a silicone spray to the parts of the drawer that are binding. You can usually identify these parts because they'll have a dark, almost polished look—from rubbing. If the drawer is the simple box type, first clear away all dust and then lubricate the sides and bottom. If it's the kind that has thin wood strips on the sides that ride in grooves, lubricate the strips. If it has a wood strip in the center on the bottom, lubricate it and the sides. In other words, lubricate wherever wood contacts wood.

If the drawer is so badly stuck that you can't get at the binding parts, you'll have to shrink the wood first. You do this with heat. One good thing to use is a *drop light*—a bulb enclosed in a little wire cage; the bulb itself is on an extension cord. Just place the bulb inside the drawer for an hour or two. You could also use a portable hair dryer, directing heat into the drawer, or a 60-watt light bulb in an ordinary lamp—in fact any source of heat. But check after an hour to see how the drawer is sliding—you don't want to dry the wood out too much.

If you can't get the drawer open far enough to blow the heat in or get the bulb in, remove the drawer above or below it and put the bulb in the corresponding compartment, or blow the heat from there. If you still can't budge the drawer, work carefully with a screwdriver to pry it out. But this shouldn't be required. When you get the drawer out, lubricate it (as described earlier).

When lubrication doesn't make the drawer slide easily, you can use sandpaper to slim it down a smidgen at critical points. First clean off the lubrication with turpentine or Spic and Span® on a damp rag. Wrap a piece of medium-grade sand-paper (found at hardware stores) around a small block of wood that you can hold in your hand. Sand, stopping and checking frequently to see how the drawer is sliding; you don't want to take off too much wood.

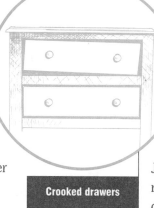

Crooked drawers

If you push a drawer in and it sticks at the last inch or so, it probably means that the bottom of each side is worn down. To correct this, remove the drawer and press in a line of thumbtacks along the paths where each edge rides. The tacks raise the drawer and let it slide easily, as if it were on railroad tracks. Of course, you'll have to raise or lower the tacks to get the drawer sliding just the way it should.

Another possible cause of a sticking drawer is that the piece of furniture is resting on an uneven floor. When this happens, one side may sag so that the compartment that the drawer goes in becomes misaligned. You can tell that this is the case if you can see uneven amounts of space around the drawer. If so, stick pieces of cardboard or wood slivers under the piece of furniture to raise it level so that the drawer (or drawers) does not rub against the compartment.

Of course, a drawer can stick simply because some object inside the drawer is jammed in the compartment. You can solve this easily if there is no partition above the drawer. Just take out the drawer above it and remove the object. Otherwise, pull the drawer out as far as you can and pick the items out one by one. Or stick a table knife between the closed drawer and the framework and poke the object free.

Drawer Closes Crooked

Another drawer problem occurs when you push in the drawer and one side goes in further than the other. This is because a piece of wood in the back of the compartment is either loose or missing, and does not stop the drawer as it's supposed to.

To cure this, forget the compartment and work on the drawer. Saw a new piece of wood as high as the back of the drawer and as thick as the extra distance it travels in. To find the latter dimension, push the drawer in and measure (with a ruler rather than tape measure) from the face of the drawer on the side that goes in too far to the front of the compartment. Glue this little block of wood onto the back of the side that goes in too far. Let it dry.

Loose Countertop Material

Plastic laminate, the hard sheeting that is used to cover kitchen and other countertops, occasionally comes loose and has to be refastened. The refastening is done with *contact cement*, a glue that sticks things together on contact. Normally, when using contact cement, you apply a coat of it to each surface (in this case, the bottom of the laminate and the top of the cabinet). Then you wait an hour or so, until the cement is dry, and press the surfaces together. They stick on contact.

However, loose plastic laminate usually isn't loose enough so that you can apply a coat of cement to each surface.

So, to make the repair, lift the laminate up as far as you can without cracking it. Load a little paint brush with a big glob of the cement and shove it in under the laminate. Press the laminate down as far as you can and immediately lift it up again. Keep the laminate propped up with a fork for an hour or so—until the cement's dry—and then take out the fork and press the laminate down against the surface, banging on it with your fist to get a good bond.

Until recently, contact cement was only available in a flammable form with harmful vapors. Now you can get a kind that is nonflammable and safe in every way. One brand is Weldwood's Home Safe Contact Cement. A pint is all you will need for the job. Leftover cement can be used on other jobs.

Wobbly Table

When a kitchen, dining-room, or other table wobbles or shakes without the slightest provocation, you have to check out a variety of things to see what's causing the problem. One common cause is that a leg is loose. On most tables there is a bolt with a nut—it looks like a square donut—on each of the legs where it joins the table. When a nut is loose, the bolt will be loose as well—and so the leg.

Just check the nuts. If there's looseness in one, use a wrench or a pair of pliers to tighten it up by turning clockwise.

Some tables have legs fastened on with screws or wingnuts. The former are fair game for a screwdriver; the latter can be tightened with your fingers. If you see another type of fastener, don't worry: Tighten as needed.

Loose table leg

Another reason for a wobbly table is that not all the legs are resting squarely because the floor is not perfectly flat. For this, try moving the table to a new position so all legs touch the floor.

If this doesn't work, it means that one leg is too short. For this, just place a piece of cardboard or a sliver of wood under the offending leg so that it has no space under it. To solve the problem permanently, cut out a piece of cardboard, wood, or other fairly solid material and glue it to the leg bottom with white glue.

No matter the repair, you'll find it easier to work with the table turned over. But if it's too heavy for this, no sweat. If a loose leg is the problem, just crawl under the table to make the repair. If you want to glue material to a short leg, just coat the shim with glue, lift the table a little, and put it in place.

Loose Casters

Loose furniture casters make it difficult, and sometimes impossible, to roll a piece of furniture around. Actually, it's not the caster that's loose but the metal socket it fits into. This socket is attached to the furniture by little metal teeth that bite into and grip the wood. The teeth lose their grip and cause the problem.

For the repair, you need four things: a hammer, a screwdriver, a little petroleum jelly, and two-part epoxy glue (an adhesive that will stick steel to wood). First, carefully pry off the socket by inserting a screwdriver under the teeth and

Coat with glue, knock in place

Anatomy of a caster

lifting. When it's off, coat the inside of the socket—the part the caster fits into—with petroleum jelly. Later, if glue oozes in there, the caster won't be accidentally bonded in place.

Mix the epoxy following label directions; then coat the outside of the socket with the glue. Insert the socket into the leg, then use the hammer to gently but firmly tap it back into place so that the teeth bite into the wood. Let it dry; then stick the caster back in place.

Loose Drawer Knob

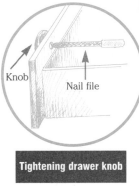

Tightening drawer knob

Pull out the drawer and hold the knob stationary with one hand. Using a nail file or screwdriver, tighten the screw inside that holds the knob on. That's it.

Electrical Maladies

The repairs least attempted by do-it-yourselfers are electrical ones. The reason is simple: fear—fear of a "shocking experience" or of possibly burning the house down.

Actually, some electrical repairs should be left to a licensed electrician. Indeed, all communities have codes that prohibit anyone but the professional from making certain repairs.

However, there are some that can be made without approval and with no danger whatsoever. And these are commonly the ones that need to be done. Let's take a look at them.

Plug Keeps Coming Out of Socket

Plugs from appliances and lamps often fall out of wall receptacles or outlets. The reason is usually that the plug prongs are bent or misshapen and can't get a grip. Or the receptacle may be worn. To solve the problem, simply bend the prongs on the appliance outward with your fingers. Stick the plug in the receptacle. Gently pull on it. Does it stick? No? Bend the prongs out a little further.

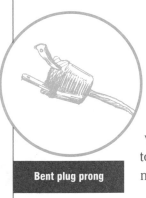

Bent plug prong

Broken Plug

When a plug is corroded, or cracked, or damaged some other way, it's a good idea to replace it. Indeed, it may be the reason why a lamp or small appliance doesn't work, and should be suspected immediately.

If you're replacing a plug on lamp wire, get a clamp type plug. To use it, first cut off the bad plug. Open the prongs or clamp device on the plug, and slip the cord into the plug slot.

Wire

Spread prongs wide, stick wire in hole...

and squeeze prongs

Push the prongs together, or push the clamp down. Inside, little teeth cut into the cord and electrical contact is made.

If you have the old-fashioned open-construction plug, snap off the fiber disk and loosen the screws to pull the cord out. Use a knife to bare a half inch of wire, then wrap the ends clockwise around the screws, and snap the disk back.

Frayed Cord

Cloth covering on electrical cords is often subject to fraying, usually close to

the plug. To repair this, simply cut the cord off at the point where the frayed section begins. Take off the fiber on the plug, loosen the screws holding the wires, and pull out the piece of cord. Discard it; then attach the cord wires to the plug as if you were replacing the plug (as described under "Broken Plug").

Cut wire at point past damage

Broken Lamp

If a lamp flickers or doesn't go on, it could be a bad bulb. If a new bulb doesn't solve the problem, check the wall plug: Are the prongs getting a good grip in the wall? How about the plug itself? Are the wires in it securely attached under the little screws? Is the plug broken? Handle any problem as previously described.

If the wall plug is okay, the trouble is inside the lamp. Pull the plug out of the wall, and set the lamp on a table where you have good working light.

Take out the bulb, and then unscrew the cap on the very top of the lamp.

Take off the shade and then the *harp*, the wire section around the bulb.

The shiny metal part that the bulb screws into is called the *shell*. On it, you'll see imprinted the word *PRESS*. Push on the word *PRESS* with your thumb or the flat part of a screwdriver, at the same time twisting the shell upward very hard. It will slip off. Inside the shell is a fiber liner

Wires on screws

shaped just like it. It may come off with the shell. If it doesn't, lift it off (this is easy to do).

Inside you'll see two wires, each attached to a little screw, as in a plug. If either is loose, tighten it up. If they're broken, cut off the cord and prepare and attach new wires, just as with a broken plug. If the socket itself is damaged, simply loosen the screws and slip out the wires. Lift the socket

Press socket down to open

off and get a replacement like it. As with a plug, tie the wires to the screws. Finally, put the lamp back together by reversing the procedure you used to take it apart. Sockets, by the way, cost about $1.30 each.

Flickering or Burned-Out Fluorescent Tube

Like regular lamps, fluorescent tubes can flicker or simply not go on. There are a variety of simple solutions for these problems.

If, when you flip on the light switch, the tube blinks repeatedly before it stays lit, that may mean that it's loose. Gently grasp it at the ends and turn it away from you to see if that seats it more securely. If it doesn't, turn it toward you to try to get it in tighter.

← Starter

Anatomy of a fluorescent lamp

If it still flickers after tightening—or tightening wasn't needed—the problem may be caused by loose sockets. The sockets (one at each end of the tube) are held on by screws on the outside ends of the metal housing. Try tightening them.

If the tube still flickers, probably a defective "starter" is causing the difficulty. This is a little barrel-shaped device that sits in a hole in the metal housing. To see it, you have to remove the tube.

Grasp the tube near the ends and turn it gently, first in one direction, then the other, until you hear a little blip. Continue to turn that way until you hear another blip. Lift out the tube. When replacing it, reverse the process.

Most starters have the word *REMOVE* imprinted on the end, with a little arrow pointing left or right. First press the starter in as far as you can; then turn it in the direction of the arrow and lift out.

Take the starter down to your hardware store and get a replacement just like it. Install it by reversing the way you took it out.

Electrician's Secret

Other indications of a defective starter are when the ends of the tube glow brighter than the middle part, or when the light switch has to be flipped several times before the tube stays lit.

If all else fails, replace the tube. A bad tube is unlikely, though, because they're designed to last hundreds of hours.

Iron Doesn't Work

When you turn on the iron and it doesn't work, it's likely that one of the wires inside the iron is loose. To find out, use a little screwdriver and remove the plate where the cord disappears into the iron. Inside you'll see that the cord splits into two wires, and that each wire has a little metal *grommet* on the end that is attached to a little screw. If there is only one grommet, the other will have fallen loose—that's the problem. So, simply slip the grommet back onto the screw shaft where it belongs and tighten the screw onto it.

Many times iron cords become frayed and require replacement. So, take the plate off in the back of the iron, loosen the screws holding the grommets on, and get another cord just like it. Then slip the grommets on the screws, tighten the screws, and replace the plate.

Door Troubles

A variety of maladies can hit a door. Following is a roundup.

Loose Hinge

If a regular door sticks when you try to close it, chances are that the top hinge is loose—the door will sag and its bottom will rub against the floor, and you'll probably see scuff marks on the floor. A loose hinge means loose screws. Tighten them up and the problem's solved.

First, open the door all the way and stick as many thin books as you can under the outer door edge. This keeps it steady while you work and stops the door from pulling on the screws as you try to tighten them.

Tighten all the screws you can see—even the ones that don't look loose—as tight as you can. (You turn the screws to the right.) This includes the screws that go through the hinge into the door and those that go into the door-opening framework (technically known as the *jamb*). Take away the books and try the door. It should work.

Sometimes you won't be able to tighten the screws well because the screw holes on the wall framework are too chewed up—there isn't enough solid wood for the screws to bite into. (This usually does not happen to holes in the door itself.)

Tighten hinge screws

To handle this problem, first wedge up the door with thin books. Take out all the screws in the hinge and turn back the hinge leaf. Pack wood putty into the bad holes. (You'll know which ones are bad because you'll never quite succeed in tightening up the screws in them. The screws will just keep turning, even though the heads are all the way in. If you look closely you will also see how chewed up they are.)

Push the putty into each hole with a finger, poking at it with the tip of a screwdriver to eliminate air pockets. Fill each hole all the way and smooth it off with your finger. Let the putty dry according to label directions.

Finally, drive in new screws where needed, the same kind as were used before but a half inch longer. Take your time and drive the screws in all the way. The combination of the putty and the extra length of the

To renew hinge holes, pack with wood putty

screws—enabling them to bite into new wood—should solve the problem.

If you can't find wood putty, you can pack white-glue-coated wooden match sticks (without the heads) into the screw holes. This serves the same purpose as putty.

Loosen screw, tighten knob

Tightening knob

Loose Doorknob

Doorknobs have an annoying way of coming loose, making it difficult and sometimes impossible to open doors. To remedy the condition, first look for a little screw on the *neck* (the narrow part) of the doorknob. Using a screwdriver, turn the little screw two or three full turns to the left to loosen it. Have someone hold the knob on the other side of the door so it can't move (or hold it yourself). Turn the knob on your side all the way to the right, pushing it forward as you do, until the front of the neck contacts the plate on the door. This may require a little muscle.

When the neck is snug against the plate, turn the knob back and forth to see how it works. If it's too tight (the latch won't come out after going in), turn the knob to your left about a quarter turn to loosen it. Then tighten up the little screw.

Cabinet Door Won't Shut

Many cabinet doors have two parts: a pronglike affair on the door and the part on the shelf that the prong fits into when you close the door. When the door doesn't shut, it's because repeated door closings have knocked the shelf part (the catch) out of line and the prong isn't fitting into it.

Door

Strike

Catch

To enable cabinet door to close—realign catch

To get the door to shut properly, all you have to do is reposition the catch. On close inspection, you'll see that it's held on by two screws that go through a slot (rather than a hole). Loosen each of the screws a half turn to the left so you can slide the catch forward. As you do, straighten it out. Try the door. Does it stay closed? No? Then reposition the catch until it does. Then tighten up the screws. To prevent a recurrence, drive another little screw against the back of the slot.

Window Troubles

The two main problems with windows are they can stick and the glass can break. Both problems are fairly easily cleared up.

Sticking Window

If you can't open (or close) a wooden window, a likely reason is that dried paint has gummed up the track it rides in. To free the window, stick a knife in where the window meets the framework. Run the knife up and down; this may cut the dried paint. Or, take a hammer and tap all around the window frame, using a little wood block or a folded towel to protect the window finish. This vibrates the window and breaks the paint seal.

Once you get a window moving, open and close it ten or fifteen times. Then

Cutting paint seal on window

apply a liberal amount of lubrication in the track. You can use wax or a silicone spray.

Another reason for a wooden window to stick is that it's lopsided in its track. You pull up, or down, and one side jams against the track.

Try to get the window level before you attempt to move it. Pull along the bottom to get it even, then carefully keep it level every time you raise or lower it. Also, lubricate the track. Repair involves taking the window down.

Sometimes a window sticks for no apparent reason. When this is the case, apply lubrication and try to get it moving.

Casement windows—the metal ones that open by turning a little crank handle— can also stick. Paint builds up on the bottom edge or the hinge screws come loose, allowing the window to sag and stick. The cure in the first case is to scrape off the paint from the bottom edge with a scraper or a butter knife. Tightening the screws will solve the second problem.

When sliding windows stick, it's usually because the lower tracks they slide in get clogged with soil. Brushing out the dirt should solve the problem. Follow this by spraying a silicone spray into the track.

Broken Windows

The hardest part of fixing a broken window is cutting a new piece of glass to fit into the window frame. However, you don't have to do it. You can get a piece cut to size free by a professional at the glass shop where you buy the new glass.

On broken window, first remove glass

First, take out the broken glass. Wear heavy work gloves. Get a grip on a broken section and gently rock it back and forth until it comes out. Repeat for other broken sections. If the glass isn't broken enough to get a grip on it, gently tap it with a hammer until it is. Wear glasses, goggles, or sunglasses to protect your eyes.

When the glass is out, scrape away the old putty from the window frame. Do a good job, going down to clean, bare wood. When the scraping is complete, brush out or use a rag to wipe out all putty crumbs.

Scrape frame clean

As you remove the putty, you'll notice little triangular pieces of metal sticking into the frame. These are *glazier's points*, and their job is to hold the glass in place. Remove them with a pair of pliers or a screwdriver. Note the places they were removed from. You can mark them with a pencil or crayon.

When the frame is clean, apply a coat of paint to it. The wood is likely to be dry and will absorb the paint rather than the new glazing compound you'll use later.

Measure the space for the glass from edge to edge inside the frame, both horizontally and vertically. When you have the dimensions, subtract $1/8$ inch from each. For

Apply paint to frame

example, if your vertical measurement is 12 inches, subtract the eighth and you get $11^7/_8$ inches. Order the glass in this size. The smaller glass gives you more space and allows the framework to expand and contract due to weather. To be sure you're measuring accurately, it's a good idea to do it three times at different points on the window.

Glass is cheap enough, so buy the right one for the job. If you're replacing glass in a multipaned window, order single-strength glass. For a single pane window, order double-strength glass.

You'll also need a little can of *glazing compound*, which is the modern counterpart of putty. Glazing compound is more expensive than putty,

Insert new glass

but it's easier to work with and is more flexible—it doesn't dry out like putty. One brand is Dap; a can costs about $1.25.

First, mix the compound in the can, with a narrow putty knife (it looks like a thin spatula). Scoop out a little on the end of your knife and apply a thin layer of it all around the window frame wood where the glass will rest.

Place the new glass all the way inside the frame. Push the glazier's points into the frame near their original

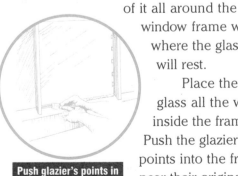

Push glazier's points in place to hold glass

holes. Each point should go in about halfway. For pushing, you can use the end of a chisel, a screwdriver, a putty knife, or a quarter. The best points to get are those with little raised sections that allow them to be pushed in easily.

Now apply the glazing compound to the window where it meets the frame. Do this by scooping out small globs of it, pressing them along on the frame in the approximate finish shape you want it to have; check the putty on other windows for this. When one frame side is done, smooth the compound out into final shape by drawing the putty knife along it.

Proceed to do the other sides of the window, one by one, as just described. Let the compound dry for half a day, then paint it and the rest of the window.

Outside Repairs

There are a number of repairs that can be done outside the house. The following is a roundup.

Crumbling Brick Mortar

As time goes by, mortar—the stuff between bricks—loosens and crumbles.

The holes should be filled for good looks and to stop further deterioration.

To do the job, five tools are required, all commonly available at hardware stores and home improvement centers: a pointing trowel, a hammer, a wire brush, a jointer (for smoothing the mortar out after it is applied), and a ³/₄-inch cold chisel.

Chisel out loose mortar

For the hole filler, a premixed mortar is best. This is a powder that comes in 10- to 80-pound bags. All you do is add water in the amount specified on the label, and mix.

First, use the cold chisel and hammer to chip out all unsound mortar— the stuff that's barely hanging on. To protect your eyes against flying chips, wear glasses or goggles. Then, use a wire brush to remove all loose, crumbly material.

Mix mortar with water (following the directions on the package), and then carry the mortar to the bricks in a pail or pan. Plop a soaking rag against the area to get it good and wet, and then scoop out

Apply new mortar— smooth with jointer

some mortar on the tip of the trowel and force it into a hole. Keep putting mortar in until the hole is overfilled a fraction of an inch; while filling, poke at the mortar to remove air pockets. Let the mortar alone for about five minutes, then draw the jointer over it to shape and smooth it so it looks like the surrounding mortar. If you smear any mortar on the bricks, clean it off right away, using the wire brush and water.

Every day for a week after you complete the job, give the patches a half-minute light spray from your garden hose. This enables the mortar to age properly.

Cracks in Concrete

Concrete steps, walks, and driveways commonly develop cracks. Indeed, sometimes it seems as if there is no such thing as concrete without cracks. At any rate, the repair is as easy as filling mortar holes. You use the same tools except that you don't need the jointer.

Start by digging out all unsound (loose) material with a cold chisel and hammer. Brush out as much material as you can with a wire brush. Douse the crack with a fine spray from the hose. Then fill the crack immediately.

The best filler for concrete is sand mix. Like mortar mix, it comes in pre-mixed form to which you add water. Start with a 20-pound bag, mixing it according to directions on the bag.

Force the fresh mix down into the crack, poking it frequently to remove air pockets. Fill the crack completely; then smooth it level with the surrounding concrete by drawing the bottom of the trowel across it.

Place a piece of burlap or an old towel on the patch. Wet the cloth with a fine spray from your garden hose. Each day for a couple of days, wet it down the same way. A brick or board will hold the burlap or towel in place.

If you have a large-area cementing job, and you are concerned with appearance, then it may well be necessary to hire a professional. The real skill that a mason brings to a job is the ability to smooth cement well, something that takes a long time to learn.

Clogged Gutters

Gutters usually become clogged in spring and autumn from leaves, twigs, bird nests, and other assorted debris. If you don't clear them, collected water can make the gutter sag. Also the water may back up and run down inside house walls.

Lean an extension ladder against the house, or against the gutter, if that's necessary for proper ladder placement. For safety, the ladder should extend a couple of feet above the gutter, if put there. Next, look down the gutter. Wherever you see debris, move the ladder into position and scoop it out with a garden trowel or other implement. You can drop the material in a plastic bucket hooked to the top rung (with a piece of hanger wire), or simply drop it on the ground and clean it up later.

Proceed around the house. When all the blockages are cleared, lug a garden hose up the ladder and run water into each gutter to clear it completely. If the water does not run quickly out the downspout, it means the downspout is clogged.

Try to clear it with a steady stream of water from the hose. If this doesn't do the job, you can use a snake, the same tool used to clear a clogged sink drain. Simply feed the pointed end of the *snake* down into the downspout. When you hit a blockage, move the snake up and down to shake it loose. Follow by shooting a stream of water down the spout. For greater water force, you can hold your forefinger halfway over the hose nozzle.

Leaking Gutters

If you can't find the gutter leaks, wait until the first rainy day; then grab your umbrella and go outside and look. Note the location of the leaks. When the weather is clear, repair them. To repair a hole in a galvanized gutter, use roofing cement and ordinary burlap. (Your local grocery store should have some.)

First, use a wire brush to remove all rust around the hole; brush down to absolutely clean metal. To make sure you get it all off, follow the wire brushing by rubbing with an *emery cloth*, a fine black sandpaper. It is available at hardware stores.

Using a spatula, scraper, or trowel, lay a good glob of cement over the hole, and spread it 3 inches on either side of the hole. The coating should be about $1/4$-inch thick.

Cut a piece of burlap as wide as the cement, and press firmly and flatly into the cement. Cover the burlap with another thin coat of cement, overlapping the edges about 1 inch each. It is important

Hole

Gutter

Trowel with cement

Burlap

Wire brush

Hole in gutter; clean hole; apply cement; lay burlap smooth; apply more cement over burlap

to get the burlap and cement flat and smooth so that water can flow by freely.

If the hole is at a joint, use the same procedure. If there is a leak in a joint, you can use a silicone caulk. Just squeeze it into the seam where sections join, smoothing it with your finger to make sure water flows.

Hole in a Blacktop Driveway

This job is done with ready-to-use cold mix asphalt patching compound, which comes in various size bags, and is used without mixing.

First, shovel out all loose rocks and debris from the hole. If the hole is more than 6 inches wide and 4 or 5 inches deep, place a large rock at the bottom. This will serve as your base, and conserve the amount of patcher needed.

Open the blacktop bag and

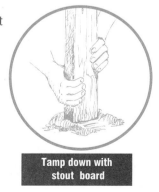

Tamp down with stout board

scoop out a shovelful. Pour it into the hole. Do this until the hole is filled to within about 1 inch of the top. Use the end of a hefty board or the back of the shovel to compact the blacktop; it's fairly soft, so you shouldn't have any trouble. When it seems thoroughly compacted, add more mix, this time filling $1/2$ inch higher than the surrounding driveway surface.

Now compact some more. You can do this with a board or shovel, but it's easier and you'll do a better job with your car. Simply drive one wheel back and forth over it until the patch is level with the rest of the driveway.

Above: Clincher mender
Below: hammer down prongs to lock on

Leaking Rubber Hose

The repair should be made with a device called a *clincher mender*. This is a brass tube, in the middle of which are encircling teeth. You can get one in a hardware store or home center. Bring the hose to the store so your dealer will give you the right size.

First, use a single-edge razor blade or a sharp knife to cut out the section of the hose with the hole. Keep your cuts

vertical. Slip one end of the device into one section of the hose and hammer down the teeth so they bite into the rubber and are flat. Slip the other end of the device into the other section of hose and hammer down those teeth.

Leaking Plastic Hose

Here, as with rubber hose, use a clincher mender, but one made of sheet brass rather than pure brass. The repair is made the same way. However, if you have difficulty sticking the tube into the end of the cut, you can soften the hose by dipping it in warm water.

Hole in Screening

Screen patch

Hail to the genius who invented screening! He made the openings in the screening small enough so bugs can't get in, but big enough so cooling breezes can, and you can even see through.

Frequently, however, holes show up that weren't part of the original design. And before you know it you've got tiny, unwelcome visitors.

The repair depends on whether you have metal or plastic screening, and the extent of the damage. If wires in metal screen are misaligned, making a "hole," push them back into position with the point of an *awl* or icepick.

A small hole—less than $1/4$-inch wide—in either type of screening can be plugged with a drop of airplane glue or household cement, such as Duco makes. For this repair, there's no need to take the screen down.

For a bigger hole on metal screening, you can buy a ready-to-use patch. This is simply a small rectangle of screening with hooks on the ends.

Take the screen down and place it on a flat surface. Place the hole over a small block of wood and tap the hole edges with a hammer to flatten them. Place the patch over the hole, and thread the hooked ends through the screening. Turn the screen over, placing the patch on a small wood block. Tap the patch hooks with a hammer so they flatten and grip the screening.

First pry out spline— for replacing screen

For a hole in plastic screening, you need to obtain a piece of scrap screening. If you don't have a piece, try a hardware store. Cut a patch about $1/4$ inch bigger than the hole. Squeeze out a line of household cement around the edge of the patch. Press the patch in place over the hole, and hold it there for a few minutes; then release it and let it dry completely.

Ripped Screen

If there's a big gash in a screen or it's otherwise extensively damaged, the only option is to replace the screening. Replacement procedures vary, depending on what the screening material is and what kind of frame it is set into.

If you're replacing metal screening in metal frames, follow this procedure: With a screwdriver, pry up a corner of the *spline*—the long thin strip of rubber that holds the screening

Spline tool

Closeup of convex wheel—use concave wheel to force spline in place, then trim with utility knife

edges in the grooves around the frame. Pull it free with your fingers, lifting out the screening.

New metal screening is available at hardware stores and costs pennies a square foot. To install it, you need a utility knife or a razor blade, plus a special screening tool that has a little metal wheel at each end, one with a concave surface and the other convex. You can get along without it, but it only costs about a few dollars and makes the job much easier.

If spine is metal, hammer it down with wood as shown

First, cut a new piece of screening 2 inches bigger on all sides than the screen frame. Lay the piece on the frame squarely so there is equal overlap all around. Using the convex wheel on the screening tool, tuck the screen into the grooves in the frame. Use short strokes.

Next, using the concave wheel, roll a piece of spline in one side. If the existing spline is in bad shape, you can get new spline at a hardware store. The advantage of using old spline is that it is already cut to the correct lengths. With

spline in one end, pull the screening taut to the opposite side and roll another piece of spline in that groove. Insert spline in one end, pull the screening taut to the opposite end, and insert spline there.

Using the metal frame as a guide, trim excess screening with a utility knife or a razor blade. If the screen uses lengths of rigid metal instead of rubber spline, follow the same steps as just described, but use a hammer and a tapered block of wood instead of the screening tool to set the strips in their grooves.

To replace fiberglass or plastic screening in metal frames, remove the spline, but cut the new piece of screening only as big as the frame. Center it on the frame and then, to get it taut, tuck it in at all four corners with 1-inch lengths of spline or *dowels* (thin round sticks available at lumberyards). Then replace the spline (whether rubber or metal) in this order: one side, one end, the other side, and the final end. In other words, clockwise or counterclockwise. Trim the excess as for metal screening; pull taut as you go.

Stapled in place, screening on wood frames

Instead of grooves and spline to hold screening in place, wooden-frame screens use tacks—or staples—on strips of wood. To replace metal screening in wooden frames, first use a putty knife (or a butter knife or screwdriver) to pry free the strips.

Cut a piece of screening that's 1 inch bigger on all sides than the old screening. Square up the new piece on the frame. Use a staple gun or tacks to fasten the screening to one side; place the tacks or staples 2 inches apart. Fold over the overlap and tack it down, placing the tacks between the ones already in.

Pull the screening taut to the opposite side and repeat the fastening procedure. Next attach the screening to one end, pull the material to the opposite end, and tack it in place. Then replace the molding, either with the nails that came out when you pried the strips free or with some new ones of the same size.

Installing fiber- glass screening in wooden frames is done the same way as metal screening. However, fasten it on in

a clockwise or counterclockwise order, starting with a side.

Miscellaneous Repairs

Loose floor board

Use nail set tool to sink nail heads

Sub floor

Joist

Angle nails for keystone holding effect

Squeaky board

Squeaky Floor

Squeaky floors are the result of one or more loose floorboards, usually just one. When you step on the board, it bends more than it should and rubs against adjacent boards. The rubbing produces the squeak. Or, it could be that one board is warped.

The answer is to nail the board down tightly so it can't move. You can use a $2^1/_2$-inch *finishing nail* or, for an even tighter job, a *spiral-fluted flooring nail*. This has a surface that is partially fluted, or grooved, and has greater holding power.

First press on the various boards to find out which one is squeaking. When you discover it, drive a nail in at the approximate point where you think it's bending. (If you don't get it exactly, no sweat.) For greater holding power, drive the nail in at a slight angle—about as much as the Leaning Tower of Pisa leans.

Step on the board. Still squeaks? Okay, drive another nail in, about 2 inches from the first, also angling it. Test for squeaking again. Still squeak? If so, drive another nail, also angled, about 2 inches in another direction from the first nail you drove in.

With the nails in, take a *nailset* (a tool that looks like an extra thick nail with a small, blunt end) and drive the heads of the nails a little bit below the surface. Then fill the depressions with wood putty the color of the wood, and sand smooth. This will hide the nailheads. Of course, if you have a rug or other covering on the floor, this last step won't be necessary.

You may be able to silence the squeak without nails. Just squirt some powdered graphite between the boards. When the board rubs, the lubrication prevents it from making noise.

Damaged Ceramic Tile

Ceramic tile is one of the toughest building materials available. However, it is not impervious to damage. It can be scratched, or broken, or chipped, and it can fall out. For good looks and to keep moisture from sneaking through behind the tiles, damaged tiles should be replaced.

This is sometimes easier said than done. You can buy replacement tiles at tile stores; however, if your tiles have been up a fair amount of time, their original color will have changed slightly and you may not be able to get ones that match.

To get a damaged tile out, use a cold chisel to chip away at the corners of the tile. Usually there's a little space under them. When all the corners are chipped out, slip the chisel under one and lift. The tile should come out easily. Scrape away all the adhesive on the wall. Mix up some plaster of paris, and set the tile in this, making it level with adjacent tiles. When the plaster is dry, use your finger to fill in around the tile with a ready-mixed grout. Smooth it out with your finger so the grout is shaped like the grout between the other tiles.

Removing ceramic tile

Finally, take a wet sponge and clean off all grout smeared on the tiles.

Usually, the grout required is white. If you need a colored grout, get the kind that can be tinted, and buy the tint separately.

Worn Resilient Tile

Resilient tile gets its name from the fact that it has some "give"—it depresses when you step on it. If one gets badly worn, cracked, or chipped, you should replace it.

You can do this with heat. Just direct the heat of a hair dryer or heat gun on the tile until the adhesive softens, then lift and pry it out.

You may not have or be able to get a replacement tile in the proper color or pattern. If this is the case, consider taking up four or five tiles in a row, or four tiles in adjacent rows, and installing tiles of a contrasting color as an accent touch. This works well in front of a kitchen sink or in the middle of a room.

Felt Lamp Pads Fall Off

If you examine the bottoms of lamps, candlesticks, vases, and the like, you'll see that they're covered by felt pads. This is to keep the item from scratching furniture.

With time, these pads either fall off or become matted with dust, furniture wax, or polish. Whatever the case, replacement is called for.

First, carefully peel off the old felt in one piece and use it as a pattern for cutting a new piece. (Felt is available at hobby stores.) If there is no old felt, or the existing material is badly damaged, or you rip it during removal, cut a new piece $1/2$ inch larger all around than the base of the item.

Apply glue to the bottom of the item and set it on the felt. You can use white glue for metal, wood, glass, or most anything, but household cement (such as Duco makes) works better for glass and metal bottoms. Use the glue sparingly— too much and it'll soak through the felt. Also, if you use household cement, don't set the item on a varnished or painted surface. The glue vapors can damage these finishes.

Since you have overlapping felt, trim it off with a single-edge razor blade or scissors—whichever works best, depending on the shape of the particular item.

If you're replacing felt on items with "feet" such as lamps with animal paws, use a double layer of felt. Follow the procedure for the first layer as described above. Stick the second layer on with just a tiny bit of adhesive.

Window Shade Trouble

For such a simple device, a shade can have a surprising number of difficulties. Following are problems you may encounter and solutions to handle them.

Sometimes a shade won't go up all the way. This is usually caused by a lack of tension in the little spring inside the shade roller. To get more tension, pull the shade down about $2/3$ of the way. Remove it from the window, and roll it up tightly around the roller. Hold it tightly rolled up and replace it in the window. Try it. It should work properly.

Sometimes a shade flies up when you pull it up. This is caused by too much tension in the little spring. To fix, raise the shade as high as it will go, remove it from the window, and then unroll it by hand halfway down. Replace the shade in the window. Try it. Still too fast? Repeat the procedure.

Sometimes a shade won't stay in place when you pull it down, but rolls back up. Take the shade down and look on the end of the roller that has a little metal bar sticking out with little gearlike affairs around it. Check for dirt. If you see any, brush and wipe it away with a rag. Then, whether or not there was dirt, squirt some

powdered graphite into the end, covering everything. Powdered graphite comes in small tubes and is commonly available at hardware stores.

Loose Toilet Paper Dispenser

When a toilet paper dispenser is attached to a plasterboard wall with screws, it invariably comes loose, because plasterboard is simply too thin a material to enable a screw to get a good bite. When this happens, discard the screws and get a pair of $5/8$-inch "Molly" bolts, as described in the hardware section, and use these to reattach it.

If the dispenser is attached to a plaster wall, you can reset it in new plaster of paris. Just pack it in, push the dispenser in place, and wipe away excess.

Damaged Bathtub Caulk

Caulk is the material used to seal the seam between the top of the bathtub and the wall. Eventually it breaks down and requires replacement. A variety of caulks are available, but silicone works best.

Before applying the caulk, clean out all the cracked, blackened, or otherwise deteriorated

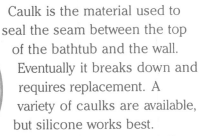
Applying caulk to tub

caulk. Use a beer can opener or a putty knife. Don't leave any crumbs.

With this done, proceed to apply the new caulk. Simply squeeze the tube. The caulk squirts out slowly from its thin spout. As it does, draw the spout along the tub-wall seam. When you've got the seam completely filled in with a solid line of caulk, smooth it out with a wet forefinger or a spoon handle. Let it dry. Follow the label for drying time before using the shower or bathtub.

Loose Toilet Seat

Every toilet seat is held to the toilet by means of nuts and bolts. When the nuts become loose, the seat is loose.

If the seat is loose, look in the back of the toilet. See the nuts? Tighten them with a pair of pliers, an adjustable wrench, or a monkey wrench, and the problem is solved.

Chipped Porcelain

Washing machines, refrigerators, sinks, and other kitchen appliances and fixtures are coated with porcelain, because it is especially hard and easy to clean.

Loose nut

Loose seat therapy

However, it can chip. When this happens, the metal below is exposed, leaving an unsightly black spot.

A spot like this can be touched up with paint specifically made for the job. This special paint is available at paint stores in small bottles in colors to match appliances and fixtures. A brush applicator comes with the bottle.

Broken Crockery

A variety of glues are available at hardware stores and home centers for reassembling broken crockery, one of the best bets being household cement. Just follow the instructions on the package to make the repair.

Squeaky Stairs

Stairs squeak because the tread, the part you step on, is loose and when pressed down rubs against the board—called a riser—that supports it. The repair is the same, essentially, as for a loose floorboard.

Have an adult stand on the loose tread to bring it into close contact with the riser. Drive the nails through the tread into the riser, for the position of the nails. You can tell that the nail is going into the riser if you encounter resistance. If the nail suddenly gets easy to drive, you know you've missed it.

Drive the nails even with the tread surface. To hide the holes, tap the nails a little ($1/16$ inch) below the surface, using a nailset. Then fill the holes with wood putty the color of the tread wood.

If the tread is covered by carpeting, you needn't drive the nails below the surface. In fact, if appearance isn't important, you can completely forget this step (no pun intended).

Carpet Spots and Stains

High on the list of household traumas is a stained carpet. Your best bet here is to obtain a spot remover, such as AFTA® or Hot Spot®, from an outlet where carpeting is sold, such as a home improvement center.

Leak in Basement Wall

On a rainy day, you may notice a leak in a basement wall. If this happens, no sweat. There is actually a product that,

when applied to the crack or hole, stops the leak in minutes.

The material is called *hydraulic cement*. To use the material to stop a leak, mix it with water until it has the consistency of putty. Wait a few minutes until it stiffens a little. Then, using a trowel or putty knife, force it into the crack or hole, and hold it there with the tool for a few minutes until it stays by itself. Add more cement the same way until the water stops flowing. When this occurs, shave the material even with the rest of the wall.

Applying hydraulic cement

Water Leaks Around Kitchen Sink

The way kitchen sinks are set into countertops makes them prone to becoming a little loose. When this occurs, there is space around the sink rim—a perfect place for water to get through.

Solve this problem with the same material used to seal off the joint between the bathtub and the wall—caulk. Just fill up the opening around the rim, using a scraper or putty knife.

Storm Door Repair

The main parts of a storm door are the lock mechanism and the pneumatic cylinder, which can be adjusted to close slowly enough so that the door does not slam, but fast enough to insure that it latches. There is also an extension spring between the frame and the door so that the door can open to a certain distance (otherwise the hinges would take too much stress and could be damaged). It is best to remove any part that you need to replace and bring it with you to the store in order to insure getting the correct part. There are quite a few variations, and the screw holes may not be in the same places on the replacement piece as they are on the existing door.

Patio Door Repair

Here, too, parts must match. You should not attempt to interchange parts, even if it seems that you can. For example, on wheels that appear to be the same size, there might be a slight difference in thickness, and even though the wheels "fit," you won't get the same fast rolling action as you would if you used the proper sized part. The manufacturer's name will often be stamped on the unit, usually on the track. This can be an aid in obtaining parts.

Garage Door Hardware

Hardware for garage doors also varies considerably, and the best procedure is to bring the old part into the store.

CHAPTER

5

According to a familiar old adage, an ounce of prevention is worth a pound of cure. This is surely true, and nowhere truer than in caring for the home. When you don't allow little things to become big things, you can save in a big way.

Painting

The adage certainly applies when it comes to housepainting, both interior and exterior. Paint protects and increases the life of your home, and even the multithumbed can do the work, and save an estimated 75 to 85 percent of labor costs.

Picking Colors

Before launching into the job, however, spend some time thinking about and deciding the colors you want. There are a number of things to consider when selecting paint colors for interior and exterior painting.

Paint is mixed in a store, and you can dab a little of the mixed paint on the same sample color chip and then let it dry. The chips are actually small paint samples, not photographic renditions, so you are looking for the mixed sample to be right on the money, or close. It should be noted, though, that if a chip is flat or eggshell sheen, the dried dab will appear different, and sometimes dramatically so because of the way it reflects light.

Be aware, too, that a paint color looks dramatically different in the store than it does on your walls. There are a number of reasons for this, including surface porosity, the way the paint reflects light, the amount of light in the room, and reflectance of colors from adjacent objects.

Surest Way to Pick Colors

To insure that the color is correct, it's best to have a small sample made and to try it on the wall. A quart is enough. Never pick colors according to the way paint looks in the can. Colors always dry darker than they appear when wet.

Ultimately, picking colors for the inside or the outside of a house is subjective. What is good for one person will be poison to another.

Today, well-stocked paint stores can computer-match most solid colors that are brought in. When I worked in a large home-improvement center I color-matched everything from a shutter to a frankfurter roll.

Interior Color Hints

The following are some tried-and-true interior color hints:

- Colors in one room should complement those used in others. For example, if you had five rooms, you wouldn't want to paint each a different color. The effect would be chaotic. Your best bet is to use complementary colors, or different shades of the same colors.

- Paint should be selected at the same time that wallpaper, flooring, and furniture are picked, if these are new or being changed.
- Colors are often selected from colors within wallpaper, or the colors in a rug or other flooring.
- A piece of clothing might be a starting point.
- A favorite painting or rug may contain a pleasing color combination to serve as a starting point.
- When a room contains multiple colors, the general rule is that the main color is used in $2/3$ of the room and other colors in $1/3$. This usually happens automatically because the walls, which contain the most square footage, are usually painted first.
- Ceilings are usually the lightest colors (usually but not always white), walls are darker, and floors the darkest element of all.
- Bold or bright, warm colors tend to make a room seem smaller. So do darker colors.
- Light pastel colors can make a room seem larger.
- If a room is too sunny, use blues and greens as a moderating effect.

Color to Cure Architectural Flaws

Color can also be used to correct architectural flaws, fooling the eye so that they are not as noticeable. Following are some situations where paint can help:

- Low Ceiling. Some ceilings are very low, and can give one a claustrophobic feeling. The basement is one such area where this problem often arises. To "raise" the ceiling, paint the ceiling a lighter color than the walls.
- High ceiling. There are a couple of ways to "lower" a ceiling. You can apply a medium or darker color on your walls and ceilings, or use a darker color on the ceiling than on the walls.
- Undersized room. If a room is very small, you can, as suggested above, use light pastel colors.
- Narrow rooms. Paint the short walls at each end a darker color than the longer walls.
- Irregular angles. If a room contains irregularities, such as a chimney jutting into a room or jogs, paint everything the same color. This tends to de-emphasize odd angles.

Exterior Color Hints

A number of color experts subscribe to the idea of having three colors on the outside: one main color and two other colors for the trim. The siding would be one color, a little on the conservative side. The front and rear doors and the windows should be another color, one that complements the siding color. The shutters, lamp post, mailbox, and house numbers can be a third color. The color would, again, be different but complementary.

In designing the color scheme, it is important to avoid having the trim or any other color that is different from the siding, stand alone from the other colors. For example, a house with beige siding, bright violet doors and windows, and yellow shutters would look chaotic. Exterior colors, again, must work together.

The following are more exterior color hints:

- Don't draw attention to downspouts, gutters, electrical conduit, meters, air conditioner units, and vents by painting them. These should be the same color as the siding or trim that they're mounted on.
- Don't draw attention to an attached garage by painting it a boldly different color. It should be the same color as the siding or a softer shade in the same color family.
- For the chimney and foundation, you can use a deeper shade of the body color; this tends to make them seem more solidly mounted.
- Medium to dark colors usually make a house appear smaller, and light to neutral colors make it look strong.

If you want to make a tall house seem shorter, paint the top a deeper tone than the bottom. This also works when the lot is small and one wants to bring the house size down, and also when the landscaping hasn't grown in and the house appears stark and overwhelming in size.

- Using a dark color to outline windows and trim will make a house look smaller. Lighter color on the trim will make a house look larger. Dark outline colors tend to pull the size of a house in; light ones expand it.
- Color ideas can come from a variety of places. Consider using a color you like from the inside of your home, or pick up a color from stonework outside or perhaps flowers or a plant. Color ideas can also come from

checking color schemes of similar-style homes in the neighborhood.

- Victorian and other period houses were painted with specific colors. If you have a house of this type and want to know what the colors were, check the library. There are books that show color schemes.
- Obtain manufacturers' color cards at paint stores and home centers. A number of these show homes painted with various combinations of colors that might work for you.
- To test combinations of colors, draw a picture of your home and color in various areas with colored pencils. Or, take a photo of the house and photocopy it, enlarge it, and then color it. The colors won't be accurate, but they will give a sense of how they will work together.
- Buy quarts of colors and apply them to various areas of the house and observe how they look overall and in various lights.

Interior and Exterior Paint

At the heart of a good paint job is the right paint. It seems elementary, but one of the most important things to be aware of when using paint is that some of it is formulated for interior use, and some for exterior; and each has different environmental problems to overcome. Some people use exterior paint indoors because they think it is tougher. After all, it is used outside and can withstand snow, rain, and wind. The fact, however, is that some of the highest grade exterior paint can be more detrimental than a poor quality interior paint.

Chemical Components of Paint

Paints contain different chemical components. Interior paint has added chemicals that make it scrubbable, stain resistant, and splatter resistant. In addition, it can be easily touched up.

Exterior paint is formulated for color retention; flexibility (to withstand expansion and contraction due to weather); and resistance to fading, mildew, and tannin bleed (a brownish chemical that can leach out of some woods). So, for example, you could use an exterior paint in the bathroom and get greater mildew resistance; however, you would sacrifice scrubbability and stain resistance.

Gloss Versus Flat Paint

A prime concern for many is a paint's washability; and the glossier the paint the more easily washed it is. On the other hand, the shinier the paint, the more light reflection—which can be annoying in some settings (such as a living room). Also, because glossy paint is thinner, it shows imperfections more readily than flatter paint.

Thus, where a paint requires greater washability but won't cause irritation, the glossier paints are preferred. Such areas include bathrooms, kitchens, and trim.

Paint for Bedrooms and Living Rooms

For bedrooms and living rooms, flat and satin flat, also known as eggshell— because it has the sheen of an egg—is preferred. Satin flat is considered washable; flat paint generally is not: Scrub it and it will come off the walls.

Some manufacturers say they make "scrubbable" flats, and this may well be true—in the laboratory. Scrubbing machines will remove soil without degrading the paint film. However, the scrubbing process may well leave what is known as a "burnish," or shiny mark, on the surface, essentially marring it. In sum, don't consider any flat paint scrubbable in a practical sense, though small mars may be removed with a damp cloth.

Oil- or Water-Base Paint?

Paint essentially comes with different bases: oil base or water base. The former thins and cleans up with mineral spirits or turpentine; the latter cleans up with water. Water-base paint, commonly called latex, dries very quickly; oil-base paint dries overnight.

The age-old question is, Which is better to use in particular situations? Years ago, this used to be fairly easy to answer, because each of the paints had its own distinct advantages.

Oil-base paint, for example, was commonly used on trim and doors, because it flowed and leveled much easier than latex, dried harder, and was much less susceptible to peeling in damp environments such as the bathroom. In fact, it used to be that some alkyds (another name for oil base) could outperform latex paints by 50 percent. In other words, latex was only half as good as alkyd.

But since the government has gotten into the picture, manufacturers have been driven into their research labs to try to come up with better latex products. And they have. Today's latex paints are comparable with oils in every way, and chances are they'll get even better.

One thing is for sure, however. Whatever type paint you buy, it should be a company's top-of-the-line, as detailed in the following section.

How to Buy Paint

The best quality indicator of paint is price. The more expensive the paint is within a particular brand, the more likely you are to get a high quality. Be assured that even companies with well-respected names sell varying grades of paint. Buy the best grade.

Top-of-the-line paint performs well. It flows better, covers better, and looks subtly but significantly better than bargain-basement or lower-quality paint. If you have to touch up a job, it's easier with better paint, and it won't stand out like a sore thumb. And the job can be done quicker.

Lead-Base Paint

Lead-base paint was outlawed for use in residences in 1976, but it is still something that must be understood and dealt with, because it still remains in many homes.

Lead is a poison that is particularly dangerous to children's health, because their bodies are small. Indeed, the American Academy of Pediatrics regards lead as one of the main hazards to small children.

Lead-base paint was used extensively in the United States until the early 1940s. It continued to be used, particularly for the exterior portions of dwellings, until 1976. In 1971 Congress passed the Lead-Base Paint Poisoning Prevention Act, and in 1976 the Consumer Product Safety Commission (CPSC) issued a ruling under this act that limited the lead content of paint used in residential dwellings, toys, and furniture to 0.06 percent.

In 1986 the EPA conducted a study that proved that over 42 million American homes still had interior and/or exterior lead-base paint. When remodeling is done, removing this lead-base material safely has become a big problem.

As moisture and UV (ultraviolet) rays from the sun bombard the exterior paint, the paint chalks, becoming a powder. This lead dust floats down through the air and gets into the soil around the foundation of the house—and can enter the house through gaps in the foundation, getting into the air we breathe.

Interior surfaces can also shed this powder, and it becomes a hazard when paint coatings are broken through during preparation for painting and remodeling, or simply by aging. And the dust is not fully removed by normal house cleaning methods.

There are a variety of ways to deal with the problem of lead-base paint, from removal to leaving it in place. Consult the EPA in your area if you think you have this problem.

Just how much paint to buy varies, because surfaces vary in their absorption, roughness, hiding ability, and so forth. In general, when calculating paint coverage, use the equation of 325 to 350 square feet per gallon. This is more realistic than the 400 square feet often given.

Volatile Organic Compounds

All solvents except for water are volatile organic compounds. When the sun strikes them, they link with the oxygen, chlorine, and nitrogen to form a gas known as ozone.

At high altitudes, ozone protects us against the ultraviolet radiation of the sun. But at ground level it is a harmful component in smog that is not good to breathe.

In recognition of this, a few years ago, the Clean Air Act started to mandate the amount of volatile organic compounds paint and stain could contain. States also applied their own restrictions. The result, in essence, is the reduction of VOC's in such coatings.

Painting Tools

A variety of tools and equipment is available for doing interior and exterior

painting. As with paint quality, bargain-basement equipment leads to bargain-basement results.

Rollers

Rollers (also called roller sleeves) are available for use with oil-base as well as water-base paints. The part that is covered by the fabric or nap is the core; and it may be plastic, phenolic-impregnated kraft paper, or cardboard.

The phenolic cores are best. They aren't affected by constant dipping in water or paint thinner and keep their shape indefinitely.

Fabric Types. The fabric or fiber on roller covers can be synthetic (for example, dacron, nylon, polyester, and orlon), natural (for example, lamb's wool, mohair, and sheepskin), or a blend. Lamb's wool, mohair, and sheepskin are designed for use with oil-base paints; synthetics are for use with latex. Lamb's wool will have an adverse reaction, just like a natural bristle brush, if used with latex; that is, it will swell and go limp. Synthetics may also be used for oil-base paint.

Nap Thickness. Sleeves also come in various nap or pile thicknesses, as well as qualities. Nap thickness runs from $3/16$ to $1^1/2$ inches ($3/16$ to $1/4$ inch are classed as short naps covers; $3/8$ to $3/4$ inch as medium; and $3/4$ to $11/2$ inches as deep). The shorter nap sleeves, $3/16$ and $1/4$ inch, are usually used to apply enamel—shiny paint (gloss or semigloss). This sleeve does not produce a glass-smooth finish but one, if examined up close, that has a slightly bumpy surface, like the skin of an orange.

For Flat and Satin-Flat Paint Application. For applying flat and satin-flat paint, the standard roller used has a $3/8$-inch nap. A $1/2$-inch roller is also used for applying flat and satin-flat paint. As you might expect, the $1/2$-inch roller brings more paint to the wall and can be useful in a situation where there is a question of whether or not you have enough paint to cover. Liebco, Wooster, and Purdy are good brands to look for.

Rougher Surfaces. The rougher the surface, the heavier or thicker the nap should be. The $3/4$-inch nap is commonly used on masonry surfaces, which may be too rough for the $1/2$-inch nap, though the latter is commonly the choice for concrete floors (which are rougher than plaster or

Sheetrock® walls but ordinarily do not require a $3/4$-inch nap).

The $11/2$-inch nap is a very good tool for painting a chainlink fence. Painting the individual wire strands that comprise the fence with a brush is a good way to drive yourself bonkers. However, if you saturate the heavy nap ($11/2$ inch) roller with paint and draw it across the wire, it will virtually paint both sides at the same time, because the paint saturated fibers will wrap around the wires; finish with light passes on the opposite side to complete the fence.

Roller Handles. Roller handles come in a variety of shapes and sizes. The standard size is 9 inches, meaning that the cage or barrel part that the roller cover goes on is 9 inches long. But you can also get handles that are 7 inches long, as well as ones that are 3 and 4 inches long.

Handles may be plastic or wood. Handles, also called roller frames, come in various types. The best is a spring cage frame with four or five thick wires. Rollers just slip on and off the handles.

$3/8$"

$1/2$"

$11/2$"

Roller covers

A good way to quality test a roller handle is simply to make side-by-side comparisons. The good ones will be made of thicker, heavier materials.

Rollers with Shields. Rollers are also available with built-on shields—trough-like sections that are designed to reduce dripping and splatter, in some cases by 90 percent. They work, but they roll more slowly than if you used one without a shield.

Most roller handles are threaded to accept threaded poles, so painting hard to reach areas is not a problem. Indeed, with a long enough pole, many houses (for example, ranches) can be painted from the ground—no ladders are required.

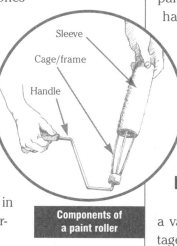

Sleeve

Cage/frame

Handle

Components of a paint roller

Trays

Roller trays are made of either plastic or metal and are commonly wide enough to accommodate a 9-inch wide roller. Your best bet is a deep, rigid plastic tray. If you compare trays, you'll quickly see the quality differences.

Grids

Professional painters commonly use a paint grid. A grid has hooks on it and hangs at a slant in a 5-gallon bucket. The bucket is kept half filled with paint, which allows the painter, usually with the roller on a stick, to dip it into the paint and roll off the excess on the grid. No trays (and constant refilling) are required.

Pads

The paint pad has proved its worth in a variety of situations. One of its advantages as a painting tool is that there is no overspray, as there may be with a roller. Also, it is faster than a brush, and it can apply paint as smoothly as a brush.

Paint pads are usually rectangular, either 6, 8, or 10 inches wide. Thousands of tiny fibers are mounted on a foam backing. One type of pad has short fibers and is designed for applying paint or polyurethane on smooth surfaces. The material is wiped on gently. Another pad has rougher fibers and is designed for painting

Grid in pail

cement block, concrete, stucco, and rough wood such as Texture 1-11. Unlike paint pads, which wipe the paint on, a light scrubbing action is used to drive the paint into all cracks and crevices.

Pads can be useful for painting shingles, depending on the type. The smooth pad is normally narrow enough to slip under

Staining pad

shingles with bottom ends, or butts (what else?), that are slightly raised. This means that the paint can be applied in one sweep, rather than having to cut into the butts with a brush.

Applicators for Decks

The best way to apply stains or clears to a deck is usually with a brush, because the material is worked into the wood by the pressure created by brush strokes. But a second-best applicator is the stain pad. This is a regular size pad, but it has a fluffy yet strong nap, perhaps an inch thick. The pad is

dipped into the material, and then, in effect, wiped on—and into the wood grain.

Most pads, like roller handles, can accept threaded poles, though these are usually force fitted into them—there aren't any threads. There are also a couple of paint pads that are used as "edgers" to cut in to close quarters.

Brushes

Brushes come in a variety of sizes. There are also some special purpose brushes that work quite well.

Generally, brushes are available in sizes that range from 1 to 5 inches wide. Sizes are commonly 1, $1\frac{1}{2}$, 2, $2\frac{1}{2}$, 3, 4, and 5 inches. They are available with square-cut ends or angled, the latter for trim work. When painting windows, particularly, the angled brushes make the job easier.

Again, quality is the byword. Good brushes hold more paint and apply it more evenly and smoothly. They make the job look better—and they save a lot of time.

Angle and square brushes

Just what size you select is a more or less arbitrary thing—within reason. A 2-inch angled brush is good for trim such as windows, and a 3-inch brush for baseboard and applying glossy paints to doors and cabinets. A roller or pad is suggested for large flat areas.

Natural and Synthetic Bristles. Brushes come with natural or synthetic bristles. The former are from animal hair, such as badgers, horses, and hogs (the best of all); the latter are manufactured.

Brushes with synthetic bristles are best for do-it-yourselfers. They can be used with both water- (natural bristle brushes, as mentioned earlier, can swell and get limp) and oil-base paint.

Brush Quality. As with rollers, Wooster, Liebco, and Purdy are good brand names for brushes. Though every new brush will shed a few bristles, when you fan bristles a few times and they continue to fall out, the brush's quality is suspect. When pressed against a surface, the bristles should bend $1/3$ to $1/2$ in relation to the tips. Also, when pressed against a dry surface, the bristles should not divide into clumps, or "fingers." If they do, they'll do that when wet, and an uneven application will result.

Paint mitt

Finally, the bristles should snap back into position after dry bending.

Other noteworthy brushes include the following:

- Stencil Brush. This looks like a shaving brush and is good for dabbing paint on carved moldings.
- Round Brush. This also resembles a shaving brush, but it has a round, long, tapered handle. It is good for painting narrow round objects, such as pipes.
- Staining Brush. Here, the bristles are very fine and the brush is 5 inches wide. This brush is geared to apply exterior stains. It can be loaded with stain and minimizes dripping of this water-thin material.
- Stippling Brush. This looks like a scrub brush with a handle made of aluminum or wood and is $3^{1/2}$ by 9 inches. The bristles are dipped into the paint and then dabbed on the surface.
- Radiator Brush. This has a long thin handle and angled bristles so that it can paint behind and between radiator sections.
- Artist's Brush. These are slim brushes that sometimes come in

handy for painting very delicate, narrow lines.

- Paint Mitt. The paint mitt is useful for painting metal or in jobs where using a brush or other applicator would take a long time because of the intricate configuration of the item (such as a wrought iron fence). To protect the hands from paint seepage, a thin vinyl glove should be worn under it.

Scraper

Brush Clamp. A brush clamp can be screwed to the end of a pole, which, in turn, has clamps for holding the brush. It enables you to get in places a ladder can't reach. If you don't have a clamp accessory, use duct tape to secure the brush to the end of a pole for hard to reach places.

Poles

Paint poles are also useful. They are made of wood, plastic, or fiberglass and come in a variety of lengths. For inside, the 4-foot length is okay; for outside, the length depends on what you

think you can handle. For most uses, 6 or 8 feet should work well.

If you buy a wood pole, get one with metal threads; otherwise the pole can become misshapen. If you already have a wood pole and this problem occurs, the pole can be salvaged by buying a device at a paint store or home center that has threads on it and can be clamped on the end of the pole.

Scrapers

A variety of paint scrapers are available. The standard scraper is 3 to $3\frac{1}{2}$ inches wide at the end of the blade and may be made of rigid or flexible metal and angled. For scraping, the rigid blade is recommended; the flexible blade is generally for applying patching material. A standard scraper has its limits, but it can accomplish most scraping jobs both inside and outside the house.

For jobs in which there is a great deal of scraping to be done, a hook-type scraper is recommended.

Hook-type scraper

They come in a couple of sizes. Essentially, they consist of a long handle on the end of a blade—a flat piece of metal with two edges sharpened and bent over. The tool is used by pulling it down across the area where paint is peeling. Its big asset is the pressure with which it can be applied; and with that plus the sharp blade, all the unstable paint comes off. Just grasp the tool with two hands, or one hand, and pull.

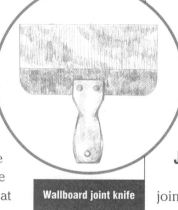

Wallboard joint knife

When one edge of the blade wears down, the other edge is available. A screw holding the blade to the handle is loosened, and then the blade is rotated to bring the new edge into play. Even better, you can get a hook-type scraper with a carbon-steel blade that can be sharpened with a file. Wire brushes may also be used for removing peeling paint.

Standard size scrapers (3 inches) are also used for applying plaster and spackling compound. Here, as previously stated, it is best to use a scraper with a flexible blade. It simply is able to apply patchers more smoothly, because more of the surface is in contact with the material, and therefore feathers the material out better than a rigid one.

Scrapers come in a variety of qualities, both with plastic and wood handles. The wood-handled version is usually better and is recommended.

Joint Knife

A close cousin to the scraper is the joint knife, so called because it is mainly used for applying joint compound when taping the joints of drywall panels. These knives range from 6 to 12 inches wide. The 6-inch size can be used for light scraping, but its basic use is to apply patcher—plaster, spackling compound, or joint compound. Its width and flexibility allow it to do a good job smoothing patching material.

Putty Knife

A couple of putty knives, so called because their main job are for applying window putty

Putty knife

(today more properly called glazing compound), are also essential. They come with plastic and wood handles. Again, manufacturers have good, better, and best lines.

If you are not good at applying glazing compound in a neat bead, one tool that works well is the combination putty knife applicator. With this, the putty can be applied more easily than with a regular putty knife, because it is shaped to use the window frame muntin (the narrow frame pieces) to guide it along as the compound is smoothed.

Wire Brushes

Wire brushes are thought of as useful for scraping peeling paint off metal, but they can also be used to scrape paint off wood. They are particularly useful where the surface is ridged and doesn't readily allow a standard scraper to be used. Here, the wire brush can be pulled down along the ridged surface; its stiff wires do a good job of removing peeling paint.

Wire brushes come in a variety of shapes, from those shaped like scrub brushes to ones with long, curved handles to ones with wide handles. Just pick the size and shape that suits your job best.

Sandpaper

Sandpaper is essentially an abrasive material bonded to a backing of paper or other material. It is, of course, a vital tool for giving patches of various kinds their ultimate smoothness.

Sandpaper is classified by the type of abrasive or grit used, its weight, and grit number (which refers to coarseness).

Four grit materials are commonly used: aluminum oxide, emery, garnet, and silicone carbide. The grits come in various hardnesses, and therefore are suitable for sanding certain materials. Garnet, which is a reddish-brown abrasive, is the softest of all and used on wood almost exclusively. Emery, a black abrasive, is used on metal. Next on the hardness scale is aluminum oxide, which is exceptionally hard and long wearing and can be used on wood, painted surfaces, and alloy steel, high-carbon steel, tough bronzes, and some hardwoods. The hardest grit of all is silicone carbide, a bluish-black sandpaper that is good on aluminum, copper, cast iron, and plastic.

Grit coarseness varies from number 12, which is very coarse, to 1200, which is super fine (the higher the grit number the smoother the material). If the sandpaper is being used in a machine, lower numbers are used than those for corresponding hand sanding.

Sandpaper also comes in "open" and "close-coat" varieties. On closed-coat papers, the grit particles are close together, covering all of the paper. This leads to the paper quickly becoming clogged with the material being sanded, such as wood. Open-coated papers have more space between grit particles and do not clog as quickly. Indeed, they can be cleaned and reused, but they are also coarser than close-coat paper.

Different kinds of sandpapers are available for wet and dry sanding. The backing on wet sandpapers is made to resist water and may be dipped into water or a light lubricating oil to effect final polishing.

Also available is a screen-type sandpaper for sanding joint compound and plaster. It looks like screening; as the surface is sanded, the dust particles escape through the holes, preventing clogging.

Sandpaper Accessories. Sandpaper can be bought by the sheet, then folded over and applied where needed. But there are a number of accessories that can make working with it easier.

One such is a sanding block. A sanding block consists of a curved block with clamps (for holding the sandpaper in place on the bottom of the block, which is faced with rubber). This device allows one to sand with greater pressure, and to apply the sandpaper more evenly.

Another type of block has a handle which can be gripped; the sandpaper is clamped on. It also has a rubber base. This type of block works the same way as the smaller one, except it's bigger and can be used for sanding wide patches or joint compound.

Sanding Stick. For sanding large areas, the sanding stick is the way to go. It has a sanding pad permanently attached to the end of a pole; but it is loosely jointed to the pad so that it can conform to the surface being sanded.

Sanding stick

Caulking Guns

Caulk, the material used to seal seams in the house (described later), is available in two basic forms: tubes or cartridges. The cartridge type is standard and is dispensed with a cartridge gun.

Cartridge guns come in a couple of versions and the byword again is quality. Even though you won't be using it all the time, it will be there for you when you need it. Cheap guns will dispense headaches. To check quality, pick various ones up and operate them. You should be able to see which is best, and price will certainly indicate quality as well.

Guns come in a number of hand-operated forms. These forms include one that has a barrel-like housing for the cartridge and another that has a framelike housing.

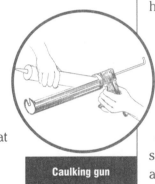

Caulking gun

Ladders

For painting the inside and outside of your home, two kinds of ladders can be used: the 6-foot stepladder and the extension ladder.

Stepladders. As with anything else, quality is important. Stepladders come in three grades: Type III or household grade, Type II or commercial grade, and Type I,

or industrial grade. Type I stepladders are rated at 200 pounds, Type II at 225 pounds, and Type I at 250 pounds. However, the tests are conducted at four times those weights.

The Type I ladder should be fine. The standard length is 6 feet; but they are available in lengths from 2 to 16 feet. A 6 footer is standard.

Ladders are made of wood, aluminum, or fiberglass. Fiberglass and wood are heavy; metal weighs perhaps half of what wood does. Although sturdy, aluminum can bend a little, which might seem disconcerting. Your best bet is go into the store and climb up and see how you like each ladder.

Extension Ladders. These are available all the way to 40 feet and, like stepladders, also are available in wood, aluminum, or fiberglass. They too come in various grades. Again, Type I should be fine. The rating doesn't guarantee top quality. Your best bet is to stick to good brands such as Werner and Keller, but get their top-of-the-line. If an extension ladder accepts replacement parts, this is an indication of top quality. Many professionals prefer fiberglass ladders for a simple reason: They don't conduct electricity, as will aluminum and wood when wet.

Dropcloths

I once knew a painter who was so good, so neat, that he didn't require drop- cloths. I must say that watching him paint in a living room containing wall-to-wall carpeting and glass-top tables and the like without pro- tecting them was a very unusual sight.

Most of us mere mortals, however, do require the use of dropcloths. A variety is available—some are water (or paint) proof; others are not.

Plastic "drops," as they say in the trade, come in various thicknesses and sizes, usually ranging from 1 to 6 mils thick. *Mils* is the term used by manufac- turers to describe the thickness. As the sheeting gets thicker, the overall size gets bigger. Hence, a 9- by 12-foot plastic drop- cloth might be 1 or 2 mils thick; and a 10- by 20-foot one might be 4 mils thick.

Plastic drops are usually recom- mended for use over furniture or other items where their "waterproofness" is a

Extension ladder

boon. However, they should not be used on the floor. Plastic is slippery and can be hazardous underfoot. For floors, paper- plastic drops are good; if you want to go to the best, get canvas drop- cloths. Canvas dropcloths come in various weights; the 8-ounce weight, while not totally liquid proof, will prevent most spat- ters from seeping through. Overlapped newspaper also works.

Nailset

Often when painting wood or dry- wall, nailheads will protrude slightly. For a neater job, these should be set below the surface, something the nailset achieves quite well. Then, the depression is spackled over.

Razor-Blade Scraper

Occasionally, paint can spatter on hard, smooth surfaces, particularly glass. When dry, this paint is easy to remove with a razor-blade scraper. It consists of a flat handle and a retractable single edge. It readily peels the paint off the surface. If you wish, you can also use regular single-edge blades, but these are not as easy to manage as the blade mounted in the handle.

Utility Knife. A utility knife is a hand-held razor knife. To use, you push a button to slide a heavy-duty blade into position for cutting.

Painting Materials

A variety of materials are required, some serving equally well for interior and exterior painting. Following is a roundup.

Caulks

As mentioned before, caulk is a sealant used to seal seams in the house. Outside, it is used wherever different materials meet, such as where windows meet siding, and inside to seal seams around the tub or where a kitchen counter meets a wall, for example.

There are a wide variety of caulks available. However, there are a few general distinctions to note. First, interior caulks should be mildew resistant, and this fact should be stated on the label. This means it contains a mildewcide that resists the formation of mildew. Exterior caulks do not necessarily contain a mildewcide.

Many caulks make excellent adhesives. For example, silicone, which happens to be the Cadillac of caulks (because it can last so long), is a tenacious adhesive that can be used for a variety of jobs.

There are many caulks that seem to have distinct applications—such as for sealing around a chimney or windows—but have, in fact, the same ingredients. Only the color may vary. Check the label. Cagey manufacturers want you to buy different caulks for different purposes when just one would do the trick in a wide variety of applications.

Following is a list of available caulks:

- Latex with Acrylic. This is available in a variety of colors and can be used for sealing around windows and doors as well as tub and wall. Note that some caulks are labeled latex but contain no acrylic, which is an important ingredient.
- Butyl Rubber. This comes in white or gray. It is an excellent caulk, because of its resilience, for use where masonry moves, such as between the house wall and a patio and driveway. it can also be used to repair cracks in sidewalks. Once applied, butyl rubber caulk, because it is so sticky, is better left alone. It will stick to the applicator if you try to tool it.

- Silicone. Silicone comes in a variety of colors as well as clear. As mentioned, it's the best caulk available and more expensive than others. It will stick to almost anything. Standard silicone caulk cannot be painted without the paint rolling off the caulk, but there are some types that can be. Check the label.

> ### Money-Saving Tip
>
> **$** Venetian-Blind Paint Guard: If you have an old venetian blind around, the slats can be used as paint guards. They are particularly good when carpeting abuts baseboard molding.

- Oil-Base Caulk. In terms of quality, oil-based caulk is low on the caulk scale. It's cheap, dries hard, and not very durable.
- Aerosol Caulk. Aerosol caulk is dispensed from a spray can, and it expands as it comes out of the can. It dries hard and waterproof. As such, it is a good filler when great gaps exist in materials, such as where shingles meet the foundation.
- Caulking Cord. Caulking cord comes segmented into six beads of various sizes. The beads are stripped off as needed and pushed in place. Caulking cord can be used inside or outside as a caulk, but it also makes an excellent filler caulk. On cracks that are particularly deep, the caulk is laid in place to fill, and then another caulk is gunned in on top of it.
- Joint Compound. Also known as joint cement, it is used to seal the seams between drywall panels; but it can also be used to fill in very shallow depressions on a surface, such as where paint has peeled.

Painter's Masking Tape

A sharp distinction must be made between regular masking tape and painter's masking tape. The former really is not suited for paint jobs, because it has tenacious sticking power, particularly as time goes by; and when removed, it can tear off the paint or wallcovering beneath it. Painter's masking tape has "easy release." The time varies, but depending on the tape, it can be peeled off after many hours without causing any damage.

One complaint about masking tape is that paint can seep in under the edge of the tape, destroying any sharp line that the painter is trying to achieve. This will happen with some tapes, but upper-end qualities, such as 3-M tape, will not allow seepage. Also Wagner makes a masking product that works well. It's called "Glass Mask" and is a soft, waxy material that is rubbed on like a soft crayon onto the glass where it meets the frame members. It protects the glass from paint, and when painting is finished, it can be peeled off easily.

Money-Saving Tip

 Paint is one of those products you can really save on by shopping around. It's always on sale somewhere, and savings can be significant. Paint sales are often held in the spring, but an even better time to shop is in January.

Paint Thinner

Also commonly known as mineral spirits, paint thinner is the most common cleaner and thinner of oil-based coatings. It is relatively inexpensive and safe to use. It is available in an "odorless" version, but this does have some odor. It is also available in various size containers, from a quart to a 5-gallon jug. Mineral spirits can

ordinarily be used where turpentine is suggested, and it costs far less.

Patchers

A variety of patchers is available for patching holes inside and outside the house. Plaster of paris, patching plaster, and spackling compounds are designed for interior use. However, wood putty and woodfillers, which are applied the same way as the interior materials, can take the rigors of weather. Such are handy for filling in nailholes and the like, as well as patching rough areas to give them a smoother look.

Plaster of Paris. Commonly known as plaster, this material is made from gypsum, a natural compound found in nature. It was first shipped to America around the turn of the century, when a huge amount of it was discovered under and outside Paris, France.

Plaster has a number of assets. It is cheap, and it dries quickly—in about ten minutes it is rock hard. In addition, it can be used as a base to fill large holes in plaster, and then topped with spackling compound or joint cement, which is easier to work with.

Patching Plaster. This works somewhat like plaster but with an important distinction: Plaster of paris will dry in ten minutes; and patching plaster has an open time of a half hour—it's much more forgiving.

Spackling Compounds. There are many of these patchers available, and they are thought of as useful for filling small holes and cracks and where a thin coating is needed. They come both powdered and premixed (the more expensive), and in two basic forms that might be called heavy and light.

A material like MH Ready Patch, which is very good, is a heavy patcher. For lightweight patchers, a whole new family exists, including Fast n' Final and Red Devil's One Time. Pick up the container and you might think it's empty— it's formulated with microscopic glass beads or bubbles in it. The advantage of these lightweight patchers is their fast drying time. Other patchers may take hours to dry (joint compound requires overnight), but the lightweights take minutes.

Care must be taken with any of these patchers. So, carefully read label instructions to see how deep they can be applied. Most can only be applied $^1/_4$-inch deep at a time, though Fast n' Final can go $^1/_2$ inch without cracking. Some people like to use something like plaster for the deeper holes first, and then use a spackling compound on top, which

makes the job easier because of the latter's workability.

Wood Putty. A variety of wood putties are available. It comes ready made in a variety of colors, as well as in a natural tannish color that can be tinted. It also comes in powder form. It is used for small repairs to wood and to hide nailholes.

Wood Fillers. Wood fillers are wood puttylike repair products for rotted wood. Minwax makes one, a two-part epoxy system that is applied with a putty knife. The same company also makes a hardener that can be injected or applied on soft or decaying wood and where it hardens to make a more suitable base for the patcher. When dry, the patcher can be sanded and worked like regular wood.

Money-Saving Tip

$ I've seen plaster of paris in 1-pound boxes as well as in 25-pound bags. Which do you think is cheaper? If you can use it, buy the large bag, but be very careful about storage. Keep it in a dry place. Plaster mixed with unintended moisture means ruined plaster.

Safety Tip

Safety is a boring subject (though one that is trumpeted throughout the book!). It's something that the do-it-yourselfer must be aware of. Following are tools and equipment that can make life easier—and sometimes longer:

- Gloves. A wide variety of gloves are available, but for ordinary painting most people favor the soft, brown cotton gloves. They protect the hands while allowing an important "feel" of the brush.

  For cleaning you can wear rubber gloves with long sleeves. However, for stripping paint, where aggressive chemicals like methylene chloride are used, you need neoprene or gloves that are specifically made for stripping (check the label). You can also get inexpensive vinyl gloves. Some people like them for cleaning and painting.

- Glasses. There is a variety of glasses available, and they are available in plastic as well as hardened, shatterproof glass. They can be bought in plain and prescription glass.

  Glasses are a good idea when power washing, chipping, or sanding. Debris can fly off a surface—right into your eyes.

- Goggles. Goggles are large glasses with protective sidepieces.

- Breathing Masks. A number of products that protect to varying degrees against harmful vapors and dust are on the market. Before purchasing any breathing apparatus, make sure it is adequate for the task at hand. And any mask should—must—fit tightly. An ill-fitting mask can leak and be dangerous, only offering the illusion of protection.

- Paper Mask. This consists of a cone-shaped white paper with a rubber band to keep it in place. It protects against dust, but not vapors.

- Filter-Type Mask. This is made of plastic and has a replaceable filter. It will do an adequate job of protecting the user against sanding dust, but not vapors.

- Cartridge Respirator. This resembles a military gas mask. It has two protruding filter cartridges and a heavy rubber strap to hold the mask to the head. If you even get involved in such things as removing lead-base paint or the like, a mask like this would be necessary. By law, the masks are marked for what they protect against.

Interior Paint Preparation

Preparation makes the job is an old adage as well as a cliché. However, it's a cliché because it's true. Preparation does make the job.

Removing—and Moving

Before doing any preparation, it's best to move the furniture out of the room or rooms you'll be painting. However, if this is not possible, move all the furniture into a close group at the center of the room—close enough so that you can reach the middle of the ceiling from your ladder.

Drape dropcloths or sheets over furniture; if you use sheets, put plastic dropcloths on first. Floors, of course, must also be covered by nonslippery drops or newspapers.

A convenient out-of-the-way work area should also be set up.

It is important that dropcloths or other coverings be laid between the work area and the area being painted. It is all too easy for shoes to pick up spattered paint from dropcloths and track it into other unprotected areas.

Masking Off

If you have an unsteady hand, use painter's masking tape to protect areas you don't want smeared with paint. Another good way to avoid getting paint on objects is to remove them. Switchplates, ceiling fixtures, wall sconces, and the like can all be removed so you don't have to "cut in" around them.

Cleaning Surfaces

At some point when convenient— either before or after dropcloths are put in place—surfaces must be cleaned. In general, cleaning is a very important step that can get short shrift. Paint simply sticks better on a clean surface than a dirty one.

The overall idea in cleaning is to do as little as you have to, but to do what needs to be done. As a general rule, kitchens and bathrooms need a washdown, and so does trim. Even though surfaces may not be obviously soiled, sometimes feeling them can reveal a greasy, oily surface, where mere looking cannot.

Dust. Some walls, such as in the living room or bedroom, just have to be dusted. A dust brush or small feather duster works well here. Be particularly aware of getting dust off the tops of wall moldings.

You can always wipe it off as you go, but it's better and quicker to do it beforehand.

If walls have to be washed, a mild laundry detergent and water works fine for removing most soil, but in some cases, such as in the kitchen, there can be a buildup of grease that must be removed. Here, TSP (trisodium phosphate, Soilax, or the like) does a good job cutting through the grease and cleaning it. You can also use Top Job or any other detergent.

Afterward, use clear water to wipe the walls down to remove any soap residue. This residue can also interfere with paint adhesion, as it works like a chalk or powder.

From the Bottom Up. When washing a wall, it's best to clean from the bottom up. This prevents dirty streaks of water from running down into uncleaned areas. These streaks are difficult to clean.

Be particularly careful when cleaning paneling. Clean it with a good quality detergent, and if it looks like there is wax buildup that is not coming off, wipe it down with mineral spirits.

Primers are a great asset when painting (discussed later), and some of them allow you to cover virtually any mars or marks on a surface. However, you should at least clean the mar or mark if it is very noticeable, to make the job

easier for the primer. You can use a scrub brush and a strong detergent, and a putty knife if there is a buildup of material, like crayon or wax.

Money-Saving Tip

$ Always plan a paint job so that no quart-size cans of paint have to be bought. By the quart, paint costs double the gallon price. For example, a gallon of paint might cost $20. Bought individually, a quart of paint might cost $10—or $40 for the gallon.

If the large economy size is available, it usually costs less—sometimes a lot less than by the gallon. The standard larger size is 5 gallons, but you can also get 2-gallon containers.

Interior and exterior stains are also sold in small and large containers. Again, avoid quarts. You can buy interior stain in half pints, quarts, and gallons. Exterior stains are usually available in quarts, gallons, and 5-gallon containers.

Mildew. Mildew reminds me of my old boss. It is a spore that thrives in an environment of dampness, darkness, and soil.

(Just kidding, of course). The bathroom is just such an environment. Mildew usually shows up in the form of clusters of black dots, but it can be green, brown, yellow, and other colors.

Mildew must be removed completely. If not, it will eventually eat its way through any paint applied over it and create unsightly stains.

Bleach—sodium hypochlorite—is the only commonly available material that will remove mildew. Sometimes it's hard to tell if a blotch is mildew or not. To tell, dab pure bleach on the blotch. If it lightens, then it is mildew. Bleach won't have any effect on plain dirt.

You can use a solution containing one part bleach to three parts water. Also, there is a wide variety of products available for removing mildew. Some of the products, such as Mil Klean by the W.M. Barr Company, are just sprayed on and rinsed off ten minutes later. Others are wiped on.

If you use any products containing bleach, it's a good idea to wear gloves and goggles. Bleach is a caustic material, and if you get it on skin, it can burn. Final treatment of the area should be a rinse with clear water.

Causes of Mildew. Mildew usually occurs where ventilation is inadequate. Either there is no exhaust fan, or the area is undersized for the volume of moisture it has to remove. If a proper exhaust fan is not going to be installed, a product called Damp Rid works well. This is simply a small container of crystals that draws moisture from the air. It lasts about six weeks before the crystals must be replaced. (This product also works well in the basement.)

Marks. If a wall is marked in some way, say by Magic Marker, tobacco stains, pencil, or other permanent marks (other than grease), you needn't spend a great deal of time trying to get them off. Best bet is to spot prime them, then paint. If a wall is heavily marked, it's best to just prime the whole area, rather than spot prime, because the primed spots could bleed through the finish coat. This could happen with a single mark, too, but it depends on how well the finish coat covers.

Peeling

Walls or ceilings may have areas with peeling paint, and it is necessary to remove all of what is actually peeling and what might peel. The finish paint will only adhere as well as the paint below it.

To test to see if the paint is sound in various areas, use a utility knife to cut a small X in the paint film. Apply a piece of transparent tape or the tape part of a Band-Aid™ to the *X* and pull it off sharply. If the paint comes off, it means it has to be removed. Try this in several areas.

If just one or two layers come off, you can simply remove the paint with a stiff-bladed 3-inch scraper, and then use a block and sandpaper (or a sanding machine) to sand down the paint to remove the roughness. If there is a buildup of paint film and the scraping results in cratering the surface a little, paint alone won't form a film thick enough to fill these cavities. For a better job, you can "float" the edges: Apply compound along the edges, feathering them to nothingness toward the inner part of each crater. Then, sand lightly.

A wide bladed 6-inch—or more—joint compound knife can be used for this job, as well as joint compound. Just spread it on thinly and smoothly. Let it dry, and then apply another coat (joint compound shrinks). Sand with 220-grit sandpaper.

Heavy Peeling. If your *X* test reveals that much or all of the paint must be removed, that the paint is peeling heavily, or that there is an indication that the only viable way to do this is by machine, a belt sander can do the job. Small models are available, which your arms will appreciate if you're sanding the ceiling.

It is advisable to wear a mask during this operation, because a considerable amount of dust will be kicked up. Plastic sheeting should also be hung over openings to prevent the dust from migrating to other areas.

Sanding

It's best to apply the patcher so smoothly that little or no sanding is required. In fact, if heavy sanding is required, it will be very difficult to end up with an area that is smooth enough to be painted.

> **Money-Saving Tip**
>
> **$** Sandpaper is sold by the package and by the sheet. Buy it by the sheet, and you can expect to save 10 to 15 percent.

Wall Liner

In some cases, you may have large sanded areas and large areas where the wall is fairly rough, and no amount of patching will make it perfectly smooth. One way to get a smooth wall is with wall liner. A variety are available; they come with instructions for use. Essentially liner covers the wall with a smooth, thin material that is paintable and can also have wallcovering installed over it. There are three kinds of liner: canvas, polyester, and fiberglass.

Canvas by Wall-Tex comes in 54-inch wide rolls and can be used when a wall is in pretty good shape. It is made with 80 percent cotton and 20 percent polyester. A close cousin is Sanitas lining, a fabric-backed vinyl that looks like primed canvas of an artist.

If the wall is textured, masonry block, heavily patched, coated with sand paint, or stippled, it's not a good idea to use liner because it will show through. But for the wall that is only moderately damaged, with paint missing and some extensive but not very bad patches, canvas wall liner works quite well. The material can be painted or covered with wallpaper.

Polyester. This is a sheet material made of polyester and cellulose. It comes in various weights, and is an excellent choice when the job is particularly tough—sandy surfaces, poor walls. It bridges gaps very well.

Textured Wall Liner. If you have very rough areas to go over, or paneling, or even concrete block, you can also use

Patching cracked plaster

textured wall liners. They are extra thick and are installed like wallcoverings. Also, they can be painted and do a particularly good job of hiding problem walls.

Cracks

Walls and ceilings may develop cracks, particularly plaster walls. The reason is house movement. As time goes by a house naturally settles, and if the movement is great enough, the wall or ceiling material can crack from the pressure. The idea is to fill the cracks in a way that eliminates further problems.

The most common place where Sheetrock® cracks is in the seams. One way to handle this is by simply applying a thin coat of joint compound over the cracked area.

Cracking is also a common problem with plaster. Unlike Sheetrock®, which is bonded firmly together with a tough paper skin (front and back), plaster walls or ceilings are homogeneous masses—one piece—with only the plaster to resist the stress from movement.

To patch a crack in plaster, first use a beer can opener or old screwdriver or the edge of a scraper to dig out the crack to a width of at least $1/4$ inch. Use a brush to sweep away all loose material, then apply the patcher. Varieties are available to choose from, as detailed earlier, but the key is the depth the patcher can be applied without danger of future cracking. Many patchers can only go $1/4$-inch deep, though a few can be applied up to $1/2$ inch. If you use the former, apply it in one or more applications no more than $1/4$-inch deep. Whatever you do, it's important to force the compound into the crack so it fills it completely (no air gaps). Slightly overfill it, then draw the scraper or joint compound knife along the crack to remove excess. When dry, sand.

If you are patching a crack that recurs between a wall and ceiling surface and molding, one way to eliminate it permanently is to use caulk as a filler material. Latex caulk works well, as does silicone; if you use the latter, get the paintable kind.

Also for cracks that recur, a product called Tuff Kote Krack Kote

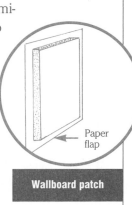

Spackling compound

Compound applied around hole

Paper flap

Wallboard patch

works well. This contains a patcher and fiberglass material that goes over it. When the wall expands, which is the cause of the problem, the fiberglass expands with it and stays intact.

Holes

Holes that occur in Sheetrock® are normally from something having impacted against the wall, such as a doorknob or a teenage fist. Sheetrock® is normally only $3/8$-inch or $1/2$-inch thick and doesn't take a direct impact well.

There are various ways to patch a hole in Sheetrock®, including installing ready-made patches. A number of these are available. One type consists of a square of sheet metal mounted on a piece of mesh with adhesive on it. A paper backing is peeled off, exposing the adhesive; and then the metal patch is placed over the hole and compound applied over it.

On holes that are bigger (6 inches or so) than such a patch can cover, there are other alternatives. One way is to use a piece of Sheetrock® to make the complete patch. First, use a utility knife to trim the edges of the hole, squaring it off as much as possible. Measure the hole, then cut a piece of Sheetrock® that is the size of the hole plus 1 inch bigger all around. Use the utility knife to trim the Sheetrock® to the size of the hole, but leave the paper covering in place.

Butter the Edges. Use spackling compound to butter around the perimeter of the hole a couple of inches, then place the patch in the hole, embedding the paper flap in the compound. Then use the joint knife to flatten the flap and remove excess compound.

When the compound is dry, apply another coat, feathering it so the patch doesn't show. Your best bet here is to run the knife across the compound in crisscross strokes.

Filler

Compound

Plaster applied to patch edges

Bigger Patches

If a large section of Sheetrock® has been damaged, the best bet is to cut a section out to the framing members. You can do this with a utility knife, cutting a squarish patch out along the top and bottom, and cutting enough Sheetrock® off

the studs (or ceiling framing members) so the patch can be nailed in place.

Cut a section of Sheetrock® to fit into the hole. Place the section in the hole, and then use drywall nails to nail it at the edges to the framing members.

Next, seal the raw edges with drywall tape and compound. Apply a 3-inch wide bead of joint compound to the cut edges. Then embed pieces of tape into it, flattening the tape by drawing a joint compound knife across it. Feather the compound. When this is dry, lightly sand it.

To avoid using drywall tape, there is also a product available known as tapeless compound. This comes ready-made in 1-gallon cans and can be applied to the wall without the use of tape. It seals and covers well.

Holes in Plaster

Holes in plaster may be small or large. Plaster or wet wall is made by first securing a base of some sort, such as wood lath (strips of wood) or metal mesh or gypsum board. Then a brown or scratch coat of plaster is applied, followed by two finish coats of white plaster.

Small holes. For small holes—a few inches in diameter—patching plaster works well. If the hole is fairly shallow—up to an inch deep—you can use patching plaster to do the job. First, wet the hole so the dry wall material doesn't suck water from the patcher, weakening it. Then half fill the hole with the patcher. When this is hard and dry, apply additional compound, slightly over-filling the hole. Then smooth and feather it with the joint knife.

If the hole is deep enough so that some filler material must first be applied before the patcher, crumpled up newspapers or steel wool can be stuffed into the hole. Once it's in place, apply successive coats (about a half inch deep) of compound until you smooth the material flush with the surrounding surface.

Really Big Holes. A very large plaster hole should be cut back to the studs. You can use a piece of Sheetrock® as a base here, just cut it to fit into the hole and nail it in place with drywall nails.

If plaster is bulging or sagging, it means that the plaster has pulled away from the lath. This is really a job for a pro.

If walls are in such poor shape that wall liner doesn't work, the best bet is to hang new drywall. This should be $1/4$-inch thick. It will cover everything, and will not

entail (usually) having to modify molding in any way.

If you are making a color change, or have a lot of patches, you should prime the walls. Primers differ from finish paint in that they hide better, provide an even coating for the finish paint, and stick tenaciously. They are problem solvers and preparers.

Many people use BIN, a shellac-base product, and Kilz Oil, which work very well, or latex-base primers. They are applied like any other paint, as detailed below. It's always a good idea to tint them to the approximate final color as suggested on the can of the finish paint.

Painting and Paneling

The type of paneling that is usually painted is the light to dark wood grain, grooved panels of fifteen or twenty years ago or more.

Though primers have tenacious sticking properties, it is suggested that you first scuff-sand the panels to provide even more tooth. Then wipe them down with a damp rag.

Apply the primer with a $3/8$-inch nap roller if the panels have no grooves and a $1/2$-inch nap roller if grooved; the extra thickness helps to get the paint in them.

Formica, Tile, and Glass

These surfaces are highly nonporous, but any of the primers suggested above—oil-base, shellac-base, or water-base—may be used (except you don't want to use BIN or any other shellac-base primer in the bathroom, because it can crack). The manufacturer of BIN suggests that it be topcoated with an alkyd finish coat, but this seems like taking an extra step when none is needed. Just use oil-base or water-base primers, and that's it.

Cracks in Concrete

Interior masonry, particularly on floors but sometimes on walls, is subject to cracking. To handle this, use a cold chisel and a hammer to deepen and widen the crack, "V-ing" it out, as painters say. This means chopping it out wide at the top and then wider at the bottom, so that the patcher can be packed in and the shape of the cavity is keyed to hold it in place.

For dry cracks, ordinary concrete patcher may be used. This comes as a powder mixed with water. Sakrete and Quik-Crete are two brands.

If the crack is wet from running water, hydraulic cement must be used. This is actually cement that hardens in a few minutes—even when a crack is wet or has water flowing in it.

Cracks in Wall Joints

Wall cracks and cracks at the floor/wall juncture may be effectively repaired. However, if a floor crack is wet, or water migrates through it every now and then (particularly during rainstorms), it's likely that the patch will eventually come loose. Water leaking through a floor ultimately cannot be stopped without using a sump pump or working to change the drainage, or the like. If painted or sealed, the coating will eventually be driven off. There's no such thing as a waterproofer for a floor, though there is for concrete walls.

Efflorescence

Efflorescence is a white powder that commonly appears on masonry walls. It is actually salts or calcium deposits that leach out of the masonry because of water seepage; when they hit the surface, the moisture evaporates and the dry deposits are left.

Efflorescence must be removed: Paint won't stick to a powder. To do this, scrub the deposits off with a brush, and then wash the area thoroughly with a 5 percent solution of muriatic acid. Allow it to dry completely before painting.

There are masonry primers and paints available for concrete walls; but I believe that for uncoated masonry walls, an interior latex primer works quite well—followed, when dry, by one or two coats of latex.

Varnished or Stained Wood

Varnished and stained surfaces, such as on old kitchen cabinets or trim, should be cleaned and scuff-sanded. Then a primer, BIN or Kilz Oil, should be used.

Dealing with Lead-Base Paint

The main problem that the do-it-yourselfer must be aware of when dealing with lead-base paint is not the particles of paint that contain lead, but the dust. If lead dust is raised (or if it falls), even the most conscientious person can miss some. It takes special care, including an appropriate mask.

Today, experts feel that the best way to deal with lead paint is to leave it alone, as much as possible. Hence, if the paint is in good condition, just prime and paint as needed.

Following are some tips on how to paint a room in which lead-base paint has been previously used. (If the house was built before the 1950s and painted thereafter, one can assume this.)

First, use heavy plastic dropcloths on the floor, and move furniture out of the room or wrap pieces in heavy plastic. To keep dust from migrating to adjacent rooms, tape plastic over doorways.

Before sanding anything, wet it down with water applied with a spray bottle. Then use the wet/dry type of sandpaper to sand the area. If there are semigloss or high gloss areas to be scuff-sanded, use a "presand," wiping the surface down with a terry cloth. This scuffs the surface without cutting it and releasing dust.

If the surface is in very poor condition and heavy paint removal rather than mere sanding is required, a chemical stripper may be used. Also, one of the wall liners may be appropriate as well as wallcovering.

When the preparation is finished, any chips or scrapings should be captured by rolling them up in the plastic, then wrapping them in more plastic, and sealing off.

Any dust must be picked up. An ordinary vacuum doesn't work. Rather, a HEPA (high efficiency particle arresting) vacuum must be rented. (It can pick up micron-sized particles.) Two vacuumings with this should clear up any remaining dust.

Money-Saving Tip

Pie Plate Dropcloth: If using a 1-gallon can, you can keep paint off the floor by gluing a pie plate to the bottom of the can to catch the drips.

Interior Painting Procedure

Once the preparation is complete, the rest of the job will seem simple in comparison. It is important to mix paint thoroughly before use. Before leaving the store where you buy it, have the dealer shake it by machine. This should be done before the paint job begins.

There are accessories for mixing paint that you can chuck into a drill; but you can, of course, do it by hand. The best way is to box the paint—pour it back and forth between containers. If you are using a 5-gallon container, you can use three 5-gallon buckets to make the pouring easier.

Paint can also be mixed with a stick. One-gallon and 5-gallon mixing sticks are available at dealers. Just dip one in and move it through the paint in a figure-eight motion.

Mixing is particularly important when the paint is oil based. Oil-base paint tends to separate into solids and solvents, and thorough mixing is required before it's used.

Using a 5-Gallon Jug with a Grid

The easiest, most efficient way to paint manually is, as mentioned earlier, from a 5-gallon container with a grid inside. Just screw the roller to a stick and work right out of the bucket.

If you are using different color paints, you could also use an empty 5-gallon container, but this would entail emptying out and cleaning the bucket for each new color.

In these instances I prefer a tray and, as noted, a deep tray. Some people use tray liners, but they are more trouble than they're worth. My main objection is that they are not very deep, and won't fit a good-sized tray, which is what should be used. If you would rather not clean when changing from color to color, you can line the tray with one continuous sheet of heavy-duty aluminum foil; avoid the thinner gauges—they can tear and defeat the purpose.

I would also suggest a wide-mouth can for working out of with a brush. The paint is easy to get at when you're using a $2^1/_2$-inch or 3-inch brush.

Paint Can Opener

The best opener I've come across for opening paint in plastic 5-gallon jugs with a lip on the side is the plastic hook-type opener. By the way, sometimes there are certain points along the lid where it is necessary to cut it loose before you can pry it free. Metal containers work differently. They usually have a cap that must be unscrewed, sometimes with a large water-pump pliers. If you want to take the entire lid off, the tabs must be pried up with a screwdriver or the like. (Note: If you have a choice between plastic and metal containers, pick the plastic; it is much less susceptible to damage and easier to handle.)

For opening 1-gallon paint cans, nothing beats the little key with a hooked-over edge. It's the cheapest opener you can get, and in my view the best.

Opener for five gallon cans

Painting Sequence

Most of the time the ceiling is painted first, because any paint that drips down on the wall can be wiped off or painted over. In general, it's best to paint against the light source. Thus, you can see light reflected off the wet sheen on the paint, and it makes it easier to see any "holidays" (missed spots).

As much as possible the light should be natural—coming from a window or windows. Sunlight is the brightest light there is. I have found painting in artificial light, however bright, tricky. On more than one occasion, I've painted at night and would swear that I covered everything, only to see some holidays in the cruel light of day.

The job can be done using a 6-foot ladder, and working off of it, or using a stick from the floor. I find working with a stick fine, but some people prefer to work off of a ladder. Whatever, the idea is to work small areas at a time—say 3 feet by 3 feet. Apply the paint one way, then another. Do two or so adjacent 3-foot square sections, and then come back and roll out the entire area with a "dry" roller. This will tend to catch any missed spots.

Keeping Paint Off Yourself

To keep as clean as possible during a paint job, wear a hat and long-sleeved shirt and long pants. You can keep paint off your face by giving it a thin coat of petroleum jelly or facial cream.

Use Enough Paint

One of the keys to doing a good job is to use an adequate amount of paint. It's good to get in the habit of going to the tray frequently: Let the paint, not you (in a sense), do the work—lay it on, roll it off.

Exactly when you "cut in" the juncture between wall and ceiling depends on whether you use a stick or work off of a ladder. If you use a stick, it is more convenient to cut in before you roll the ceiling off.

The brush line should be only an inch or so wide, just enough so you can overlap with the roller without hitting the adjacent wall. The thinness of the line helps to avoid a different look that results when paint is brush- rather than roller-applied, or vice versa. If you don't have a lot of confidence in your ability to cut in a perfect straight line, you can use painter's tape, as noted earlier.

Painting Walls

When the ceiling is done, the walls can be painted. The walls are painted in strips about 3 to 4 feet wide. Again, use plenty of paint and go into the maximum dry area with each stroke, and paint 3- to 4-foot squares. Paint an adjacent strip, then come back with a relatively dry roller and run it floor to ceiling to make the first strip smooth.

3' - 4' Squares

Wall painting procedure

Painting Trim

Trim is done last. You can do the windows and doors, and then the base molding. Here, again, don't be afraid to use paint: not so much that it runs, but enough so you don't have to paint and repaint each area. A tried-and-true technique used by painters is called painting "from the dry into the wet." You dip about $1/3$ or $1/2$ of the bristles into the paint, and then skip ahead a couple of feet from the end of the previous brush stroke and paint back into the wet paint. You can brush it out as you go.

Painting Window Framework

Painting window framework can be made easier if you use an angled sash brush and position your body to the left or right a bit so your angle on the wood allows you to see more of the wood, rather than stand directly in front of the window and have a very thin angle to paint. It's best to paint the windows from the inside out: first the narrow frame pieces(s), and then the overall framework. Use enough paint, but watch out for sagging.

If you are using semigloss or gloss paint in the kitchen or bath, the procedure will depend on your paint application. If you are using a mohair or short nap roller, you can use it the same way you'd use a $3/8$-inch or $1/2$-inch nap. As mentioned earlier, using such a roller will result in an "orange peel" finish, not perfectly smooth, but quite good looking.

If you want a perfectly smooth finish, use a high-quality brush designed for the paint you're using. Apply the paint in strokes going across the grain, and then finish with downward strokes. As mentioned, pads also apply paint smoothly.

Painting Kitchen Cabinets

The best way to get maximum control in painting (and priming) cabinets is to remove them from the hinges and lay them flat across sawhorses. You should paint the inside of the cabinets first, then the outside. If using a brush, apply the paint in light, cross strokes, and then finish with downward strokes. If you have the patience, two light coats are better than one heavier one.

Paint Disposal

The best way to dispose of paint is to use it. However, if the paint is to be discarded, the best bet is to call your local government to find out how to do it. Some localities demand that paint residue be dried out. A very good product for this is "Waste Paint Hardener," made by the Bio-Wash company.

Painting Paneling

After cleaning, scuff-sanding, and priming, follow the same procedure as for painting walls. If the panel has grooves, it would be best to use a $1/2$-inch rather than a $3/8$-inch roller.

Painting Textured Surfaces

If you are painting textured surfaces, or masonry, such as concrete floors or walls in the basement, the only viable way is to use a heavy-napped roller. The same goes for walls with a textured-paint or masonry finish. Heavier-napped rollers have longer fibers and can more easily slop into the "valleys" in a textured surface.

For normal smooth masonry walls, the $1/2$-inch nap should be fine. For block with masonry grooves, the $3/4$-inch nap works well. For heavier textured surfaces, the 1-inch nap works well.

Note that painting textured surfaces requires more paint than smooth or semi-smooth surfaces. So, this should be figured into any calculations you make.

Masonry walls should be coated with a latex primer, as noted earlier, followed by a latex finish coat. Latexes are much better able to resist the alkalinity that may still be in the masonry.

Painting Masonry Floors

Interior floors may also be painted. There is a wide variety of paints available, ranging from flat latexes and satin-flat latexes to high-gloss oils. Which you choose will depend on your end use. If the area is in the basement and being used as a shop, then you're probably better off with high-gloss oil, simply because it will clean more easily. On the other hand, if the floor is going to be used as a play area, a flatter plain is less slippery, especially when wet.

Floors can be painted with a roller. Apply a first coat, being careful that you don't work yourself into a corner. When completely dry (check the paint can), apply a second coat. In other words, the first coat is used as a primer for the topcoat.

Painted Floors. If the masonry floor is painted and there is some peeling paint, it must be stripped off—a wire brush works well. Then the floor should be spot primed and topcoated.

Running Out of Paint

If you find yourself running out of paint, end at a corner or other natural break. Leaving off in the middle of a room can lead to lapmarks.

Painting Garage Floors

The same paint that is used on a basement floor can be used on a garage floor, if you don't put a car in there. If you do, special paint should be used, special in the sense that it can stand up to tire heat. Tires can get very hot—400 degrees—and if a car is driven onto a painted floor with hot tires, the paint will lift, unless it is formulated to stand the heat.

Epoxy paint is one type of paint that is normally used, but it should specify that it can be used for garage floors. UGL also makes a floor paint that is relatively cheap (about $17 per gallon in a local home center). The manufacturer suggests that you put a coat of paste wax on the garage floor where the tires will rest, but this is not required.

Concrete stain may also be used on floors, both inside and outside. It works just like wood stain, penetrating the concrete rather than drying as a film. We don't know of any that is suggested for use on a garage floor. Also, the concrete must have been installed for at least three months and be acid etched before the stain is applied.

Painting Closets

The average interior paint job requires painting closets. Essentially, you paint each closet as if it were a small room, starting with the ceiling, then doing the walls. Most people use cheap flat paint in closets, and there's no apparent reason to get fancy.

Pouring Paint

When pouring paint from a 5-gallon bucket, pour so the paint streams past the furthest edge from the opening rather than the nearest. This maintains better paint control.

Waterproofing Walls

In the great majority of cases, water seeping through basement walls can be stopped. Manufacturers sell a variety of products for the purpose and all work, to one degree or another.

Before applying a waterproofer, however, it is necessary to find the source of the water.

Wall

Tape

Aluminum foil

Condensation test patch

Condensation

In some cases it may simply be condensation, which appears when a warm, moisture-laden air contacts a cooler surface, such as a concrete foundation wall. There are many ways to test for this.

One way is to tape a piece of aluminum foil to the wall, removing it after several days. If the room side is wet, the problem is condensation. To control this, you can cut down on such moisture-generating activities as showers, washing, drying, and the like. In addition, you can apply insulation to cold water pipes if they're sweating. Another way to remove moisture is with a dehumidifier. This does a very good job of reducing the amount of moisture in the air. Various types are available.

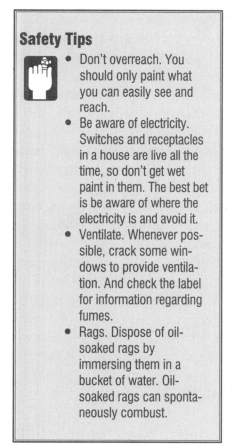

Safety Tips

- Don't overreach. You should only paint what you can easily see and reach.
- Be aware of electricity. Switches and receptacles in a house are live all the time, so don't get wet paint in them. The best bet is be aware of where the electricity is and avoid it.
- Ventilate. Whenever possible, crack some windows to provide ventilation. And check the label for information regarding fumes.
- Rags. Dispose of oil-soaked rags by immersing them in a bucket of water. Oil-soaked rags can spontaneously combust.

Seepage and Leaks

If condensation isn't the problem, then it could be seepage. Contrary to popular belief, masonry is not waterproof:

Water can and does seep through if it gets saturated enough.

Saturation is the key term. Under normal conditions, the water may penetrate masonry to some degree, but at one point—the point short of leakage—it will stop penetrating; and when the weather clears the moisture will evaporate.

There are many factors that can cause seepage in walls. Probably the most common is clogged gutters. They get clogged, or leak, or are pitched incorrectly—or a combination of the three. So the water is not routed away properly, but instead spills onto the ground next to the foundation. This saturates the soil, gradually so much so that the water starts pushing into the relatively porous masonry. As mentioned, if the saturation gets heavy enough, the water eventually finds its way into the basement.

Cracks

Aiding and abetting leakage in the basement are cracks in the foundation walls, which come as a result of stresses on the house—the house moves, and the foundation, which is fairly rigid, doesn't. Cracks often form in masonry walls where the foundation meets the slab floor, or at other joints; but in solid walls, they can form anywhere. Before applying any waterproofing material, these cracks must be fixed. The best material for repairing cracks in masonry walls is hydraulic cement, as mentioned before.

Waterproofers

There are many waterproofers on the market, including powdered and ready-mix kinds. The powdered kinds are mixed with water to create the waterproofer. In general, the powdered types are cheaper than the prepared, just as you'd expect prepared foods to cost more.

Although there are many brands available, included here are instructions for working with one brand, UGL (United Gilsonite Laboratories) Drylock, which the author has worked with successfully.

Cement and Rubber

Drylock is essentially a blend of cement and rubber, and works by expanding inside the pores of the concrete. If applied properly, the manufacturer guarantees it to withstand hydrostatic water pressure up to 4 pounds per square inch, the force of water exerted by a column of water 9 feet high. In other words, you could have a lake outside your foundation wall and the material would not yield.

Drylock may be used inside as well as outside the house on masonry surfaces such as retaining walls, cisterns, and swimming pools. When dry, the product is not toxic to people or animals. It may be used, for example, to coat a birdbath. It comes in white, gray, beige, and blue and can be tinted to light pastel shades. It can also be painted any color.

Drylock comes in three different forms: oil-base ready-mix, latex ready-mix, and powder (which you mix). The oil-base material is cheaper than the latex, but its disadvantage is its strong chemical smell; some people find this objectionable, and since the material takes around twenty-four hours to dry, it is objectionable for a long time!

The latex version, which is around $3 a gallon more, dries in a few hours. It does not a have a strong solvent smell.

The powdered version works as well as the others but is cheaper. It is available in white and in 1-pound boxes and $3\frac{1}{2}$-gallon reusable pails. The powder is mixed with water.

Application of Waterproofer

A key point to remember in regard to any waterproofer is that they can only be applied effectively to raw masonry. If the masonry has been painted, the manufacturer does not guarantee it will stick. The reason is that it would be dependent on the paint film for its ability to adhere to the wall. And, of course, a film of paint is not designed to stand up to the pressure of water.

Application of Drylock may be made with a brush or roller. A sturdy brush may be used, but the job is easier with a roller because of the rough surface. A roller with a $1/2$-inch nap can be used on most masonry. Drylock may be applied even when the wall is wet. Adhesion will not be affected.

Two coats are required. The first coat should be applied at the rate of 70 square feet per gallon, and the second coat at 125 square feet per. The average can of Drylock can cover about 125 square feet. Thus, 375 square feet of basement would require a little over 8 gallons of material.

Exterior Paint Preparation

The exterior of a home is subject to many more problems than the interior simply because it is subject to more stress. It gets no respect. Wind and rain and perhaps snow lash it, the siding and framing expand and contract, and various forms of unwanted life, such as mildew and algae take up residence on it. And then, of course, there is the sun beating down on it and the ultraviolet rays, which help to break down the finish.

The following are, a variety of what might be called commonplace problems. Included are prep steps that are normally required.

Cleaning Surfaces

As on inside surfaces, paint won't stick to a surface that is dirty or greasy or affected with mildew. You can use soap and water on dirt, but bleach is called for on mildew, as suggested earlier. Bleach also removes algae. Give the bleach five or ten minutes to work, and then rinse it off.

Cleaning Products. In the last year or so, a number of products have been introduced that manufacturers *say* make the cleaning process even easier. For example, one company, Armor-All, put out one product called Armor-All Painted Wood Wash Kit, which contains two 24-ounce bottles of the cleaner and a sprayer. The sprayer is attached to one of the bottles, and the garden hose is attached to the sprayer. The chemical is sprayed onto the surface. After five or ten minutes, the water is fed through the sprayer to rinse. The company says it sprays up to 25-feet high, and will wash away mildew, mold, and dirt.

If you find mildew or algae, the reason for the problem should be corrected. It could be bushes or trees shielding surfaces from the sun, thus allowing mildew to thrive; or it could be leaky gutters, or downspouts, or perhaps ice damming, that is creating a moisture-laden environment.

Power Washing. Another way to clean a house is with a power washer, a gas or electrically operated machine that drives water against a surface at high pressure and in great volume. It can be rented, but many homeowners buy them.

A power washer is capable of everything from removing the damaging effects of sun, which turn wood gray, to blasting paint off the siding. Since it is a powerful machine, however, you should take care with it.

If you are cleaning a painted surface and there is mildew, apply a bleach preparation first. Don't use bleach in the power washer, unless it is a store-bought product and instructions allow it. Bleach can damage internal rubber parts.

Power Washing Various Types of Siding. If you are power washing asbestos cement shingles, vinyl siding, metal siding, or other nonwood products, you can just spray away, with pressure at about 1000 psi and using 2 to 3 gallons of water a minute. However, if you are power washing a soft wood, such as cedar or redwood, you have to be extremely careful not to score the wood. Use low pressure and work up to a pressure that you can see will not score the wood.

You can also use a power washer to remove peeling paint. It's best to hold the wand so it hits the paint from the side, rather than dead on.

Power washing transfers a tremendous amount of water to the surface, so make sure the wood has a couple of days to dry thoroughly before applying primer or paint. Hold the power washer wand as close as needed to get the job done; but if the siding is clapboard or wood shingles, it's best to angle the spray so that water doesn't drive up under the shingles. Doing so can set up a moisture-laden environment that is ripe for mildew formation. It's best to spray from a ladder or scaffolding to guard against this problem.

Incidentally, power washing a house sometimes leads to the discovery that a paint job is unnecessary. Grime and mildew can be that bad!

Power washing also takes blackness and grayness off unpainted wood. (This is detailed in the sections on exterior staining and clear coating.)

Caulking

Caulking is another necessary prep step. Before caulking, all old, dried-up material should be scraped out with a beer can opener or the like. To get out any material that's crumbled, use an old brush or a dust brush that's made for the job. Crumbled caulk does not make for a solid surface.

Applying caulk from gun

To apply caulking from a gun, just cut the end tip at a slant that allows a $^3/_8$-inch bead of caulk to be extruded. Puncture the inner seal on the cartridge with a long nail or a slim piece of wood.

Insert the cartridge in the caulking gun, and then locate the tip of the nozzle on the top of the area to be caulked. Squeeze the trigger with even pressure, and draw the gun down along the crack in one continuous motion, extruding a bead that is half as deep as it is wide. The bead should have a concave shape. To insure this, you can draw a spoon along it or simply use your forefinger.

Filler Material

In some cases, the gaps are so deep that a bead of caulk alone will not do: A filler material of some sort needs to be inserted. This can be something like Mortite, which, as mentioned earlier, comes in long, beaded strips that can be removed as needed. Just press the material in place with your fingers—it will stick—and then apply the caulk. You can also use fiberglass insulation or foam backer rod, then strips of foam.

If the gaps are very big, something like "Great Stuff" (canned foam) can be used to partially fill the crack. This is squirted into the gap; it expands greatly as it dries. Foam should be applied sparingly until you get a sense of how much is required; a little, when dry, can go a long way. (For example, a spray can contains $2^1/_2$ gallons of hard foam.)

Peeling Paint

Paint that is peeling must be removed, of course, to provide a sound base for new paint. There are, as mentioned, various types of scrapers on the market.

In most cases, a stiff-bladed 3-inch scraper will do the job. If the surfaces are peeling fairly heavily, a hook-type scraper may be used. To use the tool, grasp it firmly and pull it down the siding, applying pressure as you do. This should pull off the paint. Some models of this scraper also have a knob on top for gripping with one hand, providing even more pressure.

As you go, examine the surface for areas where peeling may take place—the paint is bubbly or raised—and scrape it off. You can test suspicious areas with tape (as mentioned in the interior preparation section).

When scraping is done in this way, one is often left with a shallowly cratered surface. Here, you can use exterior spackling compound to fill in the craters, or at least apply it along the edges and feather the compound out so the edges aren't noticeable.

Holes

Wood siding and trim can be susceptible to a variety of holes. Small holes can be filled with exterior spackling compound, then touched up with a coat of the finish paint, allowed to dry, and then painted. If you have nails protruding, these can be countersunk with a nailset and hammer, and the depressions filled with compound. If the hole is small and a clear coating is going to be applied over it, then a wood filler is recommended. Although there is no such thing

as a perfect match, wood putties and fillers are available, as mentioned earlier, in a wide variety of wood colors and are easy to apply with a putty knife.

Rot

If the hole or gap is large and there is rot present, say on a window frame, then spackling compound is not enough. A product that fills the hole and prevents further problems is required. First, the rot is scraped out with a stiff putty knife, or the like, and then the filler, a two-part material, is mixed together and applied to the damaged area, just as you would any filler. After drying—it dries very hard—it is sanded, primed, and painted.

A standard wood filler for exterior (and interior) work is Durham's Rock Hard Water Putty. Another is Minwax Wood Filler (mentioned earlier).

Holes in Metal

Sometimes metal parts get holes in them, and there are a number of products, most based on epoxy, that you can use for repair. For example, you can get Oatey Epoxy putty, which comes as a soft material that you knead together before use, or liquid solder for filling small holes in gutters and the like. Also available is aluminum adhesive-backed tape, which can be wrapped around such things as downspouts. Caulk can also be used on metal, assuming the hole or crack is small enough.

Sanding

For large peeling areas, machine sanding is the way to go. A heavy-duty industrial sander using two kinds of paper, 16 grit and 60 grit, is a good choice. The 16-grit paper is for removing all the peeling paint down to the bare wood. The 60-grit paper is for smoothing the grooves left in the wood by the 16-grit paper. When you do the job, it's important not to allow any paint to remain on the surface—it will clog the pores of the 60-grit material.

What to Sand. The goal is to leave a surface that the new paint can adhere too, as well as one that looks good. In some areas, only some of the paint needs to be removed.

You could use a palm sander, a belt sander, or a rotary type. The rotary type is capable of heavily scoring the surface unless one takes care. Sanding big areas manually is tough.

Turn the machine on and bring it to the surface of the work when it's moving. Move it along the surface, holding it a few degrees (up to 10) off the surface. Don't press it flush because it tends to pull out of the hands and is hard to manage.

The action quickly takes the paint off down to raw wood, but it also leaves some grooves. Hence, you should finish sanding with 60-grit paper.

Priming Wood

You can use the same techniques for applying primer that you use for applying paint. As already mentioned, a variety of primers are available for priming wood and painted wood. Following are some recommendations.

Painted wood. If you are making a dramatic color change, say from yellow to green, a primer is a good idea. A latex primer works quite well, assuming that the wood is a nonbleeding type like pine or new wood of a nonbleeding type. To insure that the topcoat covers better it's a good idea, as mentioned earlier, to tint the primer.

If you are painting patched areas on bleeding woods, such as cedar or redwood, standard latex primer is not recommended. The water in the primer can activate tannins in the wood and send them to the surface where they will discolor the primer. Even a topcoat may not cover the discoloration.

An oil-base primer is recommended for bleeding woods, because the oils in it will not affect the extractives in the wood. There is one water-base primer, Bulls Eye 1-2-3, that is a good interior as well as exterior primer, and is also said to be good on bleeding woods.

Water Repellent First. Before applying primer or paint to raw wood, you can extend the life of a job considerably by using a water-repellent coating, such as Woodlife. It sinks into the pores of the wood and protects it from heavy accumulation of water and, therefore, rot. In tests done by the Forest Products Laboratory, the application of a water repellent prior to painting was said to have a significant positive effect.

Pitch and Knots. If the wood is exuding pitch or has knots, a stain-blocking primer is recommended. One such is BIN, a shellac-base primer that can be dabbed on and works well. But BIN cannot be used as a general outside house primer—use it just for knots.

Plywood. If the plywood is raw, a latex primer and paint system is recommended. Plywood can expand and contract and make a rigid paint, like oil-base paint, fail sooner rather than later.

Rust

The exterior of a home has a variety of metal surfaces that must be prepped for paint. The main enemy of metal is rust, which is created when raw metal and water meet.

You've probably heard the saying that "rust never sleeps." It's true. Every speck of rust must be removed or neutralized in some way, or it will return.

Wrought Iron Fencing. One of the main areas where rust is found is on wrought iron fencing. For whatever reason, the paint cracks and peels, and once water contacts bare metal, it's not long before rust is on its way. If the rust is slight, you can remove it with a wire brush. If the rust is extensive and accessible, you can also use a metal sanding accessory that is chucked into a drill. One such is made by 3-M. It consists of a hard, webbed disk and takes rust and flaking paint off quite readily. There are also other types. It is important, whatever type you use, to wear safety goggles.

Accessory to remove rust

Specks of sanded material or material from the sanding disk can fly into your eyes.

Go down to metal that is clear of rust; and before priming, wipe the metal down with lacquer thinner, which is a good cleaning solvent that dries very quickly.

Priming Metal

Bare spots should be spot primed. Oil-base primers work well, and so will Bulls Eye 1-2-3.

As mentioned, there are primers available that allow you to leave rust on the surface and not worry about it bleeding through. With these products it is suggested that you remove all flaking rust and/or peeling paint, and then apply the primer to the smooth—though still rusty—areas.

Metal windows and other items made of steel and iron can be handled the same way as cast iron fencing. Metal, after all, is metal.

If you wish, you can remove rust from hard-to-sand spots with Naval Jelly. This is a thick pinkish liquid that is dabbed on and allowed to work for thirty minutes; it is then washed off with water.

Priming Raw Galvanized Steel

Raw galvanized steel must be handled differently. This comes with an oil on it that paint will not adhere to. The galvanized steel must be allowed to weather for six months, or it can be washed off with lacquer thinner, followed by a prime coat of a zinc-rich primer specially geared for galvanized steel, and then a coat of latex paint.

Priming Concrete

There are two basic kinds of concrete that can be painted: concrete that has a coat of paint on it and concrete that is raw. This section covers raw concrete.

Cleaning the Surface. The first step in preparing raw concrete (on either the floor or the walls) for painting is to clean the surface. Use a broom to sweep the floor clean or a shop vacuum or an air compressor to blow off grit and dirt. If you use the latter, by all means wear safety goggles.

Stains on the floor must come up. Grease stains are usually relatively easy.

First, use a putty knife to scrape up any grease deposits. Then use a heavy-duty solution of water and cleaner/degreaser to remove the stains that are left, scrubbing as needed and rinsing carefully. Paint won't adhere to grease, no matter how small the spot. If the grease doesn't come up when the degreaser is used with water, it may be necessary to use it full strength.

Oil stains are worse than grease because oil penetrates into concrete; and the longer it stays, the deeper it penetrates. Hence, to clean it out you have to get something to penetrate deep into the concrete.

If there is surface oil, soak up as much as you can with a rag. Resist the temptation to wipe. Wiping results in a bigger stain, with the oil driven deeper into the concrete.

After use, dispose of the rag by sealing it off in a 1-gallon can filled with water; oil-soaked rags can spontaneously burst into flame.

Remove the rest of the oil by one of three methods. You can purchase a powdered floor-drying material at a local auto supply store. Or you can sprinkle Portland cement on the stain and allow it to stay on the stain 24 hours, before picking it up. The procedure is repeated until all the stain is gone. A third method is to purchase a commercial cleaner.

"Rust Stains" are not actually rust; they don't keep growing like real rust. So, if you are painting over rust stains, it is a simple matter to cover them with a coat of stain-blocking primer.

However, if you are using a clear sealer, you'll need to remove the stain. The material for this is called oxalic acid, which comes as a powder and is available at paint stores, woodworking supply stores, and drugstores.

The powder is mixed with water at the ratio of $1/4$ pound of acid to 1 quart of water. The mixture is applied to the rust stain and allowed to stand for an hour or so, then rinsed off with clear water while being scrubbed with a clean stiff-bristled acid brush. If all of the stains don't come off after one application, repeat the procedure.

"Etch" the Concrete. No concrete should be painted in less than ninety days after it has been poured. Reason: It leeches alkalies, which can interfere with the paint adhering. It is also a good idea to use a concrete etch. A concrete etch (made by a number of companies) roughens the concrete so that the coatings applied adhere better.

Concrete Patches. Concrete may have gaps or holes in it, and these must also be repaired before any painting is done.

If the hole is in a wall, and there is no water leakage, ordinary concrete patcher may be used (as described earlier).

Holes in Floor. If there is a hole in a concrete floor, "spalling" (flakes of concrete missing), or cracks, these also must be repaired. Concrete patcher may be used here also.

It's a good idea to allow at least thirty days to pass before painting these patches, to make sure that they have given up all the alkalies.

Prepping Stucco

Pure stucco is not painted. Prepare it in a way that calls for as little paint as possible. Unpainted stucco can last for years. Painted stucco requires periodic redoing just as any other exterior surfaces.

The first step in preparing it, then, is to clean it. You can do this with a detergent and water and a rough nylon bristle brush. Once the soil is removed, the stucco may be clean and bright—and may not need repainting.

In some instances you may also find mildew, efflorescence, and peeling paint. You can handle these as described earlier. However, it's not a good idea to power wash stucco heavily because you can knock down its texture. If there are gaps in the stucco, you can patch it with an acrylic latex caulk.

Exterior Painting Procedure

It's a good idea to stay out of the sun when doing exterior painting, not only because it can lead to problems with the paint but also because it can tire out the painter. Painting in the shade is not always possible, so if you must paint in the sun, try to do it early in the morning, when you and the siding are not getting the direct rays, and the wood is cool.

It's also a good idea to take breaks, to drink plenty of cool liquids, and to not overexert.

When painting a house or other building, paint from the top down. The theory is that if any paint drips, it will be painted over as the job progresses.

Do the siding first, and then the trim. There are bound to be some drips and spatters onto the trim, but these will be hidden when the trim is done.

Doing it this way means having to lean a ladder against freshly painted siding. This is not usually a problem if the ends of the ladder are covered with ladder mitts or cloth. If worse comes to worse, a spot can be touched up when the ladder is moved.

Dropcloths

Canvas dropcloths work best for covering up. As mentioned, they drape over things more easily and don't flutter away in the wind. You should cover every place the paint may fall. Be particularly careful to cover asphalt roofing and concrete. Because these items are porous, getting all the paint off can be a problem.

Getting paint off screens is difficult as well. Hence, it's always a good idea to remove screens or drape cloths over them.

Try not to cover plants, flowers, and bushes for too long a period of time. Being covered by dropcloths is not a natural state for vegetation, and the sooner you allow air and sunlight in, the better. If bushes and plants are brushing against a wall, you can cover them with dropcloths and tie them back with rope, or just hold them out of the way with your back as you "slither" through.

Mask Off

If you think you need to, mask off areas where you might smear paint. Good places to use masking tape are around doorknobs, around lights, along a roof line where you will cutting in siding (such as where a dormer cuts into a roof), and around posts mounted in concrete. Put tape down wherever you need a sharp, clean line—where painted surfaces meet unpainted surfaces.

When painting these cut-in areas, I have always found it best to use what is called a "dry brush"—one that holds paint but doesn't drip. Even though the painter's tape is in place to protect a surface, you don't want paint running down into it.

Wait until the paint is dry before stripping the tape off. This way the paint won't come off with the tape.

Painting Siding

The easiest way to paint siding is to do as much of it with a roller as you can. Some sidings are made so that a roller cannot cover all the surface easily. On siding of this kind, a brush or perhaps a painting pad works well.

In any case, some of the siding around windows, doors, and other protrusions (such as vents and pipes) must be cut in somewhat before a roller can be used. The cutting in should be done first. Then use the roller to get as close as you can to the obstruction.

Following is a lineup of siding types and some methods that might be used to paint them.

Asbestos Cement Shingles. This is definitely a job for a roller. One that has a $3/4$-inch nap will do a good job, but I know one painter who swears by a $1^1/_2$-

> ### The Power of Baby Oil
> Baby oil is good for removing paint spatters from skin; and, of course, it's gentle.

inch nap, saying that since it brings so much paint to the surface, the job goes more quickly.

One criticism is that a $1\frac{1}{2}$-inch nap can leave a texture kind of finish. However, backrolling (going over the painted area with an undipped roller) solves this problem.

Whichever size you choose, concentrate on getting a generous amount of paint on the surface, applying it with "W" or "M" patterns, in a 3-foot strip that goes from the bottom to the top of the siding. Do an adjacent 3-foot strip the same way, and then come back with a "dry" roller—one empty of paint—and "backroll" smooth the applied paint in the first strip.

Cedar Siding. You can use a roller on the flat type of cedar. If it is striated, you can use a cut-down brush or a pad.

Painting cedar siding is basically a wipe down job. You dip the brush into the paint, jam it up under the shingles and wipe the paint on with a downward stroke. Old-time painters often use a "stub" brush for this, which is a cut-down or worn, old brush, but a paint pad works just as well. Padco, for example, sells pads with thick, fluffy naps that might work, as well as one with a rough texture and a curved-up edge with fabric on it.

The curved-up portion is designed to jam under a course of shingles, and then is wiped on.

Clapboard. This is a little too configured to paint totally with a roller. Your best bet here is to cut in with a brush, and then paint the faces of the boards. Some painters like to use a 3-inch- or a 4-inch-wide roller on a long handle for painting the faces.

Vinyl Siding. You can paint vinyl siding the same way you'd paint wood—using an acrylic latex paint. Use a fluffy roller on it as much as possible. Tip: When painting vinyl, you should stick to lighter paint, because a darker paint absorbs so much heat from the sun that it warps the siding.

Aluminum Siding. This has a hard, baked enamel finish on it. Here, I would cut in with a brush, and then apply the paint with $\frac{3}{8}$-inch-nap roller.

You should do as much of the siding as you can working off the ground. The more you can do this way, the quicker the job will go. This means securing the roller to a pole. The standard one-piece pole is 4 feet long, but you can get them longer, as noted earlier.

I would personally not go higher than 10 feet. Beyond this the pole gets unwieldy and heavy, and the control is not there. The best bet, I think, is to use the 4-foot pole, then work off a plank set on ladder jacks, which can be rented or bought. Using a 5-gallon bucket of paint with a grid insert will aid in getting the job done quickly.

Painting Difficult Spots

Not all houses are ranch style and simple to paint. Some have all kinds of angles and such that make painting some spots difficult. For example, one difficult area is the sides of dormers or similar configurations. The roof slants; hence, it is difficult to stand on it and feel secure.

One way I've found to handle such a situation is not really for the neophyte: first lay a dropcloth or dropcloths along the roof next to the side of the dormer. Then, lean an extension ladder against the side of the house. Climb up and place half of another extension ladder or a stepladder so it lies flat and its feet rest against the top of the first extension ladder. As long as a helper holds the first ladder solidly against the ladder lying on the roof, it can't slide down. Only try this if you feel comfortable with heights and have a good sense of balance.

One way to paint a sloping roof that's fairly low is to simply lay an extension ladder along it, with the feet of the ladder

dug into the ground. You can use another ladder to climb up on the first.

Above a Porch. Another difficult spot can be above a porch or overhang of some sort, because if you set the ladder so it is above the trim, you won't be able to reach the siding. I've found that the best thing here is to cover the porch roof or overhang with dropcloths and work off the overhang. You may not be able to reach the very top of the siding; if that is the case, just lay a closed stepladder against the wall, using it as a small extension ladder.

High Up on a Peak. Another difficult spot can be high up on a peak. You may find that there's no way to rig a ladder so you can paint a peak safely. In this case, I would suggest using a brush held in a clamp. This device enables you to get into virtually any area on a house. The brush holder can be angled and locked in position with thumbscrews as needed.

Painting Trim

Exterior trim is painted the same way as interior trim. Dip the brush about one third of the way into the paint, tap it off on the inside of the can, and then apply it, brushing it out. Then, paint from the "dry into the wet": Start each succeeding brushful of paint about a foot away from the last brushful and paint back toward it.

You should use plenty of paint. If you keep dipping your brush in one third of the way, this shouldn't be a problem. Avoid excessive brushing: Apply the paint, and then lay it off as with interior painting, smoothing it out. Every now and then, look back and check for sags, and brush these out. You should do fine. Good paint is self-leveling and turns out fine with minimal effort.

As you go, there are sure to be drips on adjacent siding. You can either wipe them off with a rag moistened in thinner or swipe them flat with the tip of your brush.

Painting Windows and Doors

Just as on the inside, paint a window from the inside out. That is, open the window a few inches on the top and bottom and paint it; then open both halves (assuming a double-hung window) so you can paint the portions of the rails that are exposed. When the windows themselves are finished, paint the frame, again using the "dry into the wet" method. When the window is finished, take a look at it. If you see any missed spots or sags of paint, use the tip of your brush to brush them out. Be particularly mindful of the window sill; paint can run down over the window and collect on it.

Painting Doors

To paint a door, open it completely. (Be sure that a clean and dust-free dropcloth is pulled underneath to protect the interior from paint spatters.) How you paint depends on whether the door is paneled or flush. But the key concept is (as with trim and walls) "laying off": Apply the paint and then brush it out smoothly.

On a flush door, dip the brush about an inch into the paint, tap off excess on the inside, then paint the hinge edge of the door with sweeping strokes. When the paint is applied, bring your dry brush across it with upward strokes.

Get in the habit of checking for sags (a few minutes after

Paint first

Paint second

First strokes in painting a door

you apply paint), and brush these out with gentle laying-off strokes. Also, when painting narrow edges, don't push the brush against the edge so hard that the brush overlaps on the sides. This can lead to a brush malady called fingering—clumps of bristles are separated—and will ruin the brush. Paint the other edge, then proceed to paint the face of the door.

Paint in quarters, first applying the paint horizontally, then vertically, and then laying it off with light upward strokes. Paint an adjacent quarter the same way, and then the bottom quarters, making your final laying-off strokes overlap the previously applied paint.

If painting a paneled door, paint the edges first, and then paint from the inside out: the perimeters of the panels followed by the rails, and then the stiles. Paint the door, then paint the trim. Leave the door open until the paint dries enough so that it can be closed without marring the paint.

Finished for the Day

When you are finished for the day, there are a number of steps to take. First, take down ladders if they are placed where someone could accidentally walk into them or where kids are playing.

You should stop at a structural break—for example, at the end of a wall or up to the edge of an addition. Avoid a situation in which you are midway through painting a wall, because when you pick up your strokes of freshly applied paint, they will overlap the existing dry coat and leave a lap mark.

Cleaning Brushes and Rollers

When cleaning brushes and rollers, remove as much of the paint as you can before using solvents. To clean a brush, lay it on a sheet of newspaper. Then push down on the bristles with a scraper or joint compound knife, squeezing as much paint out of the bristles as possible. When you've got as much paint as possible removed from the brush, the next step is to wash it.

Cleaning paint brush

If latex paint was used, immerse the bristles in a solution of water and mild soap. Sometimes the soap is forgotten, but it's necessary in order to do a better

Safety Tips

Every year hundreds of people get killed and injured while using ladders. Ladder safety partially relates to using a good quality ladder. However, the following rules should be observed:

- Inspect ladders often. This is not an exercise in advanced science but in common sense. Are rails split or broken? Is something bent? Are bolts loose? If you have any question about its being totally safe, don't use it. Wrap masking tape around it and on the tape write: "Don't Use."

- Don't stretch. Only paint what you can easily see and easily reach. This may mean moving a heavy extension ladder more than you'd like, but the alternative is to take a chance on falling. Of course, some stretching will be required from time to time, but you shouldn't put yourself in jeopardy.

- Don't "jump" the ladder—move the top of it—from one position to another while on it just so you can get a spot you missed.

- Get help if you can't manage the ladder. The author once had to move a 40-foot steel extension ladder by himself along the side of a house, and it's a miracle that it didn't fall through one of the windows.

- Don't make it lean too much—or too little. The rule when leaning an extension ladder against a house is that the bottom should be one quarter of its height away from the house. Sometimes bushes and other obstructions interfere with this fine theory, but you should adhere to it as much as possible. If it's set too steep against a wall, there's always the chance it could topple back; too little and the front end could slide down the siding.

- Make sure the legs can't slide out. If the bottom legs of the ladder are set in soft earth or are otherwise in danger of sliding out, make sure they can't. For example, bang homemade pegs into the earth in front of the feet, or put weight there (a pair of concrete blocks), or, if necessary, find a way to tie the legs in place.

- Make sure the ladder can't fall sideways. This can be a problem when you are painting a house on rough terrain. The legs may not be exactly on level ground, and a shift of weight can send the ladder, and you, toppling over. If necessary, use "C" clamps to lengthen one leg to make it level with the other. Commercial extensions are also available.

- Don't stand on the top step of the ladder to reach something. Get a taller ladder.

- Don't work on a ladder in front of an unlocked door. Someone could come out and smack the door into the ladder—and down it and you go.

- Don't work outside when there's a strong wind or lightning.

- Overall, the best procedure when setting up a ladder is to climb up a few steps to see if it's stable enough to climb up further.

- If you are using an aluminum or wood ladder, by all means be careful that you are not in danger of tipping and falling into an electrical line. If the line is frayed, the shock could easily kill you.

cleaning job. Knead the bristles with your hand, and then rinse in clear running water. Wrap the brush in newspaper or its original package or its "keeper," if you have it, and hang it up.

If you need to use mineral spirits, follow the procedure above to remove as much paint as possible. Then immerse the bristles in a can of mineral spirits, kneading them with your fingers (you can wear rubber gloves if you wish). Next, immerse the brush in a can with paint thinner in it and repeat the process. Finally, immerse the brush in another can of thinner, and wash again.

The same procedure can be used with rollers, first squeezing paint out with a stick.

Water Repellent Preservative

If new wood is being painted, the application of a water repellent preservative, such as Woodlife, is recommended before the primer and paint are applied. Repellents help protect the wood against rain and dew and thus prevent swelling and shrinking. It's particularly important for a wood species such as southern yellow pine.

Water repellents can be applied by brushing or dipping. Lap and butt joints and the edges of panel products such as

Cleaning paint from roller

hardboard and particleboard should be especially well treated, because paint tends to fail in these areas first.

After applying the repellent, allow at least two warm sunny days for drying. If enough time is not allowed, any paint applied over the treated areas may be slow to dry, or may discolor, or may dry with a rough surface that resembles alligator hide. If the wood has been dipped, allow it at least a week to dry, if the weather is favorable. You should prime the wood as soon as possible after the repellent is dry.

Exterior Staining

Perhaps ten years ago, paint was just about the only thing available as a coating for exterior wood. Today, however, we have stains. Stains have come on strong, and in certain situations are, in my view, just flat out better to use than paint.

The look of stain is very different from that of paint. Paint provides a dense, opaque finish that hides the surface underneath; stains are more subtle. There is some color in what is classically regarded as a stain, but not so much that it doesn't allow the wood grain and the wood color to show through, along with the texture. There are also opaque stains available; but these, in our view and as shall be discussed later, are really paints.

Paint and stain act very differently on the surface of raw wood. Stains penetrate raw wood like sauce on a sponge cake—an average $1/8$ inch, depending on the wood species and its condition. Paint forms a film over the wood, with little or no penetration.

Because stains penetrate rather than form a film, they're less likely to peel. When moisture (one of the main reasons why coatings peel) that is trapped in the wood pushes to get out, it pushes against the film, and this leads to blistering and then peeling. Stain is "semipermeable," as they say; and when moisture pushes against it, it bleeds through, hits the surface, and evaporates.

Maintenance of Stain

Preparation for restaining is much easier than for repainting. All you have to do is clean dirt and mildew from the stain surface and apply fresh stain.

There's no need to scrape, sand, and prime as with deteriorated paint.

One type of stain is called semitransparent. It comes in a wide variety of colors. The most popular are the earth colors—browns, blacks, reds, and greens. But lighter colors, such as beige and even white, are available, as well as nonearth colors, such as blue.

Semitransparent stain is, as the name suggests, partly transparent. But applying two coats of it to wood makes it less transparent. The color is more intense

---

Stopping Periodically

There will be times during a paint job that you stop for a break or lunch. During such times, it's a good idea to safeguard tools. Also, I would immerse the roller in the paint, putting the paint in the shade. A brush can be laid flat, first wrapping it in an airtight covering such as Saran Wrap. It's not a good idea to put brushes in a pail. Doing so could put stress on the bristles and deform them. However, one manufacturer, Hyde, makes a device that can be used to temporarily hold a brush straight up in a can. It attaches to the can and has a magnet that the ferrule on the brush is placed against; thus, the brush is held in position.

simply because you're adding more pigment. Two coats are normally only good on rough-textured or weathered wood. Smooth, new wood usually can only absorb one coat of stain before becoming saturated. The excess lies on the finish; and unless it is wiped away, it can form a film that peels like paint.

Pay attention to what the manufacturer says about application. But be aware of all the possible consequences.

Another type of stain that works like a semitransparent one is called a toner, or transparent stain. This is really a clear coating with a little color in it to simulate various wood colors; but it works just like a semitransparent.

Bleed Through

Take care when restaining that the color on the wood and that in the stain you're applying are compatible. If you stain over a darker color, the darker hue will show through. You can, however, cover a lighter transparent stain with a darker one, say a beige with a dark brown.

You should also make sure that the stain you use is formulated for the area you're doing. Some manufacturers make an all-purpose semitransparent stain that can be used on siding, fencing, decks—

anywhere. However, others make a stain designed for only a specific area, such as on siding; it's not formulated for walking on. Check the label.

Semitransparents and toners are made with oil-base and latex/oil and latex formulations. I favor the oil-base types because I think they penetrate the wood better and, therefore, last longer; though the average life of these stains is usually no more than eighteen months.

Stain for Hardboard

Because they are designed to work by penetrating, semitransparent stains and toners don't work on hardboard, waferboard, oriented strand board, or other composition materials. These products are manufactured with glue, waxes, and additives that stain can't penetrate. For that same reason, you can't use semitransparent stain over paint or solid-color stain, because they are not absorbent.

Like semi's, solid-color stains dry to a flat finish. But aside from the way they work—film versus penetrator—because they contain much more pigment—are thicker—the thin film they form can peel, though the likelihood of peeling is less than with paint. Because of their film-forming nature, you can use them to coat composition products like hardboard and surfaces that are painted.

Solid-Color Stain

Solid-color stain is available in oil- and latex acrylic-base formulations. Acrylics are a better product than oil-base stains primarily because they're less likely to peel. In any film-building coating, acrylic polymers are more elastic and adhere to the substrate's surface better than oil-base polymers, which are more brittle and tend to crack.

For many years, manufacturers have formulated solid-color stains for use only on vertical surfaces like siding and fencing.

Reason: They couldn't be made strong enough to stand up to foot traffic. However, one company (Behr) has, at this writing, a formula for decks that they claim holds up because of the toughness of the acrylic resins used.

Solid-color stains come in a rainbow of colors. You'll get longer life with multiple coats. In fact, for woods like cedar, cypress, and redwood, manufacturers recommend using a stain-blocking primer under acrylic finishes. The primer prevents tannins in the wood from discoloring the finish.

It should be noted that the more solid-color stain applied, the more the natural look (or texture) of the wood is lost. At least one manufacturer, Cabot, makes a semisolid stain that is (the company says) a cross between a semitransparent and a solid-color stain. Cabot says the stain penetrates like a semitransparent, but has good color coverage like a solid color, yet with more texture showing through.

Applying Stain

The first rule for applying any semitransparent stain—any coating for that matter—is to thoroughly read the instructions. Individual manufacturers allow different application methods. If you have any doubt, use the customer service 800 numbers to get details. (Information on how to access these numbers is given in Chapter 12 called Info Power.)

In general, though, observe the following:

- Coat new wood as soon as possible. Conventional wisdom used to be that new wood, particularly pressure-treated wood, had to weather for a while before coating, to drive out moisture and provide a roughened surface. This has been found to be not true. In fact, studies by the Forest

Products Laboratory in Madison, Wisconsin, have determined that coatings should be applied as soon as a wood is surface dry. Doing this increases its life span an average 20 percent. In other words, a deck that could be expected to last twenty years without a coating could last twenty-four or twenty-five years with a coating.

- Clean all wood surfaces before applying stain. If the wood has turned gray or black, power wash it. You can also use one of the commercially available cleaners on it.

- Check to make sure that the batch numbers on the stain cans are the same. The numbers appear on the top or bottom of the cans. This will insure that each can was mixed and packaged at the same time, thus making color discrepancies from can to can less likely. Even so, pour all the stain you're using into a 5-gallon can and work out of it. Stains, like paints, are available in 5-gallon containers. Bought this way they are a little cheaper.

- The color of stain in the store will not be the same as it will be on the siding, deck, or wherever you put it. As mentioned earlier (regarding paint color), the only way to know for sure is to test a little of it on the wood. To be sure you will like the color, buy a small amount of it—a quart if you can—and apply it under a railing or in some other unnoticeable spot.

- Stain must be stirred frequently as it is applied because the solvent tends to separate quickly from the color and you want to be sure you are using it at full strength with a true color.

Use a good brush for applying semitransparent stain. It's usually the best applicator. It can also be used in conjunction with other equipment. If you spray on a semitransparent stain with a low-pressure deck sprayer, back-brush it—brush out the applied stain to make sure it's spread properly and is worked into the wood—penetration's the key. You can also use fluffy pads for semitransparent stain; rollers work well for solid-color stain, which, as mentioned, is essentially a flat paint.

- When applying a semitransparent stain, be aware that it dries quickly (flash dries). A flash-dried area that is overlapped by a second coat is, in effect, two coats—with a lapmark.

To avoid lapmarks on a deck, for example, do a board or two at a time, keeping a wet edge and working your way down the length of the board or boards until finished. You should try to work in the shade, or early in the morning, or whenever the sun is not as hot so that flash-drying is not a problem.

As mentioned, the rougher the surface the heavier the nap. Reason: As the nap becomes saturated with paint, it slops; in a sense, the paint-saturated fibers slop into all grooves, nooks, and crevices.

Do 2 boards at a time

Applying stain

Removing Stain

There are times when it is desirable to remove stain from a deck. It may have been overapplied or someone may want a color change.

Until relatively recently, there wasn't much you could do, short of using a floor sander to take it up—thereby removing wood from the deck—or waiting for it to weather out, or perhaps just getting fed up with the whole thing and painting or solid-staining it.

Fortunately, that is no longer the case. Recently, a group of products were introduced that allow you to take the stain—and more—completely off. We know of three manufacturers of such a product—Flood, Thompson, and Bio-Wash—but there are sure to be more. We tested two products: Bio-Wash's Stripex and Stripex-L. They both worked very well.

A distinction should be made between the stain-removal products and wood cleaners. Cleaners are just that: They are formulated to remove dirt and mildew and grayness from wood. But they do not have any appreciable effect on stain. The new products do. At least one manufacturer, Bio-Wash, has a remover for solid latex stain and polyurethane.

The older the stain, the better the product works. If the coating on the deck has been battered by weather, the wood is better able to absorb the stain lifters, get under the existing stain, and lift it off.

First, surrounding vegetation is sprayed down to protect it, even though Biowash's products are biodegradable. Next, Stripex is applied to the deck with a roller, and then a mist or spray of water is applied. This turns it into a gel-like substance (which, by the way is very slippery underfoot, as evidenced by yours truly falling on his backside). The product is agitated with a brush on a stick, and allowed to work for five or ten minutes. Then a

chisel or other tool is used to scrape a test area to see if the stain is loosened and lifting. If it is, a power washer is used to drive it off. A 25 degree tip at 2000 psi works well. Of course, one has be careful not to score a soft wood.

Use of the product tends to darken the wood; so after stripping, apply a wood brightener. Natural Wood Brightener is packaged with the product. Simply mix this powder with water for use. Then scrub it onto the stripped deck and power wash it off.

Out Damn Spot

Wood, particularly on decks, can be subjected to a variety of undesirable stains from such substances as barbecue sauce, wax, and vegetation. These substances must be removed prior to the application of a finished coating. Following is a lineup of problems and solutions:

- Lumber Grading Stamps. There is no solution for effectively removing these stamps, though they can be primed and painted. The solution here is to use sandpaper to abrade the letters and numbers.
- Algae and Moss. Algae and moss leave green stains that are difficult to remove completely. They develop a root structure that penetrates the wood and can regrow. The only way to control them is to apply bleach full strength as needed. Rinse the area well before applying any finish.
- Wax. When citronella and other candles are used in and around a deck, wax drippings often result. Place a mineral-spirits saturated rag on the wax spot, and keep it wet until the spot is absorbed into the rag.
- Barbecue sauce, grease, and fats. Clean with automotive degreasers and carburetor cleaners that can be rinsed with water. Don't apply these removers when the surface is exposed to direct sun—only use in the shade.
- Leaf stains. Wash with a one-to-one solution of household bleach and water.

Exterior Clear Coatings

The best way to protect wood but preserve its natural color is with a clear penetrating sealer. Unlike polyurethanes and varnishes—which give wood a clear, thick coating that is subject to cracking, peeling, and other deterioration—penetrating clear sealers do not crack. Instead, they penetrate into the wood and coat the wood fibers with a water repellent.

Blocking the Sun

Sunlight—actually UV radiation—is a natural enemy of wood. It breaks down the cells on the surface of the wood and the lignin, the substance that connects the wood fibers, graying the wood and eroding its surface over time. You can't prevent this process, but clears with UV radiation protectors can slow it down.

Clear coating protection against UV rays doesn't last long, despite what manufacturers say on the label—a year or so at most on sunlit surfaces. On vertical surfaces in the shade, you might get away with two years.

If you want to keep the wood its natural color—something usually desirable with lovely woods like cedar and redwood—you have to redo it every year or so. But even with this kind of maintenance, the wood fades and needs to be renewed with cleaner periodically.

Another type of clear has no UV ray protectors in it. This product only protects the wood against water penetration, not sun. Hence, it grays out rather quickly. Such products are cheaper, of course; but if you want UV ray protection, check the label for a statement such as "UV radiation protection" or "screens out the sun."

Picking Clears

Of the two types of clear available to choose from, pick a formulation that contains a UV ray inhibitor. Also, in all but the direst desert climates, choose a coating that contains preservatives—mildewcides and fungicides. This is especially true if you're coating a deck that's close to the ground or protecting an area that's constantly sheltered from wind and sun. Preservatives do a better job of protecting.

Not all clear sealers have preservatives, and some that do may not use the word *preservative* on the label, because to do so involves an expensive registration process (a million dollars) with the Environmental Protection Agency. Instead, companies use wording like "preserves the natural beauty of wood" or just claim to be "mildew resistant."

For a pressure-treated deck, you might consider a toner. A toner can make the wood look more like redwood or cedar.

Clears come in oil-base and latex formulations. Of the two, solvent-base clears give longer protection. Emulsions and water-base acrylics offer easier cleanup.

Applying Clears

Applying clears is relatively easy to do, but it's not the same as applying paint. Although instructions vary from brand to brand—and the label instructions should be read—the following should work. First, make sure the surface is clean and mildew free—as clean as necessary.

Coat new wood quickly. As soon as the wood is surface dry, apply the product. The longer you wait, the greater the checking and the more natural color you'll lose.

Usually, as with semitransparent stain, the brush is the best applicator. A brush drives the product into the wood better than anything else. If you wish, you can also use a fluffy pad on the end of a stick, such as Padco's.

Work with the grain. Some companies suggest a roller or sprayer. If you use a sprayer, though, be aware that's it's easy to overapply the product.

Cleaning Wood

If you are going to use a clear, it is best to get the wood back to its natural color, if it is discolored in any way. How you do this depends on the kind of wood involved, and the degree and location of the discoloration.

If the wood is cedar or redwood and has mildew, the only way to remove it is with a bleach-based product. There is a wide variety of commercial cleaners available with bleach in them.

Spray this product on the deck or the siding, and wait fifteen minutes. Then rinse it off. This should kill the mildew. You don't want to leave it on too long because it could bleach the wood.

Gray wood or brownish stains, an indication of tannins or extractives leaching from the wood, can be removed by application of an oxalic acid-based cleaner and brightener. Just spray it on and then scrub it in a bit; power wash it off. Oxalic acid pulls the tannins from wood, bringing it back to its original color.

Pressure-treated wood may be treated with a bleach-based solution, and then rinsed and power washed. (Tips for using a power washer were given earlier.) Once the wood has been rinsed, let it dry in the sun for a couple of days. Then proceed to apply the clear coating of your choice.

Back-brush

After spraying, back-brush the applied material with a brush. As with semitransparents, keep a wet edge to avoid lap marks. It's best to do three or four boards at a time, going from end to end or to a natural break.

The biggest mistake made in applying clears is to apply too much. The logic that if some is good, a lot will be better does not apply here. Some clear coatings are designed to be applied in only one coat. Otherwise the wood becomes saturated with the product, the product doesn't fully penetrate, and it lays on the surface as a puddle. It can stay that way for weeks, wet and sticky. Eventually it does dry, but to a film, which peels. Some manufacturers do recommend two coats, but where this is the case, it should be a wet-on-wet application.

Floor Sanding

In my opinion, nothing makes a room pop to life like freshly sanded floors. And today it's possible for the DYIer to do the job him- or herself—and not so incidentally, save a lot of money.

There are two ways to do the job: but regardless, always wear a breathing mask. The standard way, with a drum sander, or the newest way, with a sander that resembles a huge palm sander. Although very slow, the palm sander-type is fail-safe: It's hard to gouge the floor, the bugaboo of the standard. In my opinion, the old way is better because it's much faster. Tools for this job are strictly of the rental variety. You need a drum sander for most of the floor and an edge sander and scraper to get spots that the drum sander can't reach. You'll also need a broom or vacuum to remove sanding dust. For preparing the floor, you might need a nailset, wood putty, a hammer, sandpaper in various grits, as well as a floor finish.

Sanding floor

Floor Sanding Procedure

The body of the room should be done first, and then the edges. Start by clamping the coarsest type of sandpaper you have on the drum sander. Flip the machine on, and slowly bring it into contact with the floor. Assuming that you are doing a standard room with lengthwise narrow boards, sand lengthwise, following the grain. The sander should move forward as you contact the floor. Move it slowly across the length of the floor, but do not stop. The machine can quickly cut what amounts to a gouge, creating an uneven surface that is difficult to correct.

When you reach the other end of the room, turn the machine around and come back the other way, overlapping your first cut by a couple of inches. Try to make all the drum-width strips you're cutting the same depth—the entire floor should have the same appearance.

When you've finished your first cut, using up all of the rough-grade sandpaper, sweep or vacuum up the dust. Then repeat the sanding procedure with the medium-

Sanding edges of room

grade and then the fine-grade sandpaper. When the main body of the floor is done, you'll be left with an unsanded perimeter. Use the edge sander—this is a rotary type—to cut these areas, working your way slowly and carefully through the various grits of paper. Hold the machine tightly. Its tendency is to pull away from your grasp. Sweep or vacuum up after each sandpaper change.

When the edges are done, sweep or vacuum up all the remaining dust. You don't want any dust particles interfering with the finish.

Finish

One good finish is stain followed by two or more coats of polyurethane. You can use oil base or water base. The latter dries overnight, the water in hours. I think some water-base polys are fine. Carver Tripp is a good brand.

It's best to use a pad-type applicator on a stick. Use lamb's wool for oil base and synthetic fabric for water base.

Nonstrip Floor

If the floor is not a "strip" type but, rather, block or parquet, you won't be able to follow the grain. Here, you can follow the same procedure as above, but start with finer grits of material, as recommended by your dealer.

Note: To keep dust away from objects, remove them from the room, or tape plastic sheeting over them. You can also keep dust from other rooms by taping plastic sheeting over doorways. Inexpensive masks are available to keep you from inhaling the dust.

Money-Saving Tip

$ You should do all preparation and moving of furniture before renting the sanding machine. That way you get maximum use of the machine for the time you rent it. Also, make sure the floor is ready to be sanded: Use a nailset to drive protruding nailheads beneath the surface; nail down loose boards; fill any cracks with wood putty; and sand the patches smooth.

New Way to Sand

The newest way to sand is with the palm sander-type machine (mentioned previously). All you need to do is move the machine back and forth. Because the

sanding pad vibrates the sandpaper evenly, the chances of a gouge are remote. Other procedures are the same as for the standard sander.

Pool Care

To insure swimming fun all season long, a minimal amount of time must be devoted to the nonfun aspects of swimming pools—namely, the care and maintenance of the pool. It is a simple job if it is done properly and at the required intervals. It is when these routine tasks are neglected that trouble begins.

Need for Chemicals

One of the most important aspects of pool care is maintaining a proper chemical balance of the water. A glass of water coming out of the tap looks and (usually) tastes clean and clear. Put the same water in a 20- x 40-foot pool, and it may have a different look entirely.

That's why you shouldn't use your pool the first day you fill it up, regardless of how tempting it is and how hot the weather. The first thing you should do is turn the filter on and let it run for a day. The filter removes minerals and other solids that are present in most water. Any turgidity in the water should be removed, and the water should look sparkling clear after the first day.

From the very first day you fill your pool, its purity must be guarded by a chemical disinfectant. Some purifying agent—whether it be chlorine, bromine, or iodine—must be in there to kill disease-carrying bacteria brought into the water by bathers.

Chlorine is the most widely used disinfectant. Ideally, it should be used at one part per million (ppm), and must have at least 0.6 ppm of "free residual chlorine." The actual ratio is really very small, because 100 percent activity is gained by only one drop of chlorine for every one million drops of water.

Routine Cleaning

In addition to keeping the proper chemical balance, here are a few other suggestions that should be followed to keep your pool water clean and fresh:

- Manually skim the pool's surface with a standard "leaf skimmer," a netlike pool-cleaning tool designed especially to rid the pool's surface of leaves, bugs, debris, and other floating contaminants. Many leaf skimmers have plastic nets. Most

are equipped with long handles that enable you to reach the pool's center while standing on the pool deck.

- Brush down walls and tile. For this you'll need a stiff-bristled "tile brush" to clean near the waterline and a "wall brush" to clean the walls below.
- Clean the skimmer's basket and the hair-lint strainer. No special equipment is needed for this. Locate the skimmer basket and the hair-lint strainer in the pump, and remove the debris that has collected there. This should be done as frequently as possible— daily is preferable— or even more often during the spring and fall when there is a heavy fallout from trees and bushes. Failure to keep baskets clean results in reduced circulation of the water through the pump and filter.
- Vacuum the pool bottom. You'll need a special pool vacuum for this. There are many models and types to choose from. Consult your dealer as to the types best suited to your pool.
- Clean the filter. A dirty filter results in decreased recirculation

and consequently in dirty water. Consult the manufacturer of the filter (directions are supplied when new) for the correct procedure for your particular model. Most likely you should "backwash," or reverse the flow of water.

- Hose the deck clean. A garden hose is all the equipment you need to clean the deck. This should be done during every pool cleaning.

Pool Painting

Many pool owners leave their pools unpainted, but paint does make a pool more attractive. The trouble with painting is that you have to repaint every few years.

There are two main points regarding pool painting. The first is to be sure to use alkali-resistant paints for concrete or Gunite (a special concrete). Second, make sure that the surface is prepared properly.

The first step in preparation is to remove the water and repair all cracked or damaged areas, to present a smooth surface throughout. If the paint is just dull or worn off, a thorough scrubbing is all that is necessary. If there is peeling or flaking, it may be necessary to remove the old paint completely. If so, sand-

blasting is the best way. You can either rent the equipment or have a professional sandblaster brought in for the job. Of course this is, as they say, a megillah and a half to do—and just as expensive.

Winterizing

In most parts of North America, there are at least a few months of the year when the weather is too cold for swimming. The most important thing to remember about winterizing pools is to leave the water in. The water serves to brace the walls against pressures created by frozen or shifting earth on the outside of the walls.

Following are some other things you should do before shutting up for the winter:

- Clean the pool thoroughly.
- Lower the water to below the inlet-suction fitting.
- Remove the lights.
- Drain all the lines at their lowest points.
- Insert rubber plugs tightly in all the openings so that no water may enter.
- Fill the pool again to within 2 inches of the bottom of the skimmer opening. Make certain that the main drain valve is closed off.

- Add an extra-heavy dose of chlorine.
- Spread the pool cover, if using one.
- Place all the removed parts in a dry, warm place and properly oil, grease, or paint where necessary.
- Plug all the lines so that vermin or mice cannot enter the system.
- Remove the diving board and store it on one of its edges.
- Disconnect all the electrical energy.
- Stuff a semi-inflated bicycle tube into the skimmer to absorb pressures created by freezing and thawing.
- Check the pool from time to time. If the water has receded below the ice on top, refill it with a garden hose until the water and ice melt. Suspended ice can cause pool damage.

Correcting Water Discoloration

Discoloration of pool water can stem from a number of causes. Here are some of the causes and how to correct them.

Algae. Algae can turn water greenish and cloudy. To restore your pool to its natural sky-blue color, treat the water with the proper amount of disinfectant and an algicide. Certain algicides may cause a very fine hazy cloudiness temporarily in some water.

Red-Brown Water. The addition of disinfectants may oxidize the iron in water. Because oxidized iron is insoluble, rust particles give the water a reddish-brown color. To correct, filter continuously for about forty-eight hours. At the same time, add even more of the oxidizing sanitizer. It will oxidize any remaining dissolved iron in the water. Particles not removed by the filter will settle on the pool bottom, where they should be removed with the pool vacuum as soon as they show up to prevent staining.

Cloudiness. Windblown debris—algae spores, dust, and so forth—can cause the water to turn cloudy. Such debris may, on occasion, also change the balance of the pool water—its pH or alkalinity. To correct, adjust the sanitizer level and pH balance to remove the dirt, and clean the filter as needed.

Excessively high pH. One form of cloudiness is caused by excessively high pH, which causes the precipitation of insoluble salts. This cloudiness may not be too apparent during the daytime, but shows up as a haziness in the water at night, when underwater lights are on. Correction is easily made by restoring the water's proper pH balance (adding acid to bring the water's balance to between 7.2 and 7.6 pH).

Ice Dams

This is a perennial problem for some people, and it's good to understand why ice dams form. The reason is really simple: inadequate insulation and ventilation allow excessive heat to escape from the house, the heat melts the snow on the roof, and water trickles down until it hits the edge of the house, which is cold, and turns to ice.

People try a variety of ways to clear up the problem—including heat cables (which just sort of give the ice a different shape). The only way to solve the problem is to insulate and ventilate properly. A cool roof will not melt the snow so fast that ice dams form.

Seal Coating

It's a good idea to apply a seal coating to a driveway periodically. Just make sure the driveway is clean. Wet it down and let it dry for an hour, then brush and squeegee on the coating following instructions on the can. The best seal coating you can get is an asphalt-based kind.

The main mistake people make in applying seal coating is to apply too much. A thin coat works better—and you save money.

**HOME
IMPROVEMENTS**

CHAPTER 6

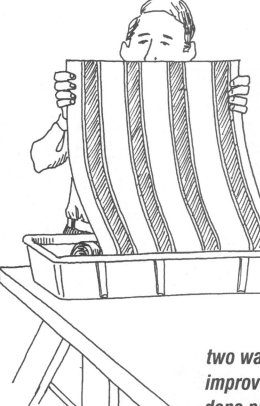

There are at least two reasons why a person wants to improve his or her home. One is to increase its value; the other is simply to make it a better place to live.

Whatever your reason(s), there are two ways to approach a home improvement: do-it-yourself or have it done professionally.

This section presents an overall guide to improvements that can give you a sense of whether you want to do them yourself and how they should be done. In addition, there are some plans for building a few projects, as well as details on how to protect yourself when hiring a contractor and when you might need an architect. There are also some suggestions on where to get the money for your projects.

Windows

There are a variety of windows one can buy, but by far the most common is the double-hung, meaning that two halves or sashes—frame and glass—slide up and down in the framework. Windows come in a wide variety of stock sizes, and are made to be installed in what is known as a "rough opening"—a framework of boards in the wall.

Windows are made of various materials. Following is a summary of the various materials used, as well as other useful information about windows.

Pure Wood

The wood used to make windows is primed and then finish painted. Like other windows, wood windows vary in quality. The hallmark of better kinds is heavier wood.

Pure Vinyl

Vinyl windows are made from vinyl parts extruded at a factory and then assembled to fit inside a window opening from which just the sash—the movable part—of the window has been removed. In other words, the framework of the window stays. Hence you get a smaller window because the new unit includes the sash and framework inside the old window.

Vinyl windows vary in quality, with many lower than the proverbial snake's keister. You have to check quality carefully by comparing one with the other, or asking around. Poor quality vinyl windows can fall apart in short order. Some contractors don't like vinyl windows because they expand and contract, and this can lead to gaps that allow weather in.

Aluminum Windows

Once these were the rage in windows, but that time has passed. The main reason is that they conduct cold, which creates condensation. Some aluminum windows have a thermal break material in them to prevent the problem, but its effectiveness is questionable. Aluminum is available in a wide variety of stock sizes and colors.

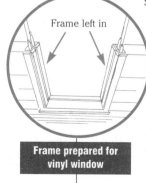

Frame left in

Frame prepared for vinyl window

Vinyl- and Aluminum-Clad Windows

These windows are covered with a vinyl or aluminum skin, and they are usually of very good quality. Most manufacturers make them in stock sizes, but at least one manufacturer (Marvin) makes them in custom sizes.

Vinyl-clad windows ordinarily come only in brown and white, but aluminum-clad windows are available in many different colors. The inside of these windows is pure wood that can be painted to match the decor. The outsides never have to be painted.

Other Windows

A variety of other windows are available, including hopper style for basements, casement windows that open with a crank handle, and bay and bow windows. Bow windows (shaped like a bow in profile) are large windows that not only increase the view to the great outdoors—because they "bulge" out of the house—but also provide increased floor space.

Insulated Glass

Whatever kind of windows you get, they should be double insulated, meaning that there should be dead air space between the two panes of glass, forming a barrier to losing heat and gaining cold. Without double-insulated glass, energy bills can be quite high, because as heat is lost, the heating system works harder to replace it, and that translates into lost fuel dollars.

Money-Saving Tip

$ If you shop around, you can save 30 percent on the price of windows. Play one outlet against another. If you get a good price from one store, ask another if they can beat it, and so on.

Doors

Wood Doors

Wood doors are for interior or exterior use and come in a couple of styles. "Flush doors" mean that the door consists of a seamless skin of wood, usually plywood on an exterior door and hardboard on an interior.

"Sash doors" are made from various parts of wood that are assembled. In this regard, they are not unlike assembled windows, hence the name. They come in a variety of styles and with or without windows, or "lights," as they say in the trade.

Wood doors come in various widths, with sizes graduating in 2-inch increments, for both width and height, and various thicknesses. For exterior use, the $1^3/_4$-inch thickness is suggested; for interior use, the $1^3/_8$-inch size should be adequate. All wood doors come unfinished, and without locks or hinges.

Some are guaranteed against failure, but they must be finished exactly as the manufacturer says (in particular, the bottom and top edges must be coated to guard against water penetration). Doors are subject to damage in transit, and they should be examined before being accepted. Hanging a wood door is very difficult to do, and should be left to an experienced carpenter.

Prehung Wood Doors

Wood doors also come prehung, meaning that they come hinged to their final framework. Then, it's just a matter of hanging the framework in the door opening, a considerably easier task. Prehung doors should be looked at as critically as free-standing ones.

Steel Doors

These are designed for exterior use only. They come in a variety of designs and are usually primed and have to be finish painted. They consist essentially of a skin of metal and of insulation. The skin can be 22, 24, or 26 gauge—the lower the number the thicker the metal; 24 gauge is okay, but 22 gauge is better.

Doors come with certain "R" factors (see Insulation section); the higher the R (or heat-resistance) factor, the better the door insulation.

Fiberglass Doors

These are also available for exterior use and simulate a wood grain texture. They can then be finished with a wiping stain.

Patio Doors

Like their standard cousins, patio doors come in a variety of materials: pure vinyl, aluminum, vinyl-clad aluminum, vinyl-clad wood, and pure wood. They are available in various sizes, with a maximum height of 6 feet 8 inches, and in widths of up to 8 feet. They also come with plain glass or multi-paned glass and in various shapes.

The Cadillacs of patio doors are the vinyl clads. These come in limited colors—brown and white. Vinyl-clad aluminum is available in a rainbow of colors. On the lower end of the scale is pure vinyl, which can be affected by weather.

A patio door can make a backyard very accessible, as well as greatly increase light inside the home, and make interior space seem greater. Small wonder it's such a popular improvement.

Garage Doors

Garage doors are available made of wood, wood and hardboard, metal, solid vinyl, and fiberglass.

The Cadillac of garage doors are those made of pure wood. Pure wood doors are designed to be painted or stained. Hardboard and wood can be okay, but the hardboard must be the tempered kind or the door can come apart. Metal is available in various thicknesses, but is not suggested in areas where kids are likely to strike it with a stray (or well-aimed) baseball. Vinyl is popular for this reason. Many of these doors have great impact resistance.

Like other items, companies can make a sow's ear look like a silk purse, so it is best to be guided by a brand name here. Three good ones are General Doors, Gadco, and Therma-Core.

Electric garage door openers also vary in quality. The higher priced ones tend to be the best. Installing a garage door is usually considered a job for a professional.

Bath Remodeling

Next to kitchens, nothing is more popular with homeowners than remodeling or creating a new bath. It pays not only in terms of resale value, but also in other ways—not the least of which is that a new bath may shorten the lines outside the bathroom in the morning.

There are a number of things to be aware of. For example, if you are building a new bath, try to plan things so the bathroom is above an existing one, or close to the existing plumbing lines. The further away, the more the cost, because that much more construction will be involved.

If you are going to be creating a new bath and are not exactly sure of how to design it, you should hire a professional designer. As small a room as it is, a bathroom is easy to design incorrectly. (Indeed, we know of one design where the door could not be opened without hitting the edge of the vanity...having a bathroom door open all the time is not exactly great design!)

Whether remodeling or creating a new bath, new "fixtures"—tub, sink, and toilet (called fixtures, I guess, because they don't move)—are required. As you've probably guessed, they come in various degrees of quality.

Money-Saving Tip

If you buy white instead of colored bath fixtures, you can save 20 percent.

The best tubs, also the most expensive, are made of enameled cast iron. You can also get them in enameled steel, which tends to be noisy.

Fiberglass tubs are also available, and these come in a variety of shapes and sizes and colors. You can also get fiberglass whirlpool tubs, which are really just tubs with plumbing that swirls the water.

Faucets and the like come separately from the tub. These also vary in quality.

Bathroom sinks, which are technically known as lavatories, are also available in a variety of materials including enameled cast iron, enameled steel, pottery, vitreous China, and cultured marble. The latter is actually plastic manufactured to look like marble. Lavatories come in various shapes and sizes, some standing on legs, some mounted on vanities, and others hanging on the wall.

Toilets are available in various shapes as well. The so-called siphon jet toilet is the most efficient.

If you buy white instead of colored fixtures, you can expect to save about 20 percent on cost. You can also save by buying plain rather than fancy fittings. The more work the manufacturer puts into producing a product, the more you can expect to pay.

When buying fixtures and fittings, it's a good idea to stay within brand names.

But be aware that different companies make different quality. American Standard, for example, offers one toilet that sells for about $60 and another that costs $800 or $900. Which do you think is going to be of better quality?

Kitchen Remodeling

This is the most popular home improvement, and it's easy to see why. Most families spend more time in the kitchen than in any other room.

A key consideration in a remodeling that involves tearing a kitchen out and installing a new one is the so-called work triangle: The stove, sink, and refrigerator should be at the corners of a triangle, preferably equilateral; and the total distance of the triangle should be more than 21 feet or less than 17 feet. The idea is that the homeowner generally "wheels and deals" between these points, making that arrangement the most efficient.

Money-Saving Tip
Shopping around can save you up to 40 percent on kitchen cabinets.

Cabinets

Cabinets for the kitchen consist of two types: base cabinets and hangers. The former rest on the floor, the latter are hung from the wall.

Stock cabinets come in various set sizes and are cheaper than custom cabinets. Custom cabinets are those made to fit exactly the space you have—thus custom cabinets are usually required to use all the cabinet space available in the kitchen. They cost two and three times the price of stock cabinets.

Cabinets may be European or American style. The former refers to cabinets that are covered by a single seamless door—"frameless." The latter are "framed"—a door fits into a framework. The European style is more modern looking and has more room than the framed kind.

Cabinets come, of course, in various qualities. Solid wood cabinets are ordinarily the best, but you can also get good quality

cabinets that are covered with plastic laminate. The best of the latter are those in which the already-built cabinets are covered with sheets of laminate. Of lower quality are cabinets made with individual sections that are covered with laminate and then assembled. The hallmark of the latter are those with joints in the cabinet parts.

> ### Money-Saving Tip
> **$** If you buy stock instead of custom kitchen cabinets, you can save up to two thirds of their cost.

Countertops

Countertops for kitchens may be "post formed"—one piece—or made in sections. This type is made by covering the countertop with a continuous piece of plastic laminate, the thin hard material commonly used to cover countertops. One advantage is that it is seamless—no seams to gather dirt. However, it is not made of laminate that is as hard as that used for the type made in sections. Also, it is only available in lengths of 12 feet, and it

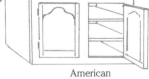

American

European

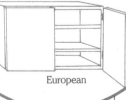

Framed (top) and frameless cabinets

cannot be used to cover odd shapes, such as a peninsula or island.

Following are some additional kitchen design ideas:

- The stove and refrigerator should not be next to one another because the stove will reflect the heat.
- The range should be on an outside wall so its ductwork will be short and direct.
- The stove should not be under a window—curtains could catch on fire.
- The dishwasher should be next to the sink; dishes can be rinsed and then loaded easily into the machine.
- There should be adequate counter space on both sides of the sink and on both sides of the stove.
- A sink is usually best located under a window.
- Open appliance doors should not obstruct doorways.

Resilient Flooring

Resilient flooring, which gets its name from the fact that it gives or depresses

Post formed countertop

when stepped on, and then "snaps" back into shape, is very popular in the home. There are two basic types: vinyl sheet flooring and tiles.

Sheet Flooring. Sheet flooring is available in 6-foot and 12-foot widths and can be cut to whatever length is needed. There are two types of sheet material: inlaid and rotovinyl. The former comes in a wide variety of patterns and colors, with the pattern and color going all the way through to the back. Hence, it wears well. It comes in a no-wax shiny finish.

Rotovinyl is its poor cousin. It's not nearly as good as inlaid because the wear layer does not go all the way through. Some rotovinyls are better than others—they have thicker wear layers.

Sheet flooring is good in places such as the bathroom or a small kitchen where it can be installed in one piece. It is glued in place—a solid, smooth foundation is the key to a successful installation. Rotovinyl can be loose laid, which makes it a good do-it-yourself project.

Vinyl Tiles. This is the other type of resilient flooring. It comes in 12-inch squares, and it may be "self stick"—where paper is peeled off to expose the adhesive—or "dryback"—adhesive is smeared on the floor and the tile set in place.

Tiles come in thicknesses of $1/8$ inch, $1/16$ inch, and $1/32$ inch. The thicker the material, the better it wears—though tiles do not generally wear as well as sheet flooring.

An exception are tiles made by Amtico. They look like pieces of finished flooring and are as easy to install as tile (on a bed of adhesive); they wear extremely well.

Openings at top and bottom of space

Holes made when closed walls are insulated

Insulation

Insulation is important not only in terms of energy saving but also in terms of comfort. A well-insulated house is usually a comfortable one.

Insulation is characterized by the "R," or heat resistance, factor. The higher the R, the more resistant the insulation is to heat transfer, which is the tendency of warm air to migrate to cold. Like a blanket keeps body heat underneath it, a blanket of insulation keeps heat inside the house.

Insulation is available in a variety of forms including short lengths called batts for filling in between studs (framing members). They have kraft paper on one side and foil-facing on the other; and

they are normally stapled in place. The foil, or impermeable side, always faces the heated side of the house so heat can't pass through.

Insulation is also available in blankets. Blankets of insulation come in 100-foot lengths and are cut to fit particular areas.

Pour-in-place insulation is also available. It's handy for such places as the attic, where it can be simply poured between floor framing members.

Rigid insulation can also be used. This is glued in place. You can also have insulation pumped into a house after it is built. In the latter case, the shingles are removed, holes are drilled through the sheathing, and the insulation is pumped in under pressure.

Installing batt or blanket insulation is definitely a job for the do-it-yourselfer. The one caveat is that you have to wear gloves, a long-sleeved shirt, and goggles to protect yourself against any of the fiberglass or rock wool that floats free.

> **Money-Saving Tip**
> Buy insulation faced with kraft paper rather than foil—it's cheaper and just as good.

Roofing

There is a variety of types of roofing available, but far and away the most common are asphalt roofing and fiberglass roofing. They function the same way, but there are differences.

The shingles start out as an organic felt or fiberglass, which is saturated with asphalt and then coated with minerals.

The most common type of shingle is the strip, which is 12 inches wide and 36 inches long and has five cutouts, or "tabs," along one edge. The shingles are available in various colors including white, black, brown, green, and red.

Shingles are installed starting from the bottom of the roof; they are nailed in place with large headed nails and over-lapped. The tabs are exposed "to the weather" when the shingles are installed.

Asphalt shingles are heavier than fiberglass ones, and more diffi-cult to cut and handle. However, it's difficult to say which is better. My advice is to choose according to the length of the warranty: twenty years is about right. Longer than that seems a bit too much; after twenty years with the same color, most people want to change their shingles anyway.

Incidentally, in most communities, you can put up to two layers or "roofs" on before the weight of the layers reaches a point where it all has to be stripped off to the wood base (called decking) before any new material is applied.

Shingles are sold in and installed in "squares," which means 100 square feet of roofing. Installing roofing is decidedly a job for the pro, unless you like the prospect of lugging 90-pound bundles of shingles onto a slanted roof and nailing them home while the sun beats down on you seven or eight hours a day.

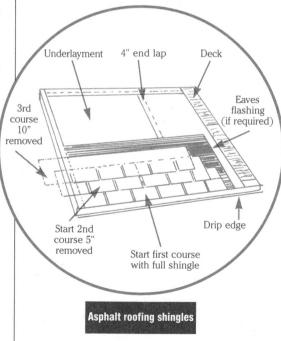

Underlayment 4" end lap Deck

3rd course 10" removed

Eaves flashing (if required)

Start 2nd course 5" removed

Drip edge

Start first course with full shingle

Asphalt roofing shingles

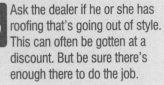

Siding

Installing the outer skin of a home, commonly known as siding, is emphatically a job for a professional...or a do-it-yourselfer seized with a need to create big problems for him- or herself. It just takes too much experience for the inexperienced to do.

There are a number of types available.

Vinyl Siding

One of the most popular is vinyl siding, which is available in a variety of configurations simulating clapboard or vertical-board siding, in various colors, and in various qualities. There is no formal grading system, but the lowest quality vinyl siding is .040 inches, is available in limited colors (cream, white, and gray), and comes in high gloss. Next comes .042-inch and .044-inch thick siding. However, the best siding is even thicker than this, and comes in a wide range of textures and designs. Like the middle range of materials, it has a low sheen.

When contracting for siding, you should make sure to determine if the trim is included. This can have a big cost effect on the job.

Also, some houses require that a backer board or other base be applied so that any bumpiness on the existing siding doesn't reflect through. Some installers may suggest tearing off existing siding, but this is rarely required. Besides, the existing siding has insulation value.

Aluminum Siding

This was once the rage, but vinyl is more popular today. Aluminum siding comes smooth and also has deeper texture and better colors than vinyl. You can get plain metal, but aluminum siding is also offered with a fluorocarbon coating that sheds dirt more readily.

Aluminum is hung like vinyl, but is more expensive. Its big bugaboo is that it dents. It also comes in various thicknesses, and the thicker the material the better.

Cedar Shingles and Shakes

People get shingles and shakes confused. Shingles are cut by machine and have a striated face. They are 18 inches long and are $3/8$ inch or $1/2$ inch thick at the butt, or bottom. They are parallel on both sides, and the butt ends are more or less square. They come in different grades: Perfections 1, 2, 3, and undercourse, with number 1 the best. There are also sawn shingles. These come 18 and 24 inches long.

Shakes are rough, cut by hand, with neither sides parallel nor butts even. In fact, they are sorted by thickness of $1/2$ inch to $1^1/_4$ inch.

Cedar is a good siding, and if left alone will weather to a gray and then black look. But the trend today is to clear coat or stain them; this can add many years of life.

Bevel siding

Board Siding

Board siding comes 4 inches to 12 inches wide, in random lengths and various thicknesses. Some boards have a rough-sawn side and a smooth side; the former is for staining, the latter for painting.

Bevel siding is tapered on the width, going from thin at the top to thicker at

the bottom; and when installed, the pieces overlap one another. Drop siding, on the other hand, is the same thickness and fits together tongue and groove, which means there is a slot along one edge of the siding into which a tongue on the other side fits.

Adding Space

As families grow, new living space becomes a necessity. Fortunately, you don't necessarily have to have major surgery done on the house, or go into hock for the rest of your natural life paying for a room addition. Sometimes there are easier ways.

One way is to convert already existing space into living area. Some suggestions follow.

Basement

If you have one, this is a logical choice. As long as you don't have a severe moisture problem, such as water seeping up through a floor, the basement can become perfectly livable with the addition of flooring, a dropped ceiling, new lighting paneling, new walls, and, perhaps for good measure, new windows to let in more sunlight.

Attic

Another good spot is an attic. As long as the floor framing (usually 2 x 8's) is solid, all you need to do is make the conversion. If the floor framing members are open, decking can be nailed in place, followed by flooring.

Attics have sloped parts, of course, and short walls (called "kneewalls"—I guess because they are only knee high or thereabouts) are constructed between roof and floor. The electricity can be supplied by tying into existing electricity, and the same with plumbing. To save money, the new plumbing, as previously noted (in the Bath Remodeling section), should be located near the existing plumbing. The less distance the remodeler has to travel, the cheaper it is.

Heating can be supplied by tying into the existing heating. Or one can also use baseboard heaters to do the job.

In the attic, insulation is also important. This can be added on the underside of the roof and between kneewalls and exterior walls. If there is existing insulation, this must be removed.

Ventilation is also important. This can be provided with ventilating units, including a fan to suck hot air out of the attic.

Stairs to the attic should be either custom made or circular rebuilt units; the latter are good because they don't take up much space. Using just a drop-down ladder doesn't work well.

Garage

Although you'd have to make accommodation for a vehicle, the garage can also be converted into living space. Just add the things that a normal room has—insulation, windows, lighting, and the like—and the space can be perfectly livable.

Divide Space

Sometimes you can divide existing space into two rooms. It's quite easy to erect a so-called divider wall to make two rooms out of one.

Structural Changes

To gain space, structural changes are sometimes the only viable way to go. The cheapest of these is to add one or more dormers, which simply means raising the

Shed dormer

Gable dormer

Dormers

roof. This creates headroom, and therefore more floorspace—space.

There are two types of dormers: gable end and shed. The gable-end type looks like a doghouse; the shed type looks like part of the roof was raised and propped in place.

As mentioned, dormers are the cheap way to go. A dormer might cost $15 a square foot; an addition could be twice that.

Room Addition

This is usually the most complex way to add space to a home; sometimes the services of an architect are required.

Essentially, adding a room is like building a small house, but the main thing is that the new addition blend with the existing house, avoiding a tacked-on look. Also, if any appliances or large items are going to be installed in the house, make sure the addition has large enough wall or window space to allow them to be brought in, or do this before the addition is built.

Skylights

A skylight may be flat or curved. The former is always glass, the latter is always plastic, raised, or bubblelike in shape. Glass skylights may be regular glass or the low emissivity type, which is energy saving. They come in various colors.

Skylights may also be fixed or movable, the latter either with a stick or motorized. Another name for a movable skylight is a roof window.

Shades and blinds are available for skylights, and can also be installed if there is an attic above. The skylight is installed in the roof; then a shaftway is built down and opened up in the ceiling.

Skylights are excellent for providing extra light and ventilation; but the big bugaboo can be installation. If not installed properly, the skylight can leak, so it really has to be done by someone who knows what he or she is doing.

Patios

The patio is center stage when it comes to outdoor living. (See also Deck section.) However, before you put a patio in, it will pay—literally and figuratively—to sit down and think and talk about it; carefully plan it with various considerations in mind. If you don't, there's always the danger of coming up with an ill-designed area, which is about as useful as a finished basement that's always damp and that you don't want to go into. Following are some considerations. (Note: Some of the information in this section can also be applied to decks.)

Accessibility

One thing to consider is the patio's accessibility from the house. It should be easy to get to. If it isn't, it simply will not be used. Also, traffic that is routed through a room to get to wherever the patio (or deck) is should not disrupt the activities of anyone in that room. If, for example, you locate the patio right outside the kitchen (as most people do), it should have a separate entrance. Otherwise, the person working in the kitchen will be disturbed.

Where's the Sun?

Another thing to consider is sun—and shade. If you're the type who likes lots of sun, then it's probably wise to locate the patio where it will be in the sun most of the day. If you don't like sun, though, you may not find it a comfortable, inviting place to go to. Perhaps you can locate it so that a part of it is shaded most of the day.

On the other hand, if you must have constant shade, and you don't have the shade available, you'll have to build an overhang of some sort to provide it.

How Big?

How big should your patio be? If you have a lot of barbecues or entertain frequently, a large structure is usually called for. If not, a smaller one is usually adequate.

How about Privacy?

It's usually a good idea, for you and your neighbors, to make the patio an "outdoor room" enclosed by fencing or shrubbery of some sort. But do consult with your neighbor before putting it in, not only to insure that the fencing is on your property, but just to be neighborly.

Wind

Wind is another consideration. This, of course, varies according to where you live. Some areas get a steady breeze; others don't. But the question is, Do you want that wind or not? Your best bet is to check the area out before you put the patio (or deck) in.

Shape

The shape the patio takes is yet another consideration. You needn't necessarily think in terms of the standard square or rectangular shape. How about an L-shape to utilize available space and get part of the structure under a shade tree? How about a round shape for the sheer good looks of it? It's your patio, and you needn't follow some mythical shape standards.

Material

The material you choose for building a patio should harmonize with your house. You wouldn't want to use weathered brick, for example, if your house is ultra-modern looking.

A variety of materials are available.

Brick. The standard size of a brick is 8 inches long, 4 inches wide, and $2^1/4$ inches thick. You may think of it as only available in a reddish color. Actually, it's available in many different colors (black, white, and tan, for example), in hundreds of shades and textures, and glazed and unglazed.

In general, brick is a good material for the do-it-yourselfer. It comes in small units, making it easy to handle. It's durable. And, it's relatively inexpensive.

On the minus side, brick is very porous. If you spill some barbecue sauce on it, it will not be an easy task getting it up.

The longest-lasting type of brick is called "well burned"; it has a deep-red color. The less durable is the so-called

green type, which is pinkish. Whatever kind of brick you buy, it's best to get it from one dealer all at once. Brick can vary slightly in color from batch to batch, and this can be noticeable on a patio.

Flagstone. This is a truly beautiful outdoor flooring material, cut from natural colored rocks. Soft yellows, browns, grays, greens, and reds are among the colors available. It can be laid with relative ease by the do-it-yourselfer, directly on soil or a sand base, or in cement. It is also the most durable patio material you can buy.

Flagstone is available in thicknesses from $1/2$ to 2 inches, and either free form, natural shape, or in rectangles. The big drawback of flagstone is price: It costs a minimum of four or five times as much as brick.

Concrete. This is such a familiar material that its virtues are perhaps not appreciated as well as some other materials. For one thing, it's durable. Also, it can be troweled or worked to a variety of textures; and by leaving the aggregate (stones or gravel that help give it strength) partially exposed, a distinctive look can be achieved. Also, it's not expensive.

On the minus side, concrete work can be backbreaking and, if you're not careful to install it properly (proper mix, grading, etc.), it can crack easily. Something that happens, even to pros.

You do not need to think of concrete as colorless. There are a number of ways to give it almost any coloration you wish, including sprinkling colored powder on the wet cement, staining it, and adding color to the concrete before it's mixed; the last is the best way.

If you live in a cold climate, consider using air-entrained concrete. This contains microscopic air bubbles that help solve the problem of cracking caused by freeze-thaw cycles. This type of concrete is also easier to work with.

Wood Blocks, Etc. Although not used for the patio itself, railroad ties, log "slices," and blocks can all be used for patio paving. Many people consider these quite handsome, a most natural and satisfying paving material. Also, wood in these forms is not expensive; many times you can pick up railroad ties, for example, from the local railroad yard (if you're willing to haul them away). And rounds, or blocks, can be chain-sawed from any trees available.

These materials are not as long lasting as stone or brick. Also, they are subject to various degrees of stress from weather and insects.

Loose Fill. There are a variety of materials that are known as loose fill: gravel, marble chips, wood chips, crushed brick, tanbark, and the like. These kinds of materials are usually used in conjunction with some other material, such as concrete or flagstone, as accent materials. You may have a patio of concrete and then islands or paths between, filled with gravel or wood chips.

As a material for forming the entire patio floor, they're really not practical. They're difficult to walk on and pieces can be kicked all over the place (and gravel and power lawnmowers don't mix).

The big advantage of loose fills is low cost. You can cover a lot of area with them cheaply. In a pinch—financial—you could get by with a gravel patio. It's simple to install. To retain it, however, you must first build some sort of concrete, wood, or brick edging. Just spread gravel out directly on a leveled soil base, tamp (pack) it down, water it so it settles some more, and re-tamp.

Decks

Decks have three great advantages, other than that they function as well, or better, than other kinds of patio areas. First, there is the beauty of wood. Wood is a natural material that harmonizes well in a natural setting. On the other hand, it also looks perfectly at home in a non-natural setting.

Second, a deck can be used to conquer problems that would be difficult with other kinds of patio construction. For example, if the terrain is hilly, an on-the-ground patio would require a big, tiresome excavating job. But installing a deck just involves varying post heights to suit the ground slope. Also, if the ground is far below the access entry, a deck can be built level to it.

Finally, wood is an easy material to work with, as long as you're careful about dimensions and use good tools. As suggested in the Maintenance section, it is important to coat the wood immediately. This can add 20 percent to its life span. (Note: Follow the suggestions given for patios regarding accessibility, privacy, and other considerations.)

Fencing

A fence can function in a variety of ways. It can give you privacy, corral kids and dogs, keep out or let in wind, and complement and accent the beauty of your home by providing a "framework" around it. But, as with other improvements, there are things to know and do.

First, tell your neighbors about your plan, if the fence will face their property or affect the quality of their lives in some way. In some cases—and not infrequently—you may be able to team up with a neighbor in building the fence, thereby sharing work and costs. For this, though, you'll have to consider only fences of "good neighbor" design: ones that look good from both sides. If you and your neighbor can't agree on costs or design, you may have to settle for building what you like just inside your property line.

Check with local building people. There are likely to be restrictions as to the kind of fence you can build, how high it can be, and where it can be located.

There are a variety of fences to select from, each with advantages and disadvantages. Following is a brief roundup:

- Brick. Because of cost, and difficulty of building for the average do-it-yourselfer, this kind of fence is usually kept on a small scale. Built too high, it can lend an undesirable "prison" look to a home, unless carefully complemented by shrubbery or plantings. On the other hand, a low brick fence can be quite attractive and is a good choice when you want to lengthen house lines.
- Stone. This shares the disadvantages of brick, but is even more costly (unless you gather the

stones yourself from some free source).

- Block. Plain concrete and cinder blocks are usually not considered good looking enough for fencing. Installation can be accomplished by a determined do-it-yourselfer.

- Designed block. Concrete blocks also come with designs, their faces "sculpted" or worked in some way, some having voids to allow breezes through. Installation is basically the same as for regular block. They make a very good looking fence (of any height you wish); but the cost is high.

- Chainlink. This is available both plain and coated with plastic of various colors. Prices vary widely, so it's best to compare them very carefully. For homes, heights of 42 inches or less are usually most attractive. Chainlink requires special stretchers to install and is a job for a professional.

- Shrubbery. There are a number of living fences you can purchase. Some are designed to grow quite thick and high, affording complete privacy. Among the types available are North Amur River privet, golden privet, boxwood, upright evergreen, and honeysuckle. Of course, these fences have to be maintained continually. If you're not the type who likes to tend to a lawn, you won't like these. If you purchase shrubs or hedges as seedlings, the cost is minimal.

- Wood. Fences made of wood afford the greatest selection. Lumberyards, building supply dealers, and other outlets carry it in two basic forms: ready-made sections (usually 8 feet) (you fasten the sections to posts that you install) and knockdown (you assemble the fence from scratch with stock pieces).

Fence Styles

A number of fence styles are particularly popular:

- Board. This is the easiest kind of fence to build. The boards are usually of 1-inch stock and of various widths, either spaced (1 inch or more) or butted. Butting, however, provides a solid front against the wind and may not be desirable in windy areas unless the posts have been most securely anchored.

  Board fences can provide any degree of privacy you wish,

depending on how far apart the boards are set. One variation on the board fence is the louvered type, with boards set between rails at an angle. This affords a good degree of privacy but lets breezes in.

- Basketweave. Basketweave fences consist of flexible boards woven between posts. It affords a solid front—and good privacy—and it doesn't look like a billboard; in fact, most people consider it quite handsome.
- Picket. This is an old standby. Its usual function is simply to dress up or "frame" the property or provide boundary lines.

    Pickets are available in a surprisingly wide range of sizes, from $1^1/_4$ to $5^1/_2$ inches wide and 2 to 5 feet long; thickness is usually an inch. If you wish, you can also get plastic and metal pickets.

- Stockade. A stockade fence is really for privacy only. It is a solid fence composed of boards that are pointed on top. Although it does work well at its assigned task, check carefully with neighbors before installing: They might consider it offensive.
- Split rail. Split rail fences have a rustic charm that is hard to beat.

Also, they're inexpensive (if today's wood prices can be termed that) as fences go and simple to make. On the other hand, they don't have any function other than looking good.

Pools

A pool can do a lot for you. Besides letting you and your family beat the heat, it can mean avoiding traffic tie-ups on the way to the beach, providing the best kind of exercise for everyone, and improving the value of your home (though it will also slightly raise taxes).

Before taking the plunge, however, you should know what's available and the advantages and disadvantages of each type. There are basically two kinds of pools: in-ground, where the pool is partially or totally in the ground, and above-ground, where the pool rests on the ground.

In-Ground Pools

In-ground types are the more expensive and the most likely to please more members of the family, because they commonly come with a deep, as well as shallow end. (Above-ground types are usually 4 feet high.)

Two kinds of in-ground pools dominate the market, accounting for over 90 percent of sales. The first is the sprayed concrete type, also called the Gunite pool. This must be installed by skilled workers. It basically involves installing a wire mesh in the excavation, then spraying concrete over it, and then applying some type of smoothing material over the concrete (the concrete itself is abrasive).

Its disadvantage as a pool is that it can crack, especially in cold climates, algae can develop, and, like all concrete pools, it has to be painted fairly frequently (anywhere from once a year to once every five years).

On the positive side, this type of pool can last a lifetime, can be installed quickly, and, because they're seamless, can be made into any shape you like, from rectangular to kidney shaped.

Gunite pools account for over 45 percent of sales. Equally popular, and definitely a do-it-yourself pool, is the vinyl-lined type.

Vinyl-lined pools come in kits (all you need to do the job is included). Basically, they consist of walls—steel, aluminum, or treated wood—and a 20- to 30-gauge vinyl liner that is draped over the walls and into the excavation, and then lined with sand and peat moss.

The advantages of the vinyl-lined pool are that it costs less than most pools and requires less maintenance. The vinyl liner can stand temperatures of 30 to 40 degrees below zero, and algae has difficulty growing on it. In addition, the vinyl never needs to be painted and you needn't drain the pool over the winter. Also, it can be installed in five days or less.

Disadvantages are that the vinyl can puncture to the point where the liner must be replaced. Most tears, however, can be repaired with an inexpensive patch kit that you can use underwater.

Above-Ground Pools

This type of pool consists of walls—steel, aluminum, or treated wood—supports, railings, and a vinyl liner. Most of them have a depth of 4 feet, but they are also available with an expandable liner that allows a depth at one end of 7 or 8 feet, making them partially built-in.

The above-ground pool has a number of advantages. First, you don't have to tear up your backyard, as you do with the in-ground type. Second, the cost is low. Third, it's an easy do-it-yourself job. Fourth, in most areas it's not counted as a home improvement, because you can take it with you if you move—taxes aren't affected.

On the minus side, above-ground pools can only be expected to last around ten years—they're not as durable as the in-ground types. Second, above-ground pools are limited to an oval or round shape. Finally, if a part needs replacement or repair, it is difficult to get the dealer to visit your home.

Pools come in a variety of sizes, usually in multiples of 4 feet. Most range from 15 by 30 feet to 20 by 40 feet. Experts feel that, assuming the pool fully occupied, each swimmer should have 36 square feet and each diver, 100 square feet.

There are a huge variety of accessories available for pools, including heaters (which can extend pool use a couple of months), slides, underwater lights, winterizing covers, vacuum cleaners, hand leaf skimmers, automatic cleaning systems, and many other things. All these, of course, add to the cost—but you don't have to install them all at once.

Home Security

It is estimated that in the next twenty years, 72 percent of all homes will be burglarized. A chilling thought. But the fact also is that you can keep yourself from becoming part of that 72 percent. Aside from having alert neighbors, owning a very vocal dog, and keeping windows and doors locked when you're away, there is a variety of hardware available that can help you keep from being a victim.

One of the things you should do is make it seem like you're home when you're away. For years now, timers have been available that turn on and shut off lights in the home automatically, when you're not there. Such devices certainly help deter potential burglars. But timers with predictable settings won't fool the determined, experienced burglar who's casing a home. The best timers to get are ones that go on and off randomly, thus avoiding the giveaway "timer-controlled effect." A number of companies make timers that can control lights randomly for twenty-four-hour periods; some, such as Internatic, make timers that can be programmed for a week.

Having exterior lights for nighttime illumination is also helpful. Some lights are turned on by sound and motion.

Door Locks

A tremendous variety of door locks are available for the home, and trying to explain mechanical distinctions can become quite complicated. Essentially though, a clear distinction can be made in terms of the latch, which is the heart of a lock in regard to security. Locks that are not very effective for security have a latch that is mechanically linked to a spring; it is short and frequently cut at an angle. Something as simple as a plastic card or "loid," as they say in the burglary trade, can be used to push the latch clear off the strikeplate so the door can be pushed open or pried open with a tool.

With a deadbolt latch, there is usually no spring; the latch is a squarish bar of metal that inserts deeply into the door and is very difficult to push or pry out. Various types are available, as follows:

- A single-cylinder dead-lock is opened and closed with a key and opened with a latch from the inside. This is a lock that's easy for children to use.
- A double-cylinder deadlock opens and closes with a key from inside and outside. It's a good lock for doors with windows in which a

Deadbolt lock

burglar could break the glass, reach in, and turn the knob. However, this type of lock can be hazardous in a situation such as a fire, where you have to get out fast. You need to know where the key is and be able to find it quickly, even if the room is filled with smoke.

- A mortise lock is difficult to pick. The entire lock mechanism is installed inside a recess in the door.
- A rim lock is a rectangular lock with one rounded end and rings through which the bolt slips when closed. It also has a knob on the inside of the lock. A rim lock is considered jim-myproof.

In the past, if you installed a deadbolt, the key to the other locks on the door would not fit. New products have changed that. Master Lock, for example, has a new universal pin system that allows your hardware store dealer to redo your new lock so the old key fits; this can be done in a minute or so. The Kwikset Grade 2 Titan lockset has a removable cylinder that can be replaced with a cylinder matching the existing lock, so the same key can be used. Depending on finish and style, locks can cost, at this writing, between $28 and $40.

To operate a deadlock, you have to turn the knob and deadlock separately, which can be difficult for senior citizens and others with decreased dexterity, or for anyone trying to get out during a fire. Schlage S200 series locksets ($115 to $170) have an inside lever that retracts both locks at the same time.

One other new lock on the market is the Alert-Lock ($115 and up) from Pease. This has a built-in alarm, and if a burglar tries to compromise it, it can emit a sound on the decibel level of a shotgun blast, depending on how it's set. A built-in red light warns burglars that the lock is armed.

Money-Saving Tip

The fancier a lock, the more you'll pay; but fanciness does not necessarily mean strength.

Note that strong deadbolts won't do much if the door or its surrounding framework is relatively flimsy. This should be kept in mind when buying a door and building the framework for it. Many burglars will kick in a door to gain entry.

Window Hardware

Double-hung windows are normally secured by a "butterfly" lock, but this is more clamp than lock and it can easily be defeated by a burglar. One good variation on this is called the "Safety Sash Lock" (around $10); it locks like a standard butterfly lock, but can't be opened.

For sliding glass doors there is also hardware available, but still effective is a slim board that's laid in the track so the sliding part of the door can't be moved.

Wallcoverings

Hanging wallcoverings (they're called that today because there are many different materials available, not just wallpaper) is well within the ability of the patient do-it-yourselfer. There are a variety of things to know about them.

Wallcoverings are sold by single roll in American or metric sizes. The former come in a variety of sizes ranging from 12 to 24 feet long and 18 to 36 inches wide.

The metric-size roll covers between 27 and 30 feet per roll; it is commonly sold in a roll $20\frac{1}{2}$ inches wide and $16\frac{1}{2}$ feet long. Rolls cover from 27 to 30 square feet—about 25 percent more than the American roll—and can range from $13^{1}/_{2}$ to $16^{1}/_{2}$ feet long and $20^{1}/_{2}$ to 28 inches wide.

Money-Saving Tip

Buy out-of-vogue wallcovering. The discounts can be great.

Wallcoverings are priced by the single roll, but standard coverings usually come in a double or, less commonly, triple roll. Some heavy industrial coverings come 48 or 54 inches wide.

Double and triple roll sizes are based on the assumption that they are going to be used on a standard 8-foot high wall. If sold by the single roll, the installer would constantly have to be splicing cut sections together, or have a lot of waste.

Money-Saving Tip

Even when buying in-vogue wallcovering, ask for a 10 percent discount. Chances are you'll get it.

Wallcoverings, as mentioned previously, come in a variety of types. Following is a roundup:

- Paper. This is a paper that has the pattern and color printed directly on it, and has a very thin coating of vinyl to protect it somewhat. But it is not normally used in areas such as the bath or kitchen, where it has to stand up to excessive amounts of soil or moisture.
- Vinyl-Coated Paper. This is paper with a coating of vinyl. It is highly washable, and comes in a huge array of colors and patterns.
- Solid Sheet Vinyl. This is a backing of paper to which a solid sheet of thin vinyl is adhered. The vinyl is imprinted with the pattern and color. This wallcovering can be installed anywhere and is easy to clean.
- Foil. This is composed of thin sheets of aluminum foil (containing the color and pattern) adhered to a paper or cloth backing known as a scrim. There may also be a layer of polyester between the foil and backing to prevent water in the wallcovering paste from contacting the foil.
- Flocked. This is wallpaper with a raised-pattern finish that might be silk, rayon, nylon, or cotton. The base of flocked wallpaper may be cloth or paper.

- Felt. This has a nappy surface that looks like the leather made from a goat. (Just what you've always wanted on your walls!)
- Suede. This also simulates leather.
- Raised Vinyl. This is also known as heated vinyl and consists of a vinyl film that has had raised patterns embossed in it with heat; it is mounted on a paper backing.
- Mylar. This is a trade name of DuPont and refers to a certain kind of polyester film that has been combined with aluminum or vinyl sheeting. It is applied over decorative wallpapers with a variety of backings. Mylar is sometimes confused with foil. The chief difference is that foil won't burn and Mylar will.
- Moire. This usually resembles solid sheet vinyl, but when light is reflected on it, it can look like a wood grain or texture.
- Grasscloth. This is made by hand. The raw material used is a native vine called arrowroot, which comes from Korea.

    The material is made using looms: Vertical strands of string (warp threading) are woven with vine strips (weft threading). Together the warp and weft are known as the netting. The netting is laminated to a paper backing and dyed.
- Rushcloth. This resembles grasscloth and is made from strands of rush, a kind of plant, woven together.
- Hemp. The raw material of this paper also comes from a plant, in this case the hemp plant. It looks like grasscloth.
- Reedcloth. This is also made by hand. It consists of reeds of different thicknesses and colors interwoven with vertical cotton threads (called the warp).
- Stringcloth. Here, delicate threads are laminated to a backing. The paper is available in a variety of colors and sizes. It differs from grasscloth in that the seams are not prominent.
- Jute. Jute is made with coarse fibers that are sometimes blended with cloth and laminated to a backing.
- Paper Weave. This resembles grasscloth. It is made of paper that has been cut into strips and then pulled to make hanks of material. Companies make the yarn into a weave, and it is then laminated to a paper backing.

- Hand Screen Prints. Silk screening is used in making this wallcovering. The process may be made by hand or machine or both. The print itself is bonded to a paper backing, like solid vinyl wallcovering.
- Hand-Printed Mural. Here, a mural is created by hanging individual strips of wallcovering that are installed in a certain sequence.

Wallpaper also comes in three different patterns, as shown in the sketch: straight-across, random, and drop. The drop is the most difficult to hang.

On each roll of wallpaper, a manufacturer imprints what is known as a "dye lot" number. When dye lot numbers differ, it means that each roll was manufactured at a different time,

Straight across match

Drop match

Random match

Wallpaper patterns

which can mean there are subtle color differences. Always buy wallcoverings with the same dye lot numbers.

Borders are also available. These are, as the name suggests, materials used to go around something, in this case to accent wall/ceiling lines, doors, windows, and the like. They come in a wide variety of styles and colors, both plain and prepasted, and can be used, like wallcovering, on papered or painted walls. They are available in 5-yard and 7-yard spools and continuous rolls.

Prepasted—or not? Some wallcoverings come plain and are installed by applying an appropriate paste or adhesive to them. Others are prepasted— their backings are coated with a factory-applied dry adhesive that is activated with water or a product called an activator (a thinned-downed clear paste).

CHAPTER

7

Home-improvement projects vary in complexity. Following are some which most people can do which will require relatively little effort and pay big dividends.

Building a Brick on Sand Patio

A brick on sand patio is simple to build. No drainage pitching is necessary, or mortar or concrete of any sort. A brick on sand patio is quite durable. If you live in an area where there is freezing, it is likely that the bricks will heave a bit as the ground swells from frost. In the spring, though, it's an easy matter to reset them, adding or taking sand from under the bricks as needed. Then again, they might settle back perfectly on their own.

Start with an Outline. Start the job by outlining the patio area with stakes and string. Then, using a spade, remove about 2 inches of soil. Break up the soil beneath with a hoe and rake it smooth; then compact it with a roller or compactor of some sort.

Next, you can install your edging. This is the material that is installed around the perimeter of the patio so that

Mortared to concrete base

Earth

8" x 8" concrete base for brick edging

One way to retain brick

the bricks, which have a tendency to push outward, cannot do so. The edging may simply be 2 x 4 redwood planks, a band of concrete, or concrete footings with bricks laid flat in mortar on top.

Next, lay a bed of fine sand 2 inches thick over the excavated area. Then, start laying your bricks in place.

Different Patterns. You can choose from a number of patterns. The running bond is the easiest to install. It is best to provide a joint about $3/8$-inch wide between bricks. Brick sizes vary, and if you butt them, you can end up with maddening misalignments and other problems. But slightly varying joint sizes can solve size discrepancies. It's also a good idea to first lay a line of bricks completely across the patio area, varying joint size as you reach the edging so you can use whole bricks instead of pieces you must cut. Once this line is laid, you can use it as a guide to laying the other bricks.

Cut Brick. If a brick needs to be cut, do the job with a broad-bladed chisel and hammer and **wear safety glasses**. Such chisels are commonly available at masonry yards.

Bricks being placed on sand

First, score the brick all around by tapping it with the chisel. Then place the brick on a board, and give it a sharp blow with the chisel blade pointing inward. A clean break should occur. If you have to cut a large number of bricks, you can rent either an electric power saw equipped with a masonry blade or a manual cutting machine called a guillotine.

When all the bricks are in position, dump more fine sand on top and brush it into the joints. When you've filled the joints as well as you can, spray the area with the fine spray from a garden hose, to settle the sand. Over a period of weeks, rain will make the sand settle some more, so have some sand handy to fill the joints all the way to the top until thoroughly compacted.

Building a Block Patio

This type of patio may be made with precast units you buy at a masonry supply house. They come in a variety of colors.

Sweep sand into brick joints

To install the blocks, first establish the perimeter of the patio with stakes and string. Decide on the height you want, and then drive one grade stake into the ground about 1 inch inside one of the perimeter lines; the top of this first stake will then serve as your guide to the level of your patio. Proceed to drive in other grade stakes, using a long straight board and level to check for evenness.

Dig the area out to about a 4-inch deep apron at the top of the stakes. To aid in getting the sand base level and speed block laying, nail 1 x 4 boards to the stakes so the tops of stakes and boards are flush.

Pour a sand base about 2 inches thick. Make a screed (smoothing board) from a long 2 x 4 and a piece of a 1 x 4 (nailed to it) as shown in the sketch. Using the staked-in-place 1 x 4 forms as a guide, level the sand over a small area, then lay two or three blocks. Level these blocks by adding or subtracting sand from beneath them. You can then continue the job, one small section a time, using the laid blocks as a guide to level. When finished, sweep sand into the joints.

Building a Flagstone Patio

There are two methods for building a flagstone patio: wet or dry construction. In wet construction you set the stone in a grout bed on a concrete slab. In dry construction you use only a sand base. The dry method is detailed here.

First, determine the size of the patio and lay it out with string and stakes. Then, excavate the ground to a depth of 6 inches. Although the edging is not essential, it does make it easier to set the stone and it retains the sand if the patio is raised above the grass. You can use a stone edging, about 1 x 6 inches, or a wood edge, either 1 x 6 inches or 1 x 10 inches, which can be staked into the earth. When setting the edging, take care to make certain it is level.

Wet and tamp the earth in the excavated area and fill with sand to approximately 1 inch from the top of the edging. Starting in one corner, begin to lay the

flagstones on the sand base, tamping each piece with a rubber hammer or a block of wood. If the stone sinks too far, pick it up and place more sand under it. If it does not sink level with the edging, move sand under it. To check the stone level, place a straight board across it and a level on top of the board.

When all the stones are laid, sweep sand into the joints. An alternative is to fill the joints with crushed stone or decorative gravel. This can enhance the beauty of the patio even more.

One thing to keep in mind when choosing flags for your patio is that larger, thicker pieces will stay level longer than smaller, thinner pieces. Also, by keeping joints to a minimum width, sand and gravel will more readily remain in place and maintenance will be relatively easy.

3'

3'

Framing jig

2x4 deck member

Nail spacers

"Jig" for making deck parquet sections

Building a Parquet Deck

First, frame a nailing "jig" or template from scrap lumber with an inside dimension of 36 x 36 inches. (This sounds more complicated than it is).

Precut 176 pieces of 2 x 4 lumber, each 3 feet long. Lightly ease the raw edges of each piece. If in direct contact with the ground, the lumber should be pressure treated with a preservative, except if cedar or heart redwood.

Using the jig, assemble sixteen parquet blocks. Allow a $1/16$-inch space between the parallel deck members. Nail each end of the deck member with two countersunk 10d nails. Be certain to use hot-dipped galvanized, aluminum, or stainless steel nails.

Lay out the deck site with stakes and line. Excavate to a depth of 6 inches; maintain a perpendicular edge and level bottom. Fill the bottom with 3 inches of gravel ($3/4$ minus gravel or alternate). Level the gravel with a hand rake. Cover the gravel with 3 inches of sand. Level sand and tamp firmly.

Lay parquets firmly in place, alternating the direction of the decking. When all parquets have been laid in place, fill the outside edge of the excavation with sand to ground level and tamp firmly to prevent parquets from

shifting. Should you wish, you may "toe-nail" (drive nails in at angles) the parquets together for rigidity.

Keep excavation edge perpendicular — 2x4 decking — 2x4 — 3" of sand — 3" of $3/4$" minus gravel

Deck cross section

Barbecues

To really get the most from your outdoor living area, having a barbecue there is about as essential as a kitchen is indoors. There are many different kinds of barbecues you can install, from brick to preassembled gas units. Your choice may depend on how it blends in with your patio or deck.

Whatever kind you choose should be located so that it is easy to get to from the kitchen and does not interfere with traffic on the patio. Also, the paths that lead to and from it should be solid—you want a sure-footed surface.

Replacing Switches and Receptacles

The first step, of course, is to turn off the power to the receptacle (or switch). To insure that you've done this, first plug a working lamp into the receptacle, turn it on, and then flick off the circuit breaker or remove the fuse that controls the outlet. When the light goes off, you'll know that the receptacle is dead—safe.

There are two main types of receptacles: those with two slots and those with two plus a V-shaped opening for a grounding prong on the plug. It is highly likely that if you live in an older home you will have the two-slot type. If so, you should probably replace it with the same type rather than a grounded kind. The reason is that replacing it with a three-slot type won't ground your electrical system, but someone seeing the three slots may think it is grounded. You could tie a copper wire between the green ground screw on the receptacle to a screw on the metal receptacle box, but in order for the system to be grounded you must also have BX (armor clad) cable with all tight connections. Our advice is to stick with what you have.

Remove Cover. Replacing either a two-slot or grounded receptacle is basically the same. First, remove the cover. One screw holds it on. It usually comes right off, though you may have to chip away a little paint around the edges or pry it off if it's been heavily painted over. No matter. Receptacle covers are commonly available in standard sizes in a tremendous array of styles; so if you

ruin the cover, it can be easily replaced.

Next, remove the receptacle from the box. The wires are stiff, so you'll have to exert a steady but gentle pull. Take it out as far as you can so you'll have as much room to work on the connections as possible.

Examine the wires. If you see that the insulation on the wires is rotted away or falls off to expose the copper wire, it's best to stop and call an electrician in to work on things. One reason is he may be able to handle the wires without destroying the insulation. If he can't, he will be there to change the wires. The latter doesn't often need to be done; but if it does, that means it's probably time to change all the wiring.

You should buy, as mentioned, the same kind (two or three slot) of receptacle as you are replacing. They are commonly available at hardware stores and electrical supply stores, and are generally white or brown. Just tell the dealer where the receptacle is used and he'll give you the proper replacement. Or, you can wait until after you've removed the old one and show it to him.

With the new receptacle in hand, remove the wires one by one on the old receptacle and attach them to the new. Set screws are used so you can loosen

Safety Tip

Whole-house wiring should be left to the pro not only because it can get dangerous but also because doing it improperly and having a fire start can void one's homeowner's insurance. However, you can replace switches and receptacles without any electrical danger.

them all the way and they'll stay attached to the receptacle. To make the job easier, you could make a little drawing indicating where the wires go on the old unit, then remove it completely and attach the new. Black wires go to the gold screws and white wires go to the silver screws.

It is important to make tight connections. On each screw, hook the wire over the screw shaft, use a needle-nose pliers to crimp it down tightly, and then tighten the screw down well. Wires should be wrapped around the screw clockwise, the same way the screws tighten. If the wires are looped the other way, tightening the screws would have a tendency to loosen the wires.

With all wires attached, gently push the receptacle back into the box. Wires should be well into the box. Try not to kink them as you push the receptacle in

or create pulling pressure on the connections.

The new receptacle comes with screws for attaching the receptacle to the box. Hold the receptacle in position with one hand and start the screws in the box holes; then snug them up. Reinstall the cover (the hole for it is also standard) with the screw, and you've just saved yourself the expense of an electrician for a dollar or so, the cost of the new receptacle.

Follow the same procedure for replacing a switch.

New Outlets. As of this writing, a new product called Electracraft was just emerging. It promises to be a boon to the DIYer who wants to add new outlets. It consists of rigid plastic sections in molding shape that snap together and have outlets built on. You just plug in the strip in a regular outlet and the strip outlets are ready to go. The product comes in beige and gray.

Replacing a Lock

Locks come with complete installation instructions. Most replacement types can be installed in the hole housing the old lock. When shopping for a replacement, the key consideration is its "backset"—the distance from the edge of the door to the middle of the knob or handle. The vast majority of locks, interior and exterior, have a $2^3/_8$-inch backset and most are installed in a $2^1/_8$-inch hole, some in a $1^1/_4$-inch hole. If the hole is backset $2^3/_8$ inches but only has a $1^3/_4$-inch hole, you can simply enlarge it. Just clamp wood over the hole and use one of the many specially sized lock boring bits available.

Some locks have a backset of 5 inches. Quickset is a popular brand. For this you have to get a new bolt. Another manufacturer, Schlage, has a link that goes between the bolt and the lock.

Providing a New Storage Area

Providing new storage area is high on the list of home improvement projects for many homeowners, and many times it can be achieved quite simply by using available hardware.

Utility Brackets. These brackets are mounted directly on the wall with screws, preferably into studs (if the studs don't fall in the proper places—studs are normally 16 inches apart, 24 inches in older homes—you can use hollow wall anchors). The shelves of your choice—which you can buy precut and prefinished—are then laid across the brackets.

Utility brackets are, as the name suggests, for utility. There is nothing particularly fancy or decorative about them, though they do come in various colors such as gold and black.

Standards and Brackets. This type of hardware allows flexibility of use. You can move the shelves to

Utility brackets

varying heights for accommodating taller or shorter items as the need arises.

Standards are vertically slotted pieces of metal that are secured to studs or wall material. They have predrilled holes for receiving screws, which are usually 6 to 8 inches apart. The bracket has a hook-shaped part on it that latches into the slots on the standards, and shelves are then laid across the brackets. Hence, if you want to move the shelves, you simply unhook the brackets and relocate them in new slots.

Standards and brackets come in various finishes and are more expensive than utility brackets. Sizes (the top part of the bracket that the shelf rests on) normally run from 4 to 18 inches in increments of 2 inches.

If you are just supporting books, rather than heavy stereo equipment, a TV, or the like, you can use hollow wall anchors to mount the standards. But if the weight you wish to support is too heavy, you run the risk of the anchor pulling out of the wall material.

Plumbline

Corner

Width of paper minus ½"

First step in hanging wall covering

Sometimes the standards and brackets from different companies are interchangeable. However, in most instances you must use the same brand.

Pilasters. These are mounted inside kitchen or other cabinets because they're not made to be attractive. There are standards, but instead of the slots being vertical, they are horizontal in order to accept small clips. Pilasters may be adjusted to some degree.

Hanging Wallcoverings

Preparing walls for wallcovering is just as important as preparing them for painting. You should prepare them the same way. (See the Maintenance section on preparation.)

Priming and Sizing. Before wallcovering is applied, it is also necessary to make sure the walls are primed and sized as needed. Priming is the process of coating the wall so there is no bleed through of the paint color through the wallcovering. Sizing is the application of a coating to insure that the wall surface is sealed and the paste on the wallcovering will not penetrate unevenly and possibly lead to failure. Sizing has one other goal: to make it easier to take off the wallcovering in the future.

A variety of primers that are also sizes are available. Shiledz is one. Your dealer should be able to tell you about others.

Paste. There are a variety of adhesives for hanging wallcoverings. However, unless you are hanging a special kind, three types will suffice: a clear acrylic paste for hanging unpasted wallcoverings; vinyl-to-vinyl paste—the strongest paste there is—for hanging borders; and activator, basically a thin, clear paste, for application to prepasted paste (which I think helps the wallcoverings adhere better).

Existing Wallcovering.

A common situation is installing wallcovering over existing wallcovering. The main thing to remember is that the old wallcovering acts as a base for the new material, and therefore must be as solid as if the wallcovering was being installed on a wall.

Check the seams of the paper. If they are lifting, secure them with seam adhesive or vinyl-to-vinyl paste. You can use a roller to make sure it adheres well. If there are open seams, apply spackling compound to them. If seams are overlapped and have a slight bump, also spackle these.

If there are bubbles or other loose spots in the paper, they should be opened up with a razor knife and affixed with adhesive, or cut out and the area spackled.

You should prime existing paper with an oil-based primer or one designed to not resolubilize—turn to liquid—the paste holding the wallcovering on. Your dealer can be helpful here.

Hanging. The first job is to figure out how much wallcovering is needed. In general, you can figure 58 square feet per double roll. Ten percent of that will be needed for waste, and you can subtract 15 square feet per window and door opening. If what you need falls between one and two rolls, get an extra double roll. You will need more or less material based on the

Soft fold, do not crease

Apply paste

Fold other end after pasting

Align edges

Method for applying paste

pattern match. As mentioned earlier, whatever rolls you buy should have the same dye lot numbers.

Plumblines. Most ceilings and floors are not straight, so it is important to first snap a plumbline. To do this, select an inconspicuous corner, such as behind a door, to hang the first strip. Measure from the corner the width of the roll less $1/2$ inch, and snap a plumbline on the wall. For example, if the wallcovering is 27 inches wide, the plumbline would be $26^1/_2$ inches from the corner; make this mark near the ceiling. Hang the plumbline from the ceiling. When the line stops moving, mark the wall where the line falls about 2 inches above the baseboard. With these two lines as reference points, snap a line that bisects them. As you reach each, snap a new plumbline as suggested.

Measure at Several Points. Measure the wall height at several points, and then add 2 inches for trimming at both the ceiling and baseboard. If, for example, the pattern is large—say a floral design—hold the roll up against the wall and determine where you want the pat-

2" overlap

Corner

Paper $1/2$" over corner

Plumbline

2" overlap

Wallcovering overlaps at top and bottom

tern to fall at the ceiling line before cutting. Lay this strip face up on a table or floor, and roll out another strip to check for a match; cut this, and then cut additional strips.

Prepasted or Not.
First, roll out the strip along the wallcovering table (or just a long table) pattern side down. Apply the adhesive to one half the strip using either a $3/_8$-inch roller or a wide wallcovering brush, working from the middle of the strip to the ends and out, covering it completely. Being careful not to crease it, loosely fold the strip on itself—wet to wet.

Repeat the procedure for the other half, applying adhesive, and then folding it back on itself. Then let it "book" relax for at least five minutes so the covering fully expands. If unpasted, also book it, whether you use activator or not.

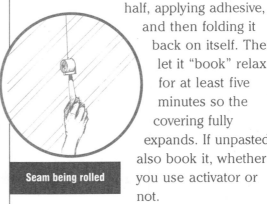

Seam being rolled

Apply the strip so the edge aligns with the plumbline and overlaps it by 2 inches at the ceiling and baseboard. Using a smoothing brush, brush outward from the center to remove bubbles and wrinkles.

Unroll the lower half of the paper and repeat the procedure. Use a sponge to clean any excess adhesive off the face of the strip.

Second Strip. Butt the first strip against the second so there is no overlap, and the pattern matches perfectly. Also, don't stretch the strip to fit—it can shrink back and open the seam.

Most of the time when wallcovering becomes loose it does so at the seams, so it's important to roll them with a seam roller to make sure the covering is in full contact with the wall and that seams are tight. Gaps mean potential weak spots.

Insurance Against Loosening. As insurance against wallcovering loosening at the seams, painter Ken Walker of Ronkonkama, Long Island, says that he uses regular paste or activator as the case may be, but also applies vinyl-to-vinyl paste to the wall at the points where the seams are. (Vinyl-to-vinyl is, as mentioned,

very strong and insures that the seams won't loosen.)

Every couple of strips, use a joint knife and a very sharp razor knife (a utility knife or one with breakaway blades works well) to trim off excess paper, using the joint skiff to hold the wallcovering tightly in the seam as you trim. As you trim, change blades frequently so you don't pull adhered paper off the wall with the movement of the blade and to make a sharp cut. As you go, use a clean sponge to clear any adhesive away.

Corners. It might seem easier to handle inside corners by simply "wrapping" the covering into them, but this is not the way to go. It can cause the covering to become slightly awry as the job proceeds.

Your best bet is to cut two pieces of wallcovering. Measure at three spots along the edge of the wallcovering— baseboard, middle, and ceiling. To the widest measurement add $1/2$ inch. Cut this width from the new strip. You can do this by snapping a cut line. Paste this strip as the others and butt it against the last strip hung.

Take the leftover part of the strip, apply paste, and then hang it on the

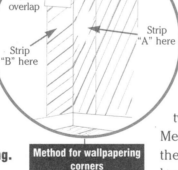

Corner
$1/2$" overlap
Strip "B" here
Strip "A" here

Method for wallpapering corners

adjacent corner, overlapping the first strip a half inch. The overlap will not be noticeable because it will match the adjacent design very well.

On an outside corner, no cutting is required. Just paste the strip and install it as other strips. Make sure it's tight and well adhered.

Openings. When you reach a window or door, the job can be continued in essentially the same way. Cut a matching strip to butt against the last applied strip, but an inch or two longer. When the wallcovering is laid over the window or door, a little more slack is needed.

When the next strip is pasted, butt it against the last-applied strip and position it over the window or door. Then use a scissors or razor to slice it diagonally Then use the joint knife to press it in snugly around the molding of the door or window, and trim off excess with a sharp blade.

Use a smoothing brush to work out the bubbles. Then trim off the excess.

Ceilings. You can install wallcoverings on a ceiling. However, there are, of course, some differences in method.

First, you should work across the short dimension of the ceiling, because this will allow you to work with shorter strips, a boon when you're working above your head. Start on the side of the room where it is going to be as much out of

sight as possible, because you won't have a match.

Cut strips a couple of inches longer than needed, apply paste, and set it up in position. To help do this you can use a broom, and a helper—definitely called for to help you get the strips in position. Trim each as you go, and roll the seams out. When finished, wipe away excess glue with a clean, damp sponge.

Removing Wallcoverings

Sometimes existing wallcoverings are in such bad shape that the only solution is to take them off. Sometimes this is easy. If it is a cloth type of paper, all that needs to be done is to grab a corner of the paper and pull it off. It comes off in one strip. It's a good idea to wash any residual glue off the wall with a cleaner (more about this later).

In doing this, however, you want to guard against damaging the wall surface. If it is plaster, there is little chance of this. However, drywall has a kraft facing paper, and this could come off—and perhaps gypsum with it—as the wallcovering is pulled off. It all depends on how the person who hung the wallcovering prepared the wall. (Often they are not prepared that well.)

Hence, it's a good idea to use a scraper to gently lift one corner and then pull the paper off with the peeling paper just about parallel with what's on the wall. Avoid pulling it straight out.

Steamer or Chemical Methods. Two other methods are available: a steamer or chemicals. If you expect to do a lot of paper removal, then a steamer is likely the cheaper way to go. Whichever method you employ, the one thing to remember is that both remove wallcovering by attacking— weakening the adhesive that bonds the covering to the wall. Once this is softened, the covering can be stripped easily from the wall.

A steamer consists of a flat-metal steam plate, about 8 x 11 inches, with holes in it, like a clothes iron. The plate is connected by a long hose to what is essentially a pressure cooker in which water is heated and turned to steam. The steam travels through the hose and emerges from the plate perforations. In use, the plate is held against the wallcovering, saturating it with hot steam. This steam resolubilizes the paste, which is water based, and the covering starts to loosen.

Fork being used to abrade wallcovering

The chemical method may be one of two types. The first is a liquid, such as DIF, that is added to water and makes enough remover for an average-sized room. The solution is applied to the wall, preferably with a deck sprayer because it saturates the wall, to a 3-foot wide area going from the ceiling to the base molding. Then, additional solution is applied to an adjacent 3-foot strip, and so on down the wall. To keep the wallcovering saturated, new solution is applied to the first strips done as the job progresses.

After a half hour of being wet, a stiff scraper is used to scrape the wallcovering off. Then more solution is used to clean off excess glue from the wall. Rags can be used as necessary.

Gel remover is more expensive than DIF, but no reapplication is required. Gel is brushed on the surface and, because it is thick, sticks there of its own accord, saturating the paper with chemical and attacking the paste. After a certain amount of time, the gel will have penetrated through the paper and attacked the paste.

After the paper is stripped, the glue that remains must also be removed. (Some types of wallcovering allow the outer plastic surface to be stripped away, leaving a backing paper in place.) Once the plastic is off, you can treat it the same way that you would treat paper: Apply solution and let it soak in, scrape, and rinse off.

Impermeable Wallcoverings. Many wallcoverings (as noted earlier) are not pure paper but are covered with vinyl or some other material. Chemical strippers will not penetrate this covering; a pathway must literally be cut for it—the paper must be scored.

This can done in a variety of ways. One way is with the tines of a fork. The tines of the fork are simply drawn across the wallcovering, breaking through the paper to the surface beneath.

Scoring can also be done with the edge of a scraper or with rough grit sandpaper. However, you need to make sure that you don't score the surface beneath the paper. If you do, you should fill in the scrapes before proceeding with new paint or wallcovering.

Another method is called the "Paper Tiger." This is a product (made by Zinsser) that has toothed wheels on it. The device is rolled over the covering, with pressure applied, and the wheels score the covering.

Once all the wallcovering is off, wash off any residual glue with chemical or gel. Removing wallcovering is a messy process no matter what you use, and it's a good idea to cover up carefully, using masking tape and

plastic drops, as well as cloth ones. It is also well to remember that plastic is slippery and can be treacherous underfoot.

Hiring Contractors

Most of the problems people have with home improvements ultimately relate to money. If consumers stayed in control of the money, there's no question the number of complaints would drop dramatically. When you hire a home-improvement contractor, the key to protecting yourself is agreeing to a plan that always keeps you just ahead of the contractor on payments.

Here's why:

- Some contractors give lower estimates than they should, for one reason or another. Maybe they do it because they want a job badly or because they just don't know what's involved. Then, when the job takes a bad turn and contractors see that they're not going to make any money, they abandon it. If, for example, only one third of the work has been done and you have given the contractor half the money, you'll be out the difference.

- Some contractors use the money you give them to finish another job, a dangerous rob-Peter-to-pay-Paul situation. Ultimately, they may not have enough money to finish your job.
- Some contractors take an advance and never even start a job, or do a day or two of work and never return. One of the worst cases involved a contractor taking $125,000 up front on a job, opening up both ends of a house for additions—leaving the house open to weather and wild animals—and never returning.

Pay as You Go

The best procedure is to make stepped payments for completed work only. List the steps at the beginning: for example, excavation, foundation work, framing, siding, roofing, insulation and drywall, electrical, and plumbing. Also, hold back some money at the end of the job. Give yourself two weeks to thirty days (depending on job complexity) to insure your satisfaction with the completed project.

Don't give an advance for supplies unless the products or materials to be used are custom made. Some contractors consider this arrangement unfair. Many think it's fine but that it is based on harsh realities.

Not giving an advance may seem unfair, but it really isn't. Established contractors buy on credit. They routinely order supplies for your job from suppliers and have to pay within thirty or sixty days. The suppliers do not demand cash on delivery from such pros, so they don't need money to pay until the bill comes due.

On the other hand, an advance is fair for custom-made products and unusual materials, such as custom kitchen cabinets or special windows, because suppliers require payment up front for such items. If it turns out you don't like the custom-made products, the contractor can't return them for credit, as he or she can stock products, and has to "eat them." That can cause massive fiscal indigestion.

But you have to make sure your advance goes to the supplier. Under lien laws, if the contractor doesn't pay the supplier, the supplier can legally come after you for the money and you can end up paying twice. The laws vary in severity, but at the least, you can end up having a lien or "claim" placed against your house so you can't sell it without paying the lien; at the worst, your property can be seized.

A contractor buying on credit, however, is probably a good customer—one who pays the bills. If he or she needs money for the supplies up front, pay the supplier directly, or write a check that requires double endorsement by the contractor and supplier. You could also ask the supplier for a lien release up front, but this would be an unusual request and chances are he or she won't agree to it.

Payment protection for yourself should extend to the contractor's workers. As the job is progressing, ask them if they're being paid. If they're not, you should stop the job immediately. Reason: Like suppliers, people who work for the person you deal with also have lien rights. Many an electrician or plumber or other worker has shown up at a consumer's door asking for payment that he or she has not received from a general contractor—whom you've already paid.

You should also know that the lien rights the suppliers or workers have can only be waived by them. Some contractors think they can waive the lien rights of suppliers or workers, but this isn't true.

Further protection

Some money should be held back, as mentioned, for two weeks to thirty days after completion of a job. How much? Most consumer affairs agencies advise 10 percent. Whatever the amount, it should

be significant, so that if the roof starts to leak, or any problems develop, the contractor will be constrained to come back and correct them.

Aside from protecting yourself as suggested above—which is far and away the most important thing—there are other things to do to insure hiring a competent, honest contractor who will do a good job at a fair price. You should research the job thoroughly to determine what you want, get multiple bids, check out contractors with consumer affairs and the Better Business Bureau, check references, visit a job or two, talk to former customers, put everything in writing in a detailed contract that has as its goal the avoidance of misunderstanding, and monitor the job as much as possible. All this requires a lot of effort, but you won't be sorry you took the precautions!

Do You Need an Architect?

The main reason you might need an architect for home improvement is, of course, design. But you also need an architect to make sure that a structure is not only built soundly but also "works" for the occupants and looks good.

Ron Boden, CEO of Jarro Building Industries East Meadow, Long Island, New York, says that an architect would definitely be required on complex projects where there is major structural work, for example, "projects that add over 400 square feet of living space." Conversely, he doesn't see the need for an architect when the work could be characterized as "cosmetic"—painting, wallpapering, roofing, siding, and the like. Kitchens and baths would also not require an architect, though they might require the services of a kitchen and bath designer. Indeed, architects use such specialists on big jobs themselves.

The main question, perhaps, of when you should hire one relates to jobs that are not that complicated designwise. In jobs where structural change occurs, such as adding dormers, simple additions or extensions, and moving interior walls, it would seem that a builder could provide the plans (which would be stamped by a licensed architect). But there is a case to use an architect on such jobs, in either a limited or an extensive way.

Noah Schechtel, a designer/builder in Babylon, Long Island, whom I have talked with, says: "The architect is trained in design. Maybe what looks like an obvious solution to a problem may create another one. For example a homeowner might automatically assume that to yield more space in his home he needs an extension or addition. But an architect may see some other possibility, like taking down a wall, or extending the house with a bay window, or switching room functions. Problem solving is his business. His solution might not only be simple—but a lot less costly. It may well be worth hiring him for an hour or two just to get his ideas."

Schechtel says the architect also brings a tremendous storehouse of knowledge about products and materials to a job. If you choose to have an architect prepare the plans, he or she will include specifications for products and materials based on the homeowner's needs and budget without the homeowner having to extensively research such things.

Clearer Bids

Architects can also help with bids. Many a homeowner has had the experience of not being able to intelligently compare bids of various contractors because each was based on slightly different designs, and each contractor would champion his or her way to build something as the best.

The architect solves that. He or she says (in concert with the homeowner) that such and such is the best way to build it. Blueprints of the architect's plans, each the same, go out to builders; and there is no confusion. All the contractors bid on the same job. As Ron Boden, puts it: "They bid on apples and apples not apples and oranges."

Supervisory Capacity

Another way an architect can serve is in a supervisory capacity. You can hire him or her to come to the job at various stages to check on how it's going. Obviously, the architect is in a better position to see how it's going than the homeowner; and if something is awry, the architect can communicate clearly what it is so it can be corrected. If you wish, an architect can be hired to be there frequently, but this is usually not required on less complex jobs.

Cost

In thinking about whether to hire an architect, cost may be a factor. When most people think "architect" they think "big money." But this need not be the case. Architects can be hired out by the hour (about $60 per) just to pick their brains, or just to do the plans—say a $500 minimum. Or they can hire out for a flat fee that includes the plans and a

> ### Architect-Approved Plans
> Whether or not you hire an architect, you will likely need plans certified by one, simply because most building codes throughout the country require it. For example, New York State requires that any job that costs more than $20,000 be certified by an architect. In my town, Huntington, New York, you must have an architect for any project that will cost more than $10,000 and will involve structural change.

few visits to the site. Or—for a percentage of the job cost——they can hire out a soup-to-nuts arrangement where full service is provided: He or she consults; makes schematic drawings (floor plans); then refines the schematics deciding on materials, details, and actual dimensions; makes construction documents; helps the homeowner decide whose bid to take; and provides weekly consultation and supervisory service.

The full service arrangement normally costs 10 to 20 percent of the building cost. If the job is $100,000, the architect gets $10,000 to $20,000. It is paid over the course of a job. Although this may seem steep, it should be noted that the architect might have saved the client a lot of money in developing the plans and in getting bids.

The idea is to dovetail the architect's services to your needs. It's the author's opinion that at the very least it would be a good idea to talk with an architect for at least a short while whenever any project involving structural changes is contemplated.

Finding an Architect

Just as you would do your homework in finding a building contractor, so too you should expend more than a little energy finding an architect. The key, says architect Jonah Zuckerman (and others we talked to) "is to find one that's right for you. One that will reflect what you want, and that will be affordable. You don't want someone to design a fort when all you need is a room or two." Indeed, Zuckerman cautions that hiring an inexperienced architect can lead to a quagmire of expenses and problems you can live without.

Boden says that it's important to get an architect who will "listen, not just make proclamations."

In seeking one out, Schechtel says that it's important to look at an architect's previous work, to search for his or her "signature. Every architect has a signature,

or style, and you want to make sure it fits with what you like." For example, you might see that one architect likes sharp, modern angles in the things she designs, but your tastes are more reserved...and so is your house.

And you should look for more than one architect, just as you would look for more than one contractor. And, as with contractors, the architect's references and competence should, as much as possible, be looked into.

Where to Look

So, where do you look for an architect? The best source for architects is the same as for contractors: recommendations. Ask friends, neighbors, and business associates if they know anyone. You might even ask a contractor who you're considering hiring if he knows someone.

Also, look around the neighborhood. Scrutinize remodelings that are similar to what you want and ask the people if an architect was involved, and, if so, who he or she is—and if they liked him or her.

Also, there is the American Institute of Architects, or AIA, an organization of architects whose members promise to meet certain standards of professionalism and ethics. Although membership in the AIA does not confer sainthood, or competence, membership in the organization does say something about the person's mindset regarding his or her profession.

And one final thing: Put whatever arrangement you make into a written contract.

Where to Get the Money for Renovation

Before you hire a contractor, you should have the money in place for what you want to do. Be aware, though, that cost might not stay firm. You might earmark a certain amount for a job, but want to add some extras, or change something once the job is under way. Remodeling attorney Reynolds Graves says that to whatever figure they arrive at they should add 20 percent. "People almost always spend more than they plan to, and you should have the money ready." Adds contractor Matt Mahoney of Mahoney Construction in Huntington, New York: "Improving their homes is like sex to some people. The more they get the more they want!"

Shop Around

The bizarre thing about loans is that very few people shop around for them.

Indeed, most people spend more time shopping for a TV or toaster than for a loan. But they should. The savings can be nothing short of stupendous.

For example, if someone borrowed $100,000 and the interest rate on it was 10 percent and the term was thirty years, they would pay about $878 per month, or a little more than three times the loan, or $315,720 over the thirty years. If you pay 14 percent interest, you would pay $1185 per month, or $307 more per month than for a 10 percent loan; and over the thirty years you would pay $426,553—four times the amount of the loan, or over $110,846 more—two or three years, salary for many people!

Secured and Unsecured Loans

All loans can be characterized as secured or unsecured. A secured loan is backed up by collateral, a house for example. An unsecured loan is not. The unsecured loans are generally more costly than secured. Following is a look at various kinds.

Home Equity Loan. Here, one borrows on the equity in a house—the market value less the amount owed. For example, if $25,000 was still owed on the house and its market value was $200,000, the market value would be $175,000 and would be available. In practice, though, the amount to be lent is factored into what the homeowner is paying out, and banks usually don't want the homeowner to be paying out more than 37 percent of monthly income on car, mortgage, and the like.

The rate you pay is based on the prime interest rate. It's usually one or two points above prime, the rate banks charge their best (and usually biggest) customers. If prime were 8.25 percent, you could pay 9.25 or 10.25 percent. But this could be more—some banks charge three and four points higher and some are adjustable, the rate going up or down depending on the prime rate. It's important when shopping for this type of loan to know what the "cap" rate is—the figure above which the loan cannot rise.

Interest on the loan is also tax deductible as long as the total debt on the house is less than $1 million (not a problem for most of us). This can be significant. For example, if you had a $20,000 loan at 12 percent, the interest would be $2400 a year. However, assuming you were in the 28 percent tax bracket, the after-tax cost would be $1728— a monthly saving of $56 or $672 per year.

Balloon Payments. Some home equity loans offer so-called balloon repayments. Here, you only pay interest back over a short period of time, then the "balloon"— the principal on the loan—all at once. This is a bad idea because if you can't refinance to get the money or get it in some other way your property will be at risk of foreclosure.

Home equity loans usually have a minimum one can borrow at one time. This is now $5000.

You should check out rates of these loans at tax time. Some banks offer lower rates then because they know borrowers will be attracted by the tax benefits.

Banks are the normal place to shop for home equity loans, but credit unions also offer them. If you belong to one, check it out. The rates are usually better than banks.

Home Equity Line. This is set up the same way as a home equity loan (variable interest, cap etc.—and it's tax deductible); but the big difference is that it is a line of credit, and you are charged interest only on what you write checks for. So, for example, if you have a $50,000 line of credit but you only write a check for $1000, you'd only pay interest on the $1000—the money you use.

Like home equity loans, lines also have fees, such as for credit check, title search, and "points." A point is a euphemism for the percentage of money the bank takes that is equal to 1 percent of the face value of the loan. If the loan is for $40,000, and each point is $300 and three points are charged, you would pay

$900. Points can vary greatly from bank to bank and should be added in when calculating the cost of the loan.

Refinance Mortgage. This means that a certain amount of money is borrowed to pay off the old mortgage, and then you can borrow up to 80 percent on the equity. Interest is also tax deductible. Interest rates are generally lower than for home equity loans, but closing costs are typically a lot higher and may offset any interest savings. Interest is tax deductible.

Home Improvement Loan. These loans are generally given for five to seven years and interest rates now range from 9 to 15 percent. Loans may be from $1000 to a maximum of $20,000. The disadvantage of these loans is the relatively short payback period, which results in high monthly payments. The loan when secured by a house is tax deductible and fees are small—just the $75 or so it costs to make a credit check.

HUD Home Improvement Loan. The FHA, under its Title I program, insures loans up to $25,000 on single-family dwellings. The loans are available at a variety of banks, and rates are about the same as for a secured home-improvement loan. The plus here is that the government insures the loan, and it will insure loans of people who don't have a lot of equity. (That's why it was created.)

> **Put It in Writing**
>
> Any changes to the original plan should be in writing, and while you may add something to it, you may also subtract something else. Don't forget to subtract these "deducts," as they're called in the trade, from the original estimate.

Unlike a regular home-improvement loan, which usually has a payback period of five to seven years, you can take fifteen years to repay this loan. This type of loan is also available for multiple-family units. Loans may be $12,000 per unit up to $60,000.

401k Loan. Under this loan, you can borrow against profit-sharing monies. The interest rate is just a little above prime, and there are no fees.

Life Insurance. If you have life insurance, this is another source to consider. Rates are low and you can borrow up to 100 percent of the cash value of the policy.

Unsecured Personal Loan. This is a very expensive loan, three to five points higher than a home-improvement loan, which is secured by the house. There is no tax deductibility, and the payback period is three to five years.

Contractor Arranged Loan. This is where the contractor arranges the loan through a bank for you. We think it's a bad idea. In essence, it eliminates shopping around, and, in some cases, the bank will pay all the money to the contractor. If the contractor doesn't complete the work—or even start it—guess who's responsible to the bank for the money anyway?

Cash. You could dip into your savings to pay for the job, but this could deplete resources you have standing by in case of an emergency. Then, if you needed cash, you'd have to use other methods to get it.

To sum up, the best way to insure an adequate cash flow for the job and the best possible loan is to shop around, taking into account the total cost of the loan—which includes fees, the amount that can be saved in tax deductions, and, of course, interest rates. It is heartily suggested that you make a little chart and then get on the phone with sharpened pencil in hand. Seeing the figures side by side will be revelatory—and can save you, as suggested earlier, a lot of money.

CHAPTER

8

The thought of repairing appliances is a scary one for a lot of people. But the simple fact is that there is plenty that one can do, and save money and get a lot of satisfaction in the process.

Small and Large Appliances

Appliances are classified as either small or large, the former includes such items as electric can openers and blenders; the latter includes such items as washers and dryers.

Repairing Small Appliances

In many cases, you may not be able to fix a small appliance. Many of today's appliances have a housing of injected molded plastic or the metal housing crimped together, and the mechanical innards can't be gotten at without destroying the housing. In such cases, you might just as well throw away the appliance.

So, too, replacement parts for some small appliances can be quite costly. For example, one magazine reported that they priced out a new carafe for a coffeemaker at $15. A brand new unit, however, could be gotten for $17.

Sometimes a repair can be done. If you have the manual that came with the appliance, check it out. Troubleshooting tips may be offered.

If this doesn't help, the manufacturer may have a customer service number you can call to get some repair advice based on the symptoms you provide. (See the section "Info Power" on how to go about obtaining this number.)

If the small appliance is not repairable by you, and you have determined that it may be repairable by a qualified service person, you have a few ways to go. In the first place, the item may be under warranty, and you can get it repaired by shipping it back to the factory or having it fixed by a repairperson who is authorized by the manufacturer of your particular product to make repairs. If the warranty period has lapsed and you still want to make a repair, you can ask for an authorized service center or take it to someone who is not authorized. In the latter case, however, it is a good idea to take it to someone who has been recommended to you.

Repairing Major Appliances

You can get even more advice on repairs of major appliances than you can on small appliances. Many companies provide good manuals and have set up 800 numbers staffed by knowledgeable personnel who can field all kinds of questions. If parts are needed, they can ship them from the factory, but it's often easier to trek down to your local home-improvement center or a store like K Mart and pick up the part. While you're there, you may find a knowledgeable salesperson who can give you advice.

Maintaining Major Appliances

One of the best things you can do to save money and avoid the inconvenience of a major appliance breakdown is to perform some simple, basic maintenance on the machines. Following is a lineup of things you can do.

Refrigerators. The cooling coils on refrigerators gather dust, pet hair, and the like. This reduces their ability to shed heat and thereby reduces efficiency and raises energy bills. Vacuuming them will make a big difference. The coils are located below the door behind a grill. If there is a heavy accumulation of grease, use a degreaser to clean the coils.

The evaporator plate should also be vacuumed. On older refrigerators, it hides behind an access panel next to

Gasket the Culprit

If a refrigerator doesn't close properly, the culprit is often food and the like that has gotten under the gasket. Lift the gasket up gently and clean under it with a toothbrush and soapy water so that it lays flat.

Rust Streaks on a Fridge

Sometimes refrigerators develop rust streaks on the inside walls. Mix a paste of baking soda and water and apply. The streaks should disappear.

the compressor motor. New models usually have it on the back of the refrigerator in the form of a grid.

Ranges. Gas ranges require more maintenance than electric ones, but in either case, a degree in brain surgery is not required to do the job. On electric models, the only maintenance requirement (but it is important) is to keep surfaces clean. The heating elements can be easily lifted out, and so can the reflecting pans beneath the heating elements. If the range has a so-called trim ring, a separate component around the pan, take care to reinstall it the same way you took it out.

On gas models, clearing clogs and dirt from various areas is the name of the game. First, the pilot light can become clogged; and second, there can be an accumulation of soot and carbon on the shield over the pilot light.

To clear clogs and dirt, first turn off the pilot light. Lift up the cooktop and hold it up with a board. Inspect the pilot light. If it's clogged, use a safety pin to gently clean it. Use a knife to scrape the carbon off the shield.

Light the pilot light. If the flame seems too short or long, follow the feed line to the control valve and adjust the flame by turning the slotted screw with a screwdriver.

Check the flame at the burners. If they're clogged, clear them with a safety pin. Finally, clean under the burners and replace the top.

Filters on range hoods also get clogged. These should be removed and rinsed with hot water once a month. Let them dry before replacing them.

Dishwashers. On these, you should first make sure the door gasket is clean. It may be clean where it's visible, but the bottom may be covered with dirt. Hold a mirror inside the dishwasher to check the bottom for dirt. Use a strong but nonabrasive cleaner to remove any dirt.

Also lift the water-level float to check for dirt. (If dirt accumulates it can get stuck, resulting in an incorrect water level.)

Also check the spray arm for an accumulation of small shreds of plastic. Remove them with a pair of tweezers if necessary.

Another good spot to check is the drain area regulator. Check for small items, and clear them if necessary. Small plastic items such as spoons can get baked onto the heating element or chip the food-grinding impellers in the drain.

Finally, make sure some water is always in the base of the dishwasher. If you seldom use it, add water periodically. You don't want the pump seals to dry out.

Washers and Dryers. One of the perennial problems of washers and dryers is that they are not level on the floor. This causes the moving parts in the machines to wear unevenly, and essentially wear out. Some appliances have self-leveling legs, but these often are just to make sure the machine is stable.

It's best to use a level to make sure the machine is evenly balanced. First, lay the level along the sides, and then along the front and back.

On a dryer, you should also clean the lint trap after each load is finished. Letting lint accumulate could lead to a fire.

Stove Filter Therapy

If the filter over the stove is dirty and greasy, clean it in the dishwasher. Or, clean it in a tub. It will work much better clean.

CHAPTER

9

Most people's concern for the environment doesn't extend to allowing bats in their belfry or roaches in the food cabinet. Keeping these creatures away is desirable for most of us, and the info that follows will allow you to do just that.

Bats

Bats are not the evil, bloodsucking airborne predators that Hollywood depicts. Although it's true that some of them can be rabid, the percentage is very small. But if you ever have to handle a dead bat, do so with gloves. You can get rabies from saliva and tissue; and if someone does get bitten, it's important to retain the bat, particularly the head, so tests can be performed on the brain to determine if the bat was rabid.

The best way to keep bats out of a house is to close up all the openings where they can get in—by applying caulk in gaps on the "seams" of the house, and plugging up obvious holes with screening, hardware cloth, and sheet metal as needed. You can also tell by observing the house at dusk or dawn. That flutter of leaves you see leaving or returning to the house ain't leaves!

Bats like to roost behind shutters. To stop this, shutters should be spaced an inch or two from the wall to allow light into dark spaces; bats don't like LIGHT.

In some buildings, it isn't possible to close all the openings. The next best thing is to shine a light in the suspected area for twenty-four hours a day for a couple of weeks during early spring and summer, when bats return to warm-weather months from caves, where they stay in winter. In some cases, ventilating an area can keep bats out. They don't like cold. Sometimes sprinkling mothball flakes or mothballs or spreading a thin layer of sticky bird repellent in areas is helpful.

Before closing up a building, make sure there are no bats, including baby bats, inside. The best time to do this is the cold-weather months.

Squirrels

Usually squirrels mind their own business, which is building nests in trees. But occasionally they will take up residence in an attic, eaves, spaces between floors, or other spots. They can be noisy and destructive.

I once had squirrels in my eaves, and after almost hiring a wildlife expert who was going to trap the squirrels at considerable cost, I hit upon a simple method. I noticed that the squirrels exited the eaves through a small hole, and as soon as they were gone, and I couldn't hear any sounds coming from inside, I covered the hole with a piece of trim. When they returned, they scampered around, outraged that they had been evicted.

If necessary, squirrels can be trapped with ordinary snap-back rat traps baited with walnut meats. But only if absolutely necessary.

Roaches

Of all the insects around, roaches are among the least loved. They hide in the house in dark places, emerging at night to run all over everything. They also carry disease, and should they get on food, it's best to just throw it out.

There are many commercial products available for killing roaches, but boric acid works very well, and is not expensive. Here we're talking about what is known as "technical boric acid." It comes colored green or blue—so it can't be confused with anything else—and is 99 percent pure,

> ### Hiring a Pro
> If you want to hire a pro for pest control, get estimates from at least three companies and make sure each is proposing the same methods so you can compare prices intelligently. If you need an unbiased opinion, contact your county's cooperative extension agent.

much more powerful than medicinal boric acid. As such, it should be handled carefully if kids or pets are around.

If roaches are in a room, sprinkle or squirt the powder into cracks on baseboards and molding; into wall openings; into openings around sinks, countertops, and cupboards; and underneath cabinets. Roaches can get into spaces $1/16$ inch wide.

Raccoons

There's not much one can do to keep raccoons from foraging through garbage cans, a favorite nocturnal activity of theirs, short of building a fence with an electrified top. The best offense is a defense: Make sure the garbage can lids are on tight and clamped down so that even if the raccoon knocks the can over, it won't be spilled.

Wasps (Hornets)

In the insect kingdom, wasps and their cousins the yellow jackets always seem to wake up on the wrong side of the bed. They'll sting you as "quick as look at you."

Eliminating them takes care. The best time to do it is at or after dusk. The wasps come back after a long day of doing what they do, and congregate in their nest. This is the best time to hit them with one of those long-range spray/stream poisons. You kill them all at once, and the danger of being stung in the process is practically eliminated.

> ### Making Ants Feel Unwelcome
> Ants have to climb up legs to get to the top of a picnic table. To prevent this, spray repellent around the bottoms of the legs.

Rodents

To keep mice and rats out of your house, it's important to first make sure that the area around the house is free of the stuff that attracts them—food. Garbage pails should be secure, and if dogs or cats eat outside, their dishes should be removed when they're finished eating.

You also want to eliminate potential nesting spots around the house. Keep the grass trimmed to 4 inches or less, and if tree branches extend closer than 8 feet to the house, trim these back.

Also, plug spots where the rodents can get into the house. So, too, areas around pipes. Chimneys should be blocked with mortar or roof cement and should have some sort of damper. It's also a good idea to cover roof ventilators and vents with metal screening. Inside, if you store food in out-of-the way places, the containers should be metal or glass.

If rats or mice get in the house—which may be indicated by rodent droppings, holes in the walls, or chewed materials— there are a variety of ways to eliminate them. The best way to kill rodents is still with a trap. It's fast and merciful. Poisons can be problematic, if you have pets or kids or if a rodent ingests poisons and then expires inside a wall.

To dispose of a dead mouse or rat, wear rubber gloves, and bury the creature in the ground. You should also take care— wear gloves—when cleaning up rodent droppings; rodents can carry disease. (Indeed, it was rodents who carried the plague that wiped out half of Europe in medieval times.)

> ### Banishing Flying Insects from Your Bedroom
> Insects that fly around the bedroom at night can be annoying in the extreme. If you have a bathroom nearby, turn on the lights and they should head toward them.

If you want to hire a pro, your best bet would be to call your cooperative extension and get an unbiased opinion.

Termites

High on the list of homeowner terrors are termites. They shouldn't be. Although they can do some damage, they can be stopped.

The sketch shows what a termite looks like. You can get a hint of their presence if you see mud tubes on the side of the foundation (their tunnels to the house), or flylike wings around the house, or insects swarming around in the spring. You should also become suspicious if poking into a suspicious piece of wood shows it's rotted.

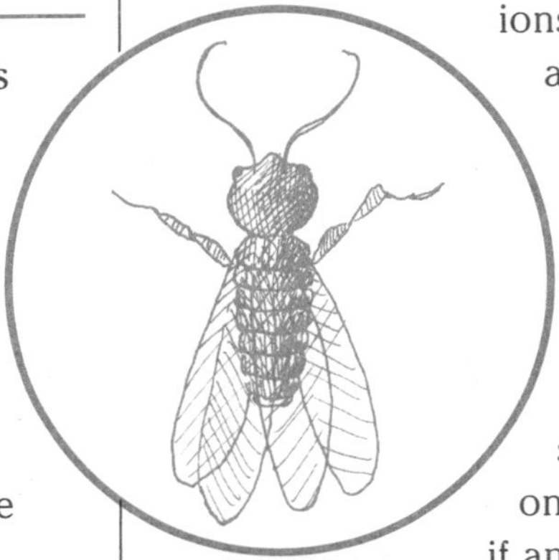

I believe taking care of termites is a job for a professional. However, I suggest that you get three opinions. In other words, assume that anyone coming to your house has larceny on his or her mind. This, more than anything else, should instruct you on just what action—if any—has to be taken.

Termite

CHAPTER 10

Emergencies in the home can include anything from a broken window in the middle of winter when you can't get to a store to a flood in the basement to a downed electrical wire outside. Following is a rogue's gallery of potential problems and how to solve them.

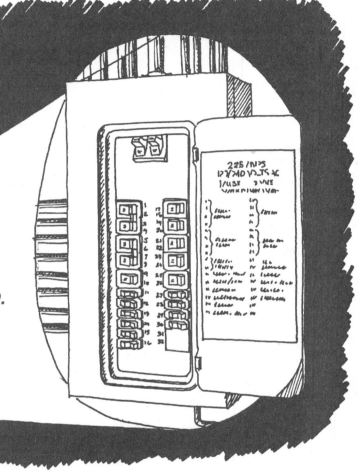

Burst Water Pipe

This is much more likely to happen in the winter than in the summer a pipe gets cold, and the water inside freezes. As water freezes it expands and bursts the pipe.

The best way of handling this is to know where the shutoff valves are that control the various water pipes. Once you do, you can turn off the valve and shut down any further flow of water.

Repair of a water pipe can be accomplished with any of a number of Fernco fittings, which can be cut and slipped over the pipe and then clamped in place to plug the leaking section. This is detailed in the "Repairs" Chapter.

There is not much you can do about old pipes wearing out and developing holes, but you can help keep pipes from bursting in cold weather by wrapping insulation around them to keep them warmer (overlapped newspaper covered with plastic

will do) or by turning the faucets on so the water trickles out—it keeps moving, and thus makes freezing more difficult.

If a pipe freezes despite your best efforts, open faucets wide to allow for expansion of frozen water. Then remove the insulation from the pipes, place rags on them, and pour hot water on the rags. It is hoped that this will melt the ice and allow it to run out of the open faucets.

Use hot water to thaw pipes

Broken Window

This usually is not a difficult repair to make. (See "Repairs.") But it sure can be if it happens when glass and repair material are not available.

An effective temporary solution is to cover the opening with plastic, whether it be a piece of clear plastic or a trash bag. Just tape it in place. It will effectively block rain, snow, and whatever else from coming in until a more permanent repair can be made.

Downed Electrical Line

The lines that are strung along telephone poles may carry electrical current or may be telephone wire. If both types are strung between poles, the electrical lines are usually the topmost ones; the telephone lines are closer to the street.

If any line falls, do not attempt to move it or touch it in any way. Assume it's live. If you can safely blockade others from going near it by setting up a barricade of chairs or the like, by all means do so. But your first response to the situation should be to call the police.

Leaking Roof

If water is coming through the ceiling material, it usually means the roof is leaking, and it should be considered an emergency. Left alone, water can do a great deal of damage inside a house.

If an area of the plaster or Sheetrock® is stained or bowed, this should be cut out as soon as possible. You don't want water-saturated ceiling material coming down on someone's head.

The next step is to find the leak, which is easier said than done. Many times the water enters at one point, and then flows down a rafter or something else to emerge elsewhere.

If it is raining, and the attic is open, poke your head up there and shine the light around. If you can see where the leak is coming from, mark it with crayon or the like; or if a hole is visible, stick a wire through to the outside so you can observe it and know where to make the repair when the weather is right.

Power Loss

When this happens, there may be a loss of power in your house only, or it may affect the general area. A look out the window to see if neighbors have lost power or a call will tell.

If the problem is just yours, you can try to flip the circuit breaker or replace a fuse as detailed in Chapter 1. If the problem is more generalized, you should call the utility company.

It's an excellent idea to have on hand candles, flashlights, or other light sources. If you live in an area subject to severe storms, you should also have on hand an emergency food and water supply, extra medicine, first-aid supplies, and extra blankets or sleeping bags, as well as fire-fighting equipment. A gas-operated generator can also be an excellent idea; it can supply more than ample power.

When the lights go out, you should flip off most light switches, as well as the furnace switch; also unplug the freezer and refrigerator. When the power goes on again it can suck (well, not literally) power through the appliances and damage them.

Also, keep the freezer door closed as much as possible to keep food frozen as long as possible. Incidentally, partially thawed food can only be safely refrozen if it contains ice crystals. Don't try to refreeze spoiled food.

If you are forced to sleep in a cold house, it's best to dress in warm but loose clothing, including a hat. From one-half to three-quarters of all body heat is lost through the head.

Ideally, you would have some sort of emergency heating equipment on hand that doesn't depend on electricity, such as a kerosene heater. However, you must take care when using such equipment; the gases emitted by them are toxic and must be vented to the outdoors.

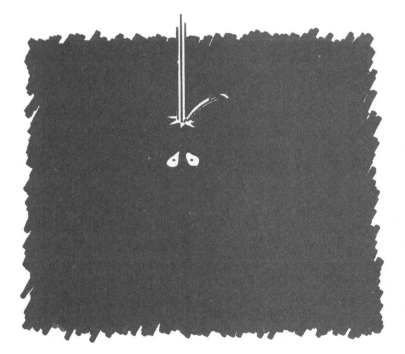

CHAPTER

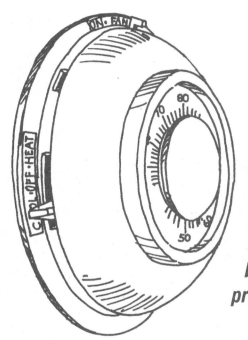

Though our devotion to energy saving is not what it was in the 1970s, when almost everyone was super aware, the truths of that time still apply: It can pay, sometimes in a big way, to engage in energy-saving practices.

Lowering Cooling Costs

Here are some ways to help keep your house cool and lower costs:

- Locate a new air conditioner on the shady side of the house or, if this is not possible, place it on the north or east wall. The idea is to keep it away from the direct rays of the sun. Also make sure there's a tight seal around the unit.
- Don't use the air conditioner anymore than is necessary, and don't cool rooms that are unoccupied.
- Keep the air conditioner off during the day. If you want to come home to a cool house, buy a timer. Connect the air conditioner through the timer. This can be set to start a half hour before you come home.
- Allow the air conditioner to "breathe." Keep draperies and furniture away from grilles and airways.
- Change or wash the air filter once a month during the summer months.
- Clean the condenser and evaporator once a year. If the unit frosts on warm days, it may mean the refrigerant is low. Refilling is a job for a service rep.
- Keep windows closed when the air conditioning is on.
- Use draperies and shades or awnings to block windows that get direct sunlight. This reduces solar radiation into the room.
- Use storm windows. These work in the winter to keep heat in, and they can work well in the summer to keep the cool air in.
- When the weather is right, turn off the air conditioner and open the windows.
- Reduce the heat in the house. Turn off light bulbs and avoid cooking, bathing, or washing clothes during the hot hours of the day. Also use irons, ovens, and heat-generating appliances in early morning or late evening. Heat produces moisture, which makes air conditioners work harder—resulting in increased electrical consumption.

Lowering Heating Costs

On any heating system, you should keep the registers, convectors, and radiators clean. Lint, dirt, and dust keep heat from flowing into the room. Also, set back your thermostat to at least 50 degrees at night or when the house is unoccupied during the day. A clock thermostat can do this automatically. Turning the thermostat down 10 degrees at night can save you over 10 percent in annual fuel costs.

Here are some additional cost-saving tips:

- Have your heating system checked out and tuned up by a pro—just as you would a car—before the heating season begins.
- If you have a steam heating system, drain and flush the low water cutoff once a month during the heating season.
- Check the water-level glass periodically to make sure there is enough water in the boiler.

For a hot water system:

- Bleed the systems expansion tank, if possible.
- Drain the system periodically to remove air that could block the flow of hot water to radiators and convectors.
- Check water pressure by observing the pressure tempera-ture gauge on the boiler.

- Lubricate the water circulating pump and motor.

For a warm air system:

- Change the system's filter at least once a month during the heating season.
- Keep registers and cold-air louvers unblocked.
- Clean and lubricate the air circu-lating fan and motor.

Improving a Heating System

There are a number of ways to improve the way your heating system functions. The improvements should be made by a professional, but they can pay big divi-dends in the future:

- Have a flame-retention head oil burner installed. This can save about 10 percent on annual fuel bills. It works by reducing the amount of heat lost up the chimney by keeping more of it in the boiler or furnace for distribu-tion throughout the house.
- Install an automatic vent damper. This is located in the smokestack

on oil- or gas-fired equipment. The device cuts off the flow of warm air up the chimney when the heating system is not operating. It can save about 5 percent on the heating bill.

Weatherstripping

One of the cheapest and most effective ways to glean energy savings is with weatherstriping, the stuff used to seal the gaps around doors and windows from the inside (like caulk does on the outside).

Weatherstriping comes in a wide variety of types and prices, from felt that is tacked or adhered on to lovely metal strips lined with foam and rubber. A trip to your local hardware store or home center should be instructive.

But the happy fact is this: Any weatherstriping will do a good job of keeping warmed and cooled air in the house, and that means money saved. It's that simple—and that profound.

CHAPTER

12

No matter how much this book helps you, there will come a time, it is likely, when the book will fail. Why? We just can't cover every conceivable question.

So what then? What does someone who needs info on his or her particular project do? The answer is to have, one might say, a menu of sources to choose from—a menu that provides (though the metaphor is mangled) a mine of information to access— and I hope, to find the answer(s) one needs.

That's the purpose of this section: to provide information sources that will answer those questions specific to your project. Fortunately, there is a variety of info available. And in most cases the info is free, or the price of a phone call. In sum, answers can be provided by customer service departments accessible via 800 numbers, companies accessible at their regular numbers, salespeople at home centers and hardware stores and other outlets, trade associations, and the library. Following is a roundup and tips on how to work this mine of information.

Customer Service Departments

Many manufacturers have 800 numbers staffed by people who are more than happy to answer technical questions on the use of their particular products. And what may seem like a deep, dark mystery to you will likely be old hat to them. I have called a zillion 800 numbers and most of the time have gotten solid answers.

Getting 800 Numbers

There are a number of ways to get such numbers. First, a list is published at the end of this chapter. Though it is subjective—I have tried to provide numbers of large as well as smaller companies—it should help.

You can also check the label on the product for an 800 number, or call the toll-free 800 directory operator, 1-800-555-1212, which carries some numbers. (Some companies with 800 numbers do not want to be listed.) Or call the store where you bought the product. They sometimes have 800 numbers, and may be more than willing to share them with you. In some cases, companies may prefer that the retailer call direct. (Sherwin Williams, for example, has an 800 number for "store" calls.) Or the retailer can call them, and then put you on the phone. This is usually the best way to go, because who can supply details on your project better than you?

And you should be prepared to furnish all the details you have. The answer may be very simple, but more often than not a detailed "Q and A" between the customer and the customer service rep will be required.

All the Gory Details

It is important to be honest. Some people are embarrassed to describe mistakes they made in using a product, and the result is that the rep can be misled—and no good answer furnished. It's like not giving all the symptoms to a doctor and then expecting him or her to provide an accurate diagnosis.

Some 800 numbers are available starting very early in the morning, and go late into the night, and on Saturdays. Some go around the clock; others are available only during normal business hours.

Incidentally, 800 numbers can be a great source for finding outlets that sell a particular product that you may be having trouble finding. All you need to supply is your address, and the vendor will be able to tell you where the closest outlet is.

Paid Calls

Many companies don't have 800 numbers, but a call may be warranted anyway. To get the number, call the store where you bought the product, or check the product package for the company address or phone number. If it's a long-distance call and you don't know the area code, you can sometimes get it from your phone book (some publish extensive area codes), or you can call information for the code (it will cost), and then dial information to get the number.

Salespeople

For the everyday run-of-the-mill repair problems, such as fixing a leaky faucet or installing a light switch, hardware store personnel can be very helpful. They deal with these questions day in and day out.

For questions relating to things that ordinary hardware stores don't normally sell (such as roofing, siding, concrete, etc.), the home center is likely to be a better source for answers. The emergence of these outlets has been a boon to homeowners needing comprehensive, detailed advice that addresses their particular concerns. Once, the salesperson might have been some gum-chewing young kid more interested in talking on the telephone (and in some companies this may still be the case); but today, home centers employ carpenters, plumbers, electricians, and others who have deep product knowledge and experience.

Often, a project will require follow-up questions. In such situations, establishing contact with a knowledgeable salesperson is like having a free consultant.

No Nirvana

Such places are not perfect. Some sales personnel do not know a great deal, and some dispense wrong information rather than admit they don't know something.

So who do you look to for the best information?

It would be nice if we could assume that the gal with the gray hair has the most knowledge, but this is not always true; the gal with the curly red hair might be the one you need to see. Also, some people may be expert in one area, say carpeting, but may not know much about installing ceramic tiles.

You can approach this in two ways: You can walk into a department, say flooring, and ask, "Who's your guru on ceramic floor tile?" (or whatever), or you can call the store manager before visiting the store and ask him or her who's best. The store manager will know, because he or she knows who gets paid for what.

You don't necessarily have to go into a store. Many people will answer questions over the phone. Or you might ask them if they're busy and when's the best time to talk on the phone. Or maybe they'll call you when they can.

Nor do you necessarily have to deal at a store to ask a question. On more than one occasion, I have gone through the Yellow Pages and called a variety of outlets other than home centers and hardware stores (for example, paint stores, window stores, paneling stores, and

Using the Yellow Pages

The Yellow Pages can be useful in information gathering. You can find specific kinds of outlets, and also get a lead on a parent company should you want it. Most outlets list their main line of brand name products, such as Eljer or Sherwin Williams, and you can easily access it.

To make the Yellow Pages easier to use be aware (if you're not already), that it reads alphabetically like a dictionary, and there are also main subject headings on the tops of the pages. Also, some sizable Yellow Pages have a separate index that can save even more walking for your fingers.

masonry yards) to ask very specific questions. And most of the time I have gotten answers. My reasoning in calling such places is that any outfit that deals with the same product day in and day out is likely to know it quite well.

Trade Associations

Trade associations can be helpful. These are organizations whose members are companies who make common products. The association performs a variety of functions, and one is to provide information to members and sometimes to the general public. They have engineers on staff who give the answers, or have access to highly knowledgeable people.

Although they do not have 800 numbers, some have told me they will consult (free, of course) over the phone. (See "Trade Associations" below.)

> ### Bring a Visual Aid with You
> If you go into the store with a question, bring a visual aid with you, such as the item itself, if practical (Leave the cast iron tub home!), a sketch, or a Polaroid or regular photo of the item. The salesperson will appreciate it.

The Library

"Many people come into the library," says reference librarian Raymonda Crowe of Harborfields Public Library in Greenlawn, New York, "and they haven't any idea of what's available or how to access it."

Indeed, the library can be a rich source of information. In addition to magazines and newspapers, libraries carry all kinds of how-to books, some of them in circulation and others in the reference collection. And many libraries also have how-to video collections, and more.

Your local library may also be able to access books and periodicals from other libraries, both ones in circulation and those that are part of the reference collection. "We'll also go out of state to get a book," Raymonda says (something I can attest to).

The quality of the books vary. Some have zero quality. Others, such as those comprehensive tomes that pretend to cover anything and everything related to a home, are pretty but don't usually have the detail one needs. (I remember one that showed how to hang a door with four sketches and two paragraphs of instruction...Yikes!)

Some are good. Your best bet is to take a number of them out on the topic you're interested in, and peruse them. The wheat will quickly separate from the chaff.

To simplify your life, and to insure that you have the best shot at getting what you need, start with the reference librarian for help. These people are like well-trained bird dogs at finding information, and they can help you home in on (no pun intended) what you need much more quickly, it's safe to say, than you could alone.

Other Sources

Other sources may simply be people you know who have expertise in a particular area, or who may know someone who does and will talk with you. Jim down the block, for example, may have been doing his own home improvements for years. He could prove to be a solid source. Or Susan may have a brother who's a roofing contractor who can answer your questions. Think about it. You may be surprised by the number of people you know who know something.

800 Numbers

Following is a list of companies who have customer service departments with 800 numbers. Many companies sell products under a variety of brand names, but if you peruse the package, you'll find the name of the parent company on it, which is the way the companies are listed here.

In some cases, the number listed will get you right to the technical person you're looking for. For example, if you call the Dutch Boy number for technical help, the number will bring you right to that person. In other cases, where a company makes a wide variety of products, there may be an overall 800 number; and when you call in, the operator will connect you to the proper technical person, or give you another 800 number to call.

Please note that the product(s) column is not intended to detail all the products a company makes but, rather, the major ones they make.

Tools and Hardware

Company	Number	Product(s)
American Tool Company	1-800-767-6297	Hand tools
Anchor Wire	1-800-262-3526	Hanging devices, picture hooks
Baldwin Hardware Corporation	1-800-566-1986	Mortise locks
Black and Decker Power Tools	1-800-762-6672	Power tools and accessories
Boss Manufacturing	1-800-447-4581	Gloves, protective clothing
Campbell Group	1-800-358-7335	Power washers, paint sprayers, compressors
Clicker Corporation	1-800-442-5425	Replacement garage door openers, transmitters
Coleman, Powermate	1-800-445-1805	Power washing machines
Crawford Products	1-800-225-5832	Peg hooks, storage devices
Crown Bolt Inc.	1-800-767-2658	Bolts and screws
Dremel	1-800-437-3635	Rotary and bench-top power tools
Desa International	1-800-323-5190	Chain saws, among other tools
Dewalt	1-800-4-DEWALT	Power tools
Door Products Inc.	1-800-445-6136	Door hardware
Fiskars, Inc.	1-800-500-4849	Hand tools
Freud USA	1-800-334-4107	Power tools
Gainsborough Hardware	1-800-845-5662	Door hardware
Genie Company	1-800-995-1111	Garage door openers, shop vacuums
Liberty Cabinet Hardware	1-800-542-3789	Drawer slides, furniture hardware
Karcher, Alfred	1-800-537-4129	Power washers
Makita	1-800-4MAKITA	Power tools
Norton Company	1-800-377-0331	Sandpapers, surfacing products
Olympic Tools	1-800-888-8782	Striking tools, other hand tools
Ryobi	1-800-867-9624	Power tools
Stanley	1-800-622-4393	Hardware
Stanley Tools	1-800-262-2161	Tools
Tec Inc.	1-800-654-3103	Construction adhesives

Plumbing and Related Products

Company	Number	Product(s)
American Standard	1-800-223-0068	Faucets, fittings, tubs
Amerock Corp.	1-800-435-6959	
Deflect-O Corporation	1-800-669-4399	Drier vents, designer hooks
Desa International	1-800-323-5190	Indoor space heaters, kerosene heaters, power tools, generators
Eljer Industries	1-800-872-7277	Fixtures and fittings
	1-800-423-5537	Faucets only
Enforcer Products Inc.	1-800-241-5656	Drain clearing products
Fernco	1-800-521-1283	Flexible fittings
Franklin Brass	1-800-421-3375	Bathroom accessories
General Marble Corp.	1-800-432-4114	Bathroom "furniture"—marble tops, vanities, medicine chests
Jameco Inc.	1-800-326-3603	Fittings
Jancyn Manufacturing	1-800-252-6296	Cesspool and drain treatment products
Keller Industries	1-800-333-4586	Shower doors (among other things)
Moen Incorporated	1-800-321-6636	Faucets and sinks
Nibco Hardware	1-800-323-3570	Valves and fittings
Oatey	1-800-321-9532	Plumbing hardware and cements
Price Phister	1-800-732-8238	Faucets
Sterling Group	1-800-558-7782	Stainless steel sinks

Paint, Wallpaper, and Related Products

Company	Number	Product(s)
America's Finest	1-800-642-8468	Paint
W.M. Barr	1-800-643-7993	Paint strippers
Behr Process	1-800-854-0133	Paint
Darworth Company	1-800-624-7767	Caulks and sealants
Dutch Boy	1-800-642-8468	Paint
Eisenhart Wallcoverings	1-800-726-3267	Wallcoverings

Paint, Wallpaper, and Related Products (continued)

Company	Number	Product(s)
Flood Company	1-800-321-3444	Wood coatings
Glidden Company	1-800-221-4000	Paint
Masterchem Industries	1-800-325-3552	Paint primers
Minwax	1-800-523-9299	Wood finishes
Sears, Roebuck	1-800-9 PAINTS	Paint
Thompson & Formby	1-800-647-9352	Wood coatings and strippers
Wagner Spray Tech	1-800-328-8251	Paint applicators, paint sprayers

Electrical Products

AFC Cable	1-800-225-8588	Armored and metal-clad cable
Carlon	1-800-547-4349	Conduit, enclosures, accessories
Gamak	1-800-237-6263	Circuit breakers, fittings, weather-proof devices
Halex	1-800-749-3261	Fittings
King Technology	1-800-633-0232	Silicone-filled weatherproof connectors
Leviton Mfg.	1-800-824-3005	Switches, receptacles, wall plates, dimmers
Square D Company	1-800-432-2599	Load centers, circuit breakers, wire, grounding bars
Thomas and Betts	1-800-888-0211	Various electrical products
Wiremold Consumer Products	1-800-621-0049	Metal and plastic raceway

Building Products

Alcoa	1-800-962-6973	Vinyl and aluminum siding
Builders Edge Inc.	1-800-969-7245	Gable vents, exhaust fans
Celotex	1-800-CELOTEX	Roofing, insulation, siding, drywall
Certainteed	1-800-782-8777	Insulation, roofing, siding, windows
Emco Industries	1-800-933-3626	Storm doors

Building Products (continued)

Company	Number	Product(s)
Gibson Homans	1-800-433-7293	Roof and driveway tar, self-stick wallcovering
Instafoam Products	1-800-800-3626	Expanding foam
LTL Home Products	1-800-360-1585	Woof shutters, dividers, folding doors, bifold doors, windows, house wrap
United States Gypsum (USG)	1-800-874-4968	Drywall, joint treatments, joint compound, joint tape, patchers
ODL, Inc.	1-800-253-3900	Glass doors, mahogany
Owens Corning	1-800-766-3464	Roofing, insulation, door frames, skylights
Screen Tight	1-800-768-7325	Porch screening systems
Silver Line Building Products	1-800-299-9501	Replacement windows, patio doors, specialty windows and doors
SNE Enterprises	1-800-826-9594	Wood and vinyl windows, patio doors
Stanley Doors	1-800-521-5262	Steel doors
Velux America	1-800-969-7245	Roof windows, skylights, and accessories
Wing Industries	1-800-341-9464	Doors, fixed shutters, and windows

Wall and Floor Products

Company	Number	Product(s)
Alladin Carpet Mills	1-800-544-7992	Carpeting
Armstrong	1-800-233-3823	Flooring, roofing, and much more
Bretlin, Inc.	1-800-Bretlin	Carpet runners
Chesapeake Hardwood	1-800-446-8192	Wall paneling
Clairson International	1-800-874-0008	Closet shelving

Wall and Floor Products (continued)

Company	Number	Product(s)
Congoleum	1-800-234-8811	Resilient flooring
Dal Tile	1-800-283-4069	Ceramic tile
Newell Home Hardware	1-800-232-6395	Decorative shelving
Duo Fast	1-800-838-6327	Nails, tools, staples
Felker Operations	1-800-365-4003	Masonry, diamond, and tile-cutting saws
General Felt Industries	1-800-631-0845	Carpet padding
Mannington	1-800-638-7929	Resilient flooring
Nafco	1-800-227-4662	Resilient flooring
Shaw Industries	1-800-441-7429	Carpeting

Miscellaneous

Company	Number	Product(s)
Amerock Corp.	1-800-435-6959	Wide variety of products
Angelo Brothers	1-800-999-2226	Fans and light fixtures
Bemis Manufacturing	1-800-547-3888	Wide variety of products—gutter, toilet seats, cutlery, and more
Dimango Products	1-800-346-2646	Chimes, home security products
Eclectic Products	1-800-767-4667	Adhesives
Gardner Asphalt	1-800-367-3219	Driveway and roof coatings and repair products
General Electric	1-800-255-8886	Silicone caulk
Georgia Pacific	1-800-284-5347	Wide variety of building products
Loctite	1-800-321-9188	Adhesives
Macklanburg Duncan	1-800-854-8454	Caulks and weatherstrip
Merrilat Industries	1-800-624-1250	Kitchen cabinets
Norton Company	1-800-377-0331	Sandpaper
Z Brick	1-800-828-0253	Facing brick

Trade Associations

Company	Number	Product(s)
APA: The Engineered Wood Association	1-206-565-6600	All kinds of information on plywood, OSB, Glulam, and other structural products
Brick Institute of America	1-703-620-0010	Information on building with and repairing brick
National Concrete	1-703-713-1900	Information on building with and repairing block
Masonry Association Manufacturers Association	1-901-526-5016	National Oak Flooring Information on repairing, installing, and finishing oak flooring
National Wood Flooring Association	1-500-443-WOOD (25 cents/min)	Information on repairing and finishing all kinds of hardwood flooring
National Particleboard Association	1-301-670-0604	Information on working with particleboard
Portland Cement Association	1-847-966-6200	Information on repairing and installing concrete

Index